Plotinus on Intellect

Plotinus on Intellect

Eyjólfur Kjalar Emilsson

CLARENDON PRESS · OXFORD

OXFORD
UNIVERSITY PRESS

Great Clarendon Street, Oxford OX2 6DP

Oxford University Press is a department of the University of Oxford.
It furthers the University's objective of excellence in research, scholarship,
and education by publishing worldwide in

Oxford New York

Auckland Cape Town Dar es Salaam Hong Kong Karachi
Kuala Lumpur Madrid Melbourne Mexico City Nairobi
New Delhi Shanghai Taipei Toronto

With offices in

Argentina Austria Brazil Chile Czech Republic France Greece
Guatemala Hungary Italy Japan Poland Portugal Singapore
South Korea Switzerland Thailand Turkey Ukraine Vietnam

Oxford is a registered trade mark of Oxford University Press
in the UK and in certain other countries

Published in the United States
by Oxford University Press Inc., New York

British Library Cataloguing in Publication Data
Data available

Library of Congress Cataloging in Publication Data
Data available

Typeset by Laserwords Private Limited, Chennai, India
Printed in Great Britain
on acid-free paper by
Biddles Ltd, King's Lynn, Norfolk

ISBN 978–0–19–928170–1

10 9 8 7 6 5 4 3 2 1

Acknowledgements

Some parts of this book have been in the making for a long time and I am grateful to a number of people who have assisted me on the way. The oldest parts originate in work done during my junior fellowship year at the Center for Hellenic Studies in Washington, DC, in 1990–1. The issues dealt with here were not my main project at the centre, but I worked on this nevertheless. I am grateful to the centre in general for letting me be there and for the pleasant and inspiring company of the other fellows and staff during my stay, not least the director, Zeph Stewart, a marvel of a man.

As for the rest of the book, bits and pieces have been presented as lectures in many places. I have benefited from questions and remarks from many people whose names, in some cases, are unknown to me, some perhaps forgotten. I wish to express my thanks to these all the same. I have also been rather too unrestrained—or so I have sometimes felt at least—in imposing my Plotinian interests, ideas, and even pages, upon colleagues and friends. Among the many who have read and discussed with me some chunks of drafts of this book, or just discussed the ideas with me in an engaging way, I would like to mention and thank the following in particular: Edgars Narkevic, Laszlo Bene, Dominic O'Meara, Pavlos Kalligas, Dmitri Nikulin, Pauliina Remes; and among colleages at the University of Oslo: Håvard Løkke, Panos Dimas, Christel Fricke, Øivind Andersen, and Olav Gjelsvik. The following have either read and commented on the bulk of the material or been engaged and engaging discussion partners throughout, or both: Alexandrine Schniewind, Carsten Hansen, Camilla Serck-Hanssen, Svavar Hrafn Svavarsson, and Michael Frede. To all these I am especially and deeply grateful. Thanks also go to the two anonymous readers for OUP whose comments were helpful, though in different ways, and to Eirik Welo and Ólöf Embla Eyjólfsdóttir, who have assisted me at the final stages by checking references and compiling the indices. It may have become a worn commonplace in acknowledgements such as here to thank one's family, an obligatory courtesy whose sincerity—as is common with courtesy—is not beyond question. Nevertheless, I take the risk of thanking my family whose good company has made the process of writing this book much more pleasant than it would otherwise have been.

Contents

Introduction

Before I set out to introduce this book as such, it may be worthwhile to
have a bird's eye view on the world according to Plotinus. With this in
place, the introduction to the contents of the chapters to come can be seen
in its proper context.

Plotinus conceives of reality as hierarchically ordered. At the top there is
the One, also called the Good. It is the simplest or most unified 'thing' there
is. It is so unified, in fact, that it contains no distinctions whatsoever. This
implies that it isn't really correct to call it a 'thing', as I just did: it is 'beyond
being' in the sense that there is nothing it can be said to be, nothing that
can be predicated of it as such. In this context 'being' presupposes some
particular form that limits the being in question, and a limit presupposes
distinctions. None of this applies to the One. So if in spite of this we insist
on calling it a thing, we must realize that it is no ordinary thing and in many
ways defies the logic of things. It goes together with this view that the One
cannot be thought or known: to think or to know something is to think or
know what it *is*, to know the being of the thing thought about. The One
doesn't even know itself, because self-knowledge requires some distinction
between knower and known, and if it were to know itself, it would have
to know itself as something non-simple. This absolutely simple One is the
cause of everything else. How does Plotinus arrive at such a first principle?

If we are to make any sense of the sensible world around us as a whole
and of individual things in it such as the animal species and their parts
and attributes, we must posit intelligible principles, Platonic Ideas. This
prompts Plotinus to posit a level of intelligible principles above the sensible
realm. This quest for principles is a quest for something which explains
the features of the sensible realm. Moreover, true to Plato and many other
Greek thinkers, Plotinus demands that his principles possess the features
they are to explain in other things in such a way that the question does not
arise with respect to the principles why they possess these features. Take
the sensible horse as an example: some matter or mass has taken on the

form of a horse and moves and comports itself in the equine way. This must ultimately be accounted for with reference to an intelligible item which is horse by virtue of itself and whose equinity needs no explanation. Considerations about the human soul lead to an analogous result: our powers of sense-perception and reasoning presuppose an intellect whose cognitive power is quite free from all the limitations characteristic of our human cognitive powers of sense-perception and discursive reason.

Thus, both considerations of ontology and considerations of cognition lead to the positing of intelligible principles. In this context Plotinus makes a clever move: at the intelligible level, being and knowledge, ontology and epistemology, are unified. That is to say, the intelligibles, the Platonic Ideas, exist as the thoughts of a universal intellect, which is at once the principle of cognition and of being. This unification will be one of our main concerns in the chapters to come.

The realm of the universal intellect—henceforth referred to as 'Intellect'[1]— is characterized by a much higher degree of unity than the sensible realm. For one thing, it is non-spatial and it is atemporal. As such it is free from the dispersion involved in space and time. Moreover, the intelligibles make up a kind of system of organic unity so that each intelligible item in some way presupposes or 'refers to' the others. Nevertheless, Intellect is not absolutely one. It contains internal differences. Hence, its unity is a borrowed feature. Therefore, by virtue of the principle of metaphysical causation mentioned above, something which has unity all by virtue of itself is needed to account for the unity of Intellect. This is what necessitates the supposition of the One above Intellect. Below Intellect in the hierarchy and before the sensible realm is Soul. This is the intelligible principle that is the immediate cause of the sensible and the principle of perception and thought for human beings. These three, the One, Intellect, and Soul, make up what is known as the three principal hypostases.

In this book, I try to leave the Soul out as much as possible. This is not at all because I don't deem the topic of Soul worthy of inquiry but simply because it would complicate matters immensely if it were to be covered in addition to the difficult topics that we shall address. Luckily, this neglect

---

[1] Following custom I capitalize the word 'intellect' when I take it to refer to the fully actual second hypostasis: this is called 'Intellect', without the definite article. I use this restrictively, however. So when I am talking about any intellect whatsoever, including Intellect, or when it is, say, a question of both the so-called inchoate intellect (see p. 70) and Intellect, or when I don't wish to prejudge the question or when I am not sure which intellect is at stake, I prefer to say simply 'the intellect'.

of Soul ought to be quite unproblematic: the Plotinian hypostases are supposed to be such that an account of a lower one indeed presupposes an account of its cause but not the converse: the One and Intellect should be self-sufficient in relation to Soul, and hence we should be able to talk about them (though not so much can be said about the One except indirectly) without bringing in Soul.

Admittedly, however, the matter may not be quite so simple. Plotinus' views on the One and on Intellect are expressed in words, in language. As such they are expressed from the viewpoint of a human soul. That human point of view, which in the hierarchy belongs to the order of Soul, will thus be with us, even if our subject is Intellect (or for that matter the One). For this reason at least, the sphere of Soul cannot be quite ignored in a discussion of Intellect.

In any case, the One, Intellect, and Soul come in an order of dependence and each has its characteristic degree of unity. Plotinus sometimes expresses this in a formulaic way by saying that the One is merely 'one', Intellect 'one many', and Soul 'one and many'. It was seen by Bréhier (1924: 59) and brilliantly proved by Dodds (1928) that these formulas and Plotinus' formal distinctions between his three hypotheses are derived from the first three hypotheses of Plato's *Parmenides*, counting 155e–157b as a separate hypothesis.

Let this suffice as the barest outline of Plotinus' thought. The bulk of this book is a study in aspects of the second hypostasis, Intellect, which, as we have seen, is at once the sphere of perfect knowledge and of true or real being. The exception here is the first chapter, 'Emanation and Activity', which deals with a pervasive phenomenon in Plotinus' thought: the manner of being for each of the hypostases and the manner of generation of the level below a given one. This topic is indeed highly relevant for the subsequent chapters but it is not limited to Intellect.

The very idea of the Plotinian Intellect strikes me as at once fascinating and enigmatic. We may describe it as an ideal knower, something that knows and understands what there may be to know and understand in as full a sense as one could possibly postulate. From this perspective Intellect constitutes an interesting limiting notion, one that becomes all the more interesting because Plotinus is wary of pitfalls that might render Intellect's knowledge less than perfect. Thus, he is not satisfied with merely insisting on Intellect's perfect knowledge. He makes an effort to investigate what sort of properties and relations to its object a perfect knower must have. Into these considerations enters the concern to make Intellect immune to the threat of sceptical arguments. To regard Intellect as an ideal knower seems to me to be a fruitful perspective that helps explain some of its stranger features. At the same time, the notion of an ideal knower is in itself philosophically interesting. Though the themes focused on vary, the supposition that Intellect is an ideal knower colours my whole approach to the problems in Chapters 2–4.

An ideal knower has according to Plotinus several interesting features. Here are some of the more significant ones. (1) It knows its object non-representationally, i.e. it knows the very thing itself as opposed to some image or proxy for this object. (2) Its act of knowing involves a distinction between thinker and thought, knower and known. (3) Its object must contain internal differences. (4) It is unerring. (5) Its knowledge is holistic, i.e. it knows all the features of its object and knows them at once in a single act.

It follows from (1), (2), and (3) for reasons that will become fully clear in Chapter 3 that the knowledge in question is self-knowledge.

So the sort of knowledge Intellect has is in fact its self-knowledge. Plotinus' notion of self-knowledge, as I expound it in Chapter 2, though having clear Platonic and Aristotelian flavours, is in significant ways quite different from anything we find in Plato or Aristotle or, for that matter, in other philosophers before Plotinus or after. Intellect's self-knowledge is at once a self-constitution and knowledge of what the subject of the thought is. That is to say, before the intellect begins to think—in some logical rather than temporal sense of 'before'—it has no determinate identity. Its identity only comes about through its thought in which both the subject and the object are constituted. Moreover, this identity comes about in such a way that the thinker knows its identity by a kind of first personal knowledge. That is to say, not only does it know the content of what happens to be it itself, it knows that it, the thinker, is this content. This, I believe, is new in relation to what Aristotle has to say about self-thinking in *Metaphysics* XII or *De anima* III, 4–5, on which Plotinus otherwise clearly depends in these aspects of his theory of Intellect.

The self-constituting aspect of this account may give an impression of what we may for lack of a better term call an existentialistic element in Plotinus' thought. Phrases like 'I am what I freely make of myself' might seem to be apt for describing Intellect's lack of restraint in its thinking whereby it makes itself, somewhat like the Sartrean Orestes in *The Flies*, who freely defines himself through his actions. In an analogous way, one might think that Intellect said: 'I think I am F, hence I am F.' Its thought is after all not determined by any antecedent, external object which it has to match. What it thinks is its own, free creation.

While it is true that Intellect defines itself, this impression of absolute freedom is misleading. For in a very important sense the thought of Intellect is determined by the One, though not in such a way that the content of Intellect depicts the One as an ordinary external object of thought or perception. Intellect is indeed called an image of the One and bears a resemblance to it, but it is not an image that faithfully represents this intended object of its gaze. There is a radical loss involved in the picture Intellect gets as a result of its attempt to see the One. So the One, even if antecedent to Intellect, is not an antecedent object against which Intellect can test its thoughts. Yet, Intellect's thoughts are determined by the One, and thus determined by something which is beyond Intellect's reach. We are here faced with what at least for me is one of Plotinus' deep, disconcerting, but possibly true insights: thought, however successful, ultimately leaves something of its intended object untouched. It remains out of its reach.

Plotinus sometimes describes Intellect as a god or as divine. For those of us who have grown accustomed to a notion of a Christian God, who indeed is supposed to be a benevolent thinker, it may be all too easy to conceive of the Plotinian Intellect along the same lines. This is of course not entirely unjustified, if only because the notion of the divine in major thinkers in the Christian tradition such as St Augustine, who in turn have shaped our conceptions, has indeed been heavily coloured by Plotinus' notion of Intellect. We should, however, be on our guard in transferring features of the Christian God to Intellect. The latter, for instance, lacks all the personal characteristics of the former.

Another concept that it is natural to compare Intellect with is that of Reason. I am then thinking of Reason as it appears in rationalists such as Descartes and Spinoza, and in Kant, and even in common, everyday conceptions. We say, for instance, that something stands to Reason or that Reason forbids this or that. Reason is in such locutions conceived of as one impersonal and common thing that is identically shared by all who are at all rational; and it is shared in such a way that we can appeal to it when the question arises what is and what isn't, what is right and what is wrong. It seems to me that as an epistemological principle, at least, the Plotinian Intellect has the same function as Reason. Intellect too is impersonal and shared; what it shows to be the case serves as a norm for what there is. There is a difference, however, in that Plotinus took Intellect to be not only the principle of knowledge and understanding, but also the principle behind the sensible world around us: the latter too, though in itself void of consciousness and thought, is rational in a way, because it behaves rationally. Another difference is that as opposed to what we commonly think about Reason, Plotinus thought that in order to serve in its normative role as a measure of correct thought and of what there is, Intellect must itself think. It is not clear that Reason itself is a thinker who thinks anything at all, even if we say that Reason demands, forbids, and dictates certain things.

Plotinus may not have been the first to raise the issue, but he is surely the first extant thinker to directly and seriously address the question of the limits of thought. His conclusion is, as we have seen, that thought has absolute limits. The first stage after the One is a stage of thought. This thought strives for something it cannot have. Plotinus lays down some conditions for thought, tries to say what the minimal conditions for there being thought are. He is willing to embrace the idea that thought may be timeless, of many things at once, even that it is non-representational and doesn't exhibit propositional structure. In this he is of course much more generous or optimistic about thought than, say, almost all contemporary philosophers. It seems that there are two crucial conditions that thought, nevertheless, must satisfy according to him: thought involves a subject and an object and the object must be somehow varied. The apprehension of the One that Intellect has is bound to satisfy these two conditions, which means that the apprehension doesn't capture the One as it is in itself. The One itself is not bound by these conditions. It is free from them in two ways: it does not itself think, for thinking implies a duality, nor is it possible to think it, because the object of thought presupposes a duality (or plurality) too: a totally undifferentiated something, as the One is in itself, is not a possible object of thought.

The fact and role of the One is indeed crucial to the whole of Plotinus' philosophy. In the chapters to come the One is often impending and implied but the issues surrounding it are only touched upon (most directly in Chapter 2). I wish to stress here that what Plotinus has to say about Intellect must be seen against the context of the One which marks the limits of thought. At the same time, for this very reason, I am wary about saying too much about the One, which indeed is beyond any thought and linguistic expression.

II

Each of this book's four chapters has its own prehistory in previous publications. Thus, the two first chapters are in some sense descendants of 'Remarks on the Relation between the One and Intellect in Plotinus', my contribution to John Dillon's Festschrift, *Traditions of Platonism* (Emilsson 1999). This was my first attempt to deal with these aspects of Plotinus' metaphysics. Although some insights remain, the original piece has been expanded and radically transformed beyond recognition. Very little, if anything, of the original is left. The third chapter is an expanded and much revised version of 'Cognition and its Object', which originally appeared in the *The Cambridge Companion to Plotinus* (Emilsson 1996) and of which a shorter version appeared in *Archiv für Geschichte der Philosophie* 77 as 'Plotinus on the Object of Thought' (Emilsson 1995). The fourth chapter is a much expanded and thoroughly rewritten version of 'Discursive and Non-Discursive Thought', which appeared in *Non-conceptual Aspects of Experience* (Emilsson 2003).

As this prehistory indicates, my concern with the main theme of each chapter was not originally conceived as a part of the whole which is the present work. I expect that the chapters still reflect this to some extent: even if cross-references between them are fairly frequent, each may be considered as a more or less independent essay on its topic. Some years ago it crossed my mind, however, that there were several threads that connect these studies of mine so that something would be gained by bringing them together. Thus, the idea of the book was conceived.

Even if I cite and otherwise draw on Plotinus' *Enneads* quite indiscriminately, the reader will note that one treatise in particular, V.3, which is very late (number 49 on Porphyry's chronological list of Plotinus' treatises) and to which Porphyry gave the title 'On the knowing hypostases and that which is beyond', seems to be especially favoured: parts of my text, especially in Chapters 2 and 3, may even read like a commentary on certain passages from this treatise. In a way this is almost incidental, however. I surely make no pretensions of presenting an interpretation of this treatise in general. The main reason why the treatise V.3 turns up so frequently on these pages is simply the fact that it is a treatise that discusses some of my main questions at length and in depth. There are other treatises which also do that, however, especially VI.7 and to a lesser extent some other treatises of *Ennead* V and III.8 and VI.2. I do make use of all these treatises. For some reason—perhaps it is the well-focused way in which Plotinus treats his topics in V.3—I have tended to fall back on it as my main reference. This is, however, in no way premeditated.

The first chapter, 'Emanation and Activity', deals with the interrelated concepts of double activity and emanation. Though important aspects of the conclusions of this chapter are highly relevant for the rest of the book, some of the details may not be so very relevant. In this regard this first chapter stands somewhat apart. Given, however, the significant role these notions play in the *Enneads* in general and that they are indeed highly relevant in all three subsequent chapters, I felt I had better do my best to straighten out the issues of double activity and emanation.

At the outset I presented a rough outline of the Plotinian hierarchy with the One at the top. It was also said that the One is the cause of everything else. Nothing, however, was said about the way in which it causes everything else. It is here that emanation and double activity enter the picture. We might say by way of first approach—though this statement will be radically modified and supplemented—that the way in which the One causes Intellect is by emanating, and that this too is the way in which Intellect causes Soul and Soul in turn the sensible realm. Thus, emanation would appear to be the manner of causation by which the different stages of the hierarchy are created.

Such a theory of emanation is of course one of Plotinus' claims to fame. Nevertheless, it is by no means clear that the *Enneads* contain anything that deserves the label 'a theory of emanation'. There is surely no one word in Plotinus' Greek of which 'emanation' would be the most natural rendering. What we do find, though, in numerous places is 'emanative metaphors', as I shall call them, of fire heating, snow cooling, light-sources illuminating, springs overflowing, and so forth. He also has a notion of procession (*proodos*), which often is combined with such emanative metaphors. A procession in this context means that a cause or principle 'proceeds' so as to make something 'lesser' out of itself. These are the sources of the attribution of a theory of emanation to Plotinus. While these emanative metaphors certainly play a quite important role in Plotinus' philosophy, it would in my view be misleading to make out of them 'a theory of emanation'. For Plotinus' talk of illumination, overflow, and so forth is quite obviously metaphorical.

On the other hand, Plotinus employs a notion (or a theory) that has been called 'the doctrine of double activity'. This doctrine, which is stated in Aristotelian terminology, may be said to be an abstract or philosophical expression of the point of the emanative metaphors. That is to say: as fire, say, has an internal activity of its own, in virtue of which it is fire, while also emanating heat to its environment, so the Plotinian principles are characterized by an internal activity as well as by an external one by which the level below the given principle is constituted. It is shown how the so-called double activity is a way of discussing in philosophical terms what Plotinus' celebrated emanation metaphors also are intended to convey. So what 'emanates' corresponds to the external activity, while that from which it 'emanates' corresponds to the internal one. This double act doctrine is to be regarded as the general account of causation of the stages in the hierarchy.

The notions of internal and external acts are also intimately connected to another pair of notions which are well-known trademarks of Platonism, viz. 'paradigm' and 'image'. As we already have had occasion to note, the internal act corresponds to the paradigm, whereas the external act corresponds to its image. The external act is indeed an image, a less perfect manifestation, of the original internal act. As I see this, Plotinus is through his doctrine of the two acts saying something about the relationship between causes and effects, Platonically understood. Plato too discusses this relationship, but mostly by means of considerations from below, from the viewpoint of the recipient that is said to imitate or participate in its cause. There is little in Plato about this relationship from the viewpoint of the cause, except for some suggestive but cryptic remarks in the *Timaeus* and the allegory of the Sun in the *Republic*. It is as if Plotinus is seeking to fill out the picture here according to his own understanding of Plato, of course. I take up those aspects of Plotinus' views on activity that link it to the emanative metaphors as well as its relationship to the Platonic notions of paradigms and imitation.

The chapter starts by making a list of the features that seem to be essential to the double act doctrine in order to determine what the doctrine really amounts to. This, however, involves us in a difficulty. It turns out that

Plotinus seems to wish to say that any internal act is both self-contained in the sense that it does not essentially involve anything outside (below) itself. At the same time, he maintains that the internal act is the cause of the external one that is supposed to follow from it by necessity. So one central question of this first chapter is whether Plotinus can consistently maintain both that the internal act is self-contained and that it causes the external act. This whole issue turns out to be rather complicated. It forces us to glance into contemporary action theory and it leads us into a discussion of some difficult passages in Plotinus' account of Aristotle's categories in VI.1. Here we find Plotinus' most detailed account of some of the central notions relating to this issue.

Stated succinctly, the conclusion about the relationship between the internal and the external act is that there is only one act involved, at least in the sense that there is only one exertion: the agent of the internal act doesn't do anything in addition to what it does in engaging in the internal act in order to produce the external one. Nevertheless, it remains somewhat unclear whether in Plotinus' view the external act is a different description of the internal one, in terms of its effects outside itself, or whether he regards it as a different event, though a direct and necessary consequence of the internal act. The fullest passage on the matter, V.4.2, suggests rather the latter.

I spend quite a few pages on Plotinus' example in VI.3 of the relationship between walking and leaving a trace. Here he describes walking as an absolute (*apolytos*) activity, which nevertheless produces an external effect (a trace, *ichnos*). I suggest that this may serve as a model for the relationship between the internal and the external acts in general: the external act is absolute in the sense that in itself it is not transitive, in itself it is not the doing of something unto another. This, however, is compatible with its leaving a trace of itself in something else.

The second half of the chapter deals with the sources of Plotinus' double act doctrine, a matter of some scholarly controversy. I argue that: (1) The sources are Aristotelian and Platonic, not Stoic in a relevant way as some scholars have suggested. (2) The Aristotelian influence, however, does not primarily lie in the model of first and second acts as instantiated by 'teaching' and 'being taught', as has been suggested; it lies rather in Platonic elements in Aristotle instantiated by his account of the relationship between the prime mover and the first movable. (3) The Platonic sources for this doctrine are not to be sought in one or two Platonic passages that gave Plotinus an idea on which he expands (as some accounts suggest). Rather the double act doctrine is to be seen as Plotinus' general interpretation of Plato's account of the relationship between causes (principles) and what they are causes (principles) of, e.g. the Ideas and what participates in them, the soul and actions in the sensible world. So double activity is something Plotinus sees all over in Plato, though he tends to describe it partly in Aristotelian terminology.

In the second chapter, entitled 'The Genesis of Intellect', I address questions relating to the derivation of Intellect from the One. The One has an external act, often described in the literature as inchoate intellect (Plotinus sometimes calls it 'Sight not yet seeing'). This inchoate intellect converts or turns back towards the One. It cannot apprehend the One as it is in itself and must be satisfied with an image of it. This image is turned into the actualized intellect, which also is the sphere of true being (the Platonic Ideas).

We encounter here one of the most difficult and confusing topics in all of Plotinus' philosophy. The first section of the chapter lays out the outline of Plotinus' view, as I see it, presents the essentials of my interpretation of it, and raises questions to be addressed in subsequent sections.

The emergence of Intellect amounts to the emergence of otherness and, thereby, of plurality. Actually, when Intellect has come about, plurality of two kinds seems to have emerged: the duality of subject and object of thought, and the plurality within the object; for, Plotinus argues, thinking requires a subject/object distinction and an object of thought must be a manifold. In the second section of the chapter I take up the question whether and how these two kinds of otherness or plurality are related. I eventually argue that they can indeed be seen as two sides of the same coin, that neither of them is primary in relation to the other, and that each presupposes the other.

The argument for this conclusion involves us in several other difficult and delicate issues. We face for instance the question why there cannot be a subject/object distinction without any diversity in the object. In context this means: why cannot the inchoate intellect have the One in its simplicity as its object? To be sure, this would not be an object of *thought*. We may go along with Plotinus in holding that any object of thought must be diversified. Still, there may seem to be room for a kind of 'mental' relationship to something simple which is not thought.

These questions lead us to consider the nature of the inchoate intellect's apprehension of the One in its conversion and to compare this with some passages where Plotinus seems to suggest a mystical union with the One. I come to the conclusion, following Bussanich (1987), that the so-called mystical union is a rather different affair from the inchoate intellect's grasp of the One. The latter indeed turns out to be a grasp that cannot be held. It is something which must be postulated in order to safeguard the idea that the content of Intellect indeed is an appearance of the One, but it is not, as it were, a position that can be rendered stable: even if the inchoate intellect sees the One in its simplicity, it cannot hold on to this vision.

In the final section of the chapter I return to the question about the relationship between the two kinds of otherness, the otherness of subject and object and the otherness within the object. I suggest here that the two kinds really coincide in the case of Intellect's self-thinking, which is supposed to be what the thinking of Intellect consists in. That is to say: when Intellect thinks its contents, the Ideas, it thinks in the first person. If this were to be rendered propositionally—in Chapter IV I discuss the question whether Intellect thinks propositionally and come to a negative conclusion—Intellect's thought would have to be rendered by 'I am being', 'I move (am motion)', and other such statements in the first person whereby Intellect asserts its identity. In general these thoughts have the form 'I am F', where 'F' holds the place of any of Intellect's content. This suggestion turns out to have excellent textual support. If it holds, Plotinus' notion of self-thinking is significantly different from that of Aristotle, on whom he, however, heavily relies here, and importantly different from what is usually suggested in the literature. Moreover, it solves the problem we set out from in this chapter, namely, how the two kinds of otherness are related. For if the 'first thought' is 'I am F', there is a differentiation between subject and object, corresponding to the 'I' and the 'I being F'. But there is also a differentiation within the object of the thought in that the object is 'I being F', which is not a simple object but a variegated one.

The upshot of this interpretation is that for Plotinus self-consciousness is an integral aspect of Intellect's thought in a straightforward way: its thoughts are essentially first-personal self-identifications. There are doctrines of thought claiming that any thought is accompanied by an awareness of self or that any thought takes place from a subjective point of view. Plotinus might or might not have accepted such views. The view I ascribe to him, however, concerning Intellect's thought is different and more radical than these: it says that the primary kind of thought asserts about its subject what it is and that it does so in such a way that the subject cannot fail to think that the assertion indeed is about itself.

In the third chapter I deal with the internal structure of Intellect. In particular the following themes are discussed: (1) Plotinus' internalization of the objects of Intellect's thought (intelligibles, Platonic Ideas, being). I argue that he sees this as necessary if knowledge of being itself is to be possible, for he holds that any cognition of objects external to the cognizing subject at most yields cognition of the object through the object's external act; hence, this is at most cognition of an image of the object. If the object is to be known by its internal activity, it must be internal to, in a sense identical with, the cognizing faculty. (2) I discuss what this internality of the object of thought to Intellect amounts to: Plotinus has to find a fine balance between abolishing the distinction between subject and object entirely, in which case his intellect would seem to collapse into the One, and keeping subject and object so separated that he will face the problem he himself raises for theories that maintain an external object. I suggest that he attempts to solve this by a theory according to which the activity of thinking is the basic notion. Thinker and object emerge as necessary moments of the activity. (3) How does this account, which in many respects reflects Aristotle, relate to the account given in Chapter 2 of Intellect's self-thinking as a first-personal self-identification? I argue that there is no inconsistency between the two accounts. The account of Chapter 2 in itself contains elements from the 'Aristotelian' account and what is new in it can be accommodated to such an account. (4) I discuss Plotinus' strange doctrine that each object of thought also is an intellect. It is shown that the preceding account, which takes the act of thought as the basic concept, can help us make sense of this. (5) I address the role some sceptical arguments may have played in the development of Plotinus' account of Intellect. Some of the moves he makes in his doctrine of Intellect appear as if designed to secure 'knowledge of the real', at least for a divine mind, in the face of sceptical arguments. It is as if Plotinus wished to endow his Intellect with characteristics that would render it immune to any sort of sceptical attacks. This is evident in two passages in particular: in V.3.5, where the issue whether Intellect can know itself is considered against the background of a sceptical objection that claims self-knowledge to be impossible because it is bound to be knowledge of a part by a different part; and in V.5.1, where Plotinus argues for his Internality Thesis on the ground that unless the intelligibles are internal to the Intellect it would be unable to recognize them, since *ex hypothesi* they are its standards of judgement for anything. I shall return to these points later in this introduction. (6) Finally, I address the question in which sense Plotinus may be labelled an idealist. It seems to me that there is no good reason for denying him that label. For Plotinus 'the real', or 'true being', was surely in an important sense mental. That the One is 'beyond thought' does not strike me as a decisive argument against the case for idealism, since the One is after all, among other things, a quasi-mental entity.

Plotinus distinguishes between discursive thought (*dianoia, logismos,* et al.) and non-discursive thought (*noêsis, theôria*). In the fourth chapter I summarize and contrast the properties of both of these modes of thought. Many of the defining characteristics of non-discursive thought have actually emerged in previous chapters. Non-discursive thought is supposed to be (*a*) immediate, (*b*) all at once of the whole sphere, (*c*) of its object itself as opposed to an image of it, (*d*) unerring, (*e*) free from search. It turns out that these characteristics are not just gratuitously connected. That is to say, it is no sheer coincidence that if a mode of thought is non-representational it is also immediate, all at once of the whole sphere the object belongs to and unerring. And vice versa with discursive thought. Not that all the characteristics Plotinus attributes to discursive and non-discursive thought, respectively, follow upon one another by strict logical necessity. They nevertheless form two quite natural clusters so that one can readily see that if something has one of them it may seem natural to attribute the others to it.

One debated issue here that has not been touched upon so far is whether non-discursive thought, i.e. Intellect's thought, is propositional or not. Anthony Lloyd (Lloyd 1970; 1986) and Richard Sorabji (Sorabji 1982; 1983) come to very different conclusions on this question. I take issue with both of them on the ground that each wrongly assumes that complexity of thought amounts to the propositional nature of thought. So I argue, against Lloyd, that non-discursive thought is indeed complex, and against Sorabji that though complex, it need not be propositional. Instead, I propose that we should take the visual metaphors Plotinus is so fond of in describing non-discursive thought seriously: non-discursive thought is in important respects like vision. It is wrong, or at least misleading, to describe ordinary vision as propositional.

This vision-like character of Intellect's thought leads us to the question of the holism of intellect, the view that the intelligibles make up a system in which each one owes its being to its place in the system and in which 'each reflects all'. In order to come to grips with this, I explore an analogy with the sciences Plotinus sometimes uses. As a scientist does not know the theorems of his science in isolation but the knowledge of one theorem is supported by the knowledge of others and of the science as a whole, Intellect knows the intelligibles as a tightly woven web where each item presupposes every other.

Chapter IV ends by some remarks about the question why, according to Plotinus, non-discursive thought is the basic kind of thought and in what sense discursive thought may be said to depend on it. It turns out that there are two senses in which it might be said that non-discursive thought is the primary kind of thought. First, it is the ideal kind of thought in the sense that it is the most complete or perfect kind of thought conceivable. This, however, doesn't by itself render it primary in the sense that it is a cause or precondition of discursive thought, which is a view Plotinus also adopts. I make some suggestions about how he conceives of this dependence. In particular I argue that the contrast between discursive thought by means of images or representations and non-discursive thought of the things themselves is to be seen on analogy with the difference between knowledge by direct experience and knowledge by means of reports. So understood non-discursive thought is no doubt primary in the sense of being a precondition of discursive thought.

III

I would now like to turn to a different matter: the methodology and in general the approach to the texts used in this book. I can foresee two kinds of readers who might reproach me for different, indeed opposite, kinds of shortcomings. I wish now to present a little justification of my way of going about the material to each kind. Whether or not this will appease them is of course a different matter.

There are the philosophically oriented readers who, if they should happen to read the pages to come, may recognize a certain philosophical spirit on them but at the same time feel that their expectations are constantly frustrated by a lack of detailed analysis and by more or less inconclusive conclusions, philosophically speaking. These readers would probably like to have seen somewhat fewer textual citations and not a word about the World-Soul and other obsolete entities. I can imagine they would have wished me to pursue the logic of the derivation of the rest from the One more stringently; they would have liked me to make out of the account of double activity something that they could more readily compare with contemporary theories of causation and action; they would like to have seen me analysing the holism I attribute to Plotinus in greater detail, where I would show how it compares with contemporary holism about belief and meaning; and so forth. While I see their point, I must say in my defence that I am not at all in the business that these wishes are expecting of me. I occasionally make use of contemporary philosophical theories where I have happened to find them useful in my attempt to understand what Plotinus is saying, but only to the point of rigour that the texts seem to me to allow for. And I am definitely not at all concerned with making him up to date, trying to present his thought as a viable alternative today or anything of the sort (which, of course, is not to imply that he may not be).

A different kind of reader, the historically-philologically oriented one, may accuse me of being ahistorical, of taking Plotinus too much as if he were a professor at another contemporary university whose thought can be expounded in more or less contemporary philosophical terms, largely ignoring his place and time, remote and immediate predecessors, and the spiritual mood of his age. Well, I would not find such a criticism quite fair, because I do seek to take such things into account, even to a greater extent than may be explicitly shown on the pages. I see the point, however. Indeed, I have very few references to the middle Platonists, the Gnostics, Alexander of Aphrodisias, the Stoics, and other such close background thinkers for the *Enneads*. Even Plato and Aristotle are not particularly prominent on the pages to come, though I do bring them up now and then for comparison and contrast. With the exception of the account of double activity in Sections 7 and 8 of Chapter 1, I am not at all concerned with giving a genealogical account of the views expressed in the *Enneads*.

Our understanding of the very nature of the *Enneads* as a text has been vastly improved by many excellent recent studies, though I believe that here too quite a bit remains to be said. There is still some purely philological work to be done on the *Enneads*: there are quotations, references, and echoes of previous writers still to be detected and analysed. But in particular, I think that more work, primarily philological and historical in method, that seeks to determine Plotinus' intentions and aspirations with his writings, showing us what sort of philosopher he took himself to be, may bear fresh fruit. This may best be done in studies of and commentaries on individual treatises such as are and have been appearing at an increasing rate.

Allowing for all this, the large bulk of recent as well as older Plotinian scholarship is more historically-philologically than philosophically oriented. Some of the more philosophically inspired literature is not well informed. It seems to me that Plotinus can well stand a philosophically focused treatment such as Plato and Aristotle and, by now, the Hellenistic philosophers have often been subjected to. Others have indeed attempted this, and there are many examples of excellent work on Plotinus that provide a fine balance between philosophical and philological considerations. I am indebted to several such studies and do not at all claim the status of a pioneer. Yet it is not at all common to write on Plotinus by a sustained philosophical argument and discussion with his texts. I am not aware of any previous book with the focus on his notion of Intellect that does this—though Anthony Lloyd's *The Anatomy of Neoplatonism* (Lloyd 1990) may come close. With full respect for other kinds of approach, it seems to me that the one adopted here is evidently worth trying. It goes with this kind of approach that an ongoing discussion of sources, the identity of possible adversaries, and other such matters would spoil the flow of reasoning and possibly distract the reader from what really is my primary concern. This will serve as my apology for writing this book in the way it has been written. I shall, however, proceed to make some remarks, not by way of apology, on the kind of writing we find in the *Enneads*, about the difficulties involved in interpreting it, and about my approaches to the problems involved.

IV

The *Enneads* were presumably written in the course of Plotinus' last seventeen years (cf. Porphyry, *Life of Plotinus* 4 and 2), starting when he was approaching 50 and must be assumed to have been fairly mature in his thought. There have been attempts at showing a change of mind or at least significant doctrinal developments in his thought. While there is little doubt that the early treatises—I am not questioning Porphyry's chronological list—tend to be simpler in their structure and way of argumentation than the later ones, attempts at showing a radical change of mind have largely been unsuccessful.

This fact does not, however, prevent Plotinus from saying different and at least prima facie incompatible things about the same subject from time to time. It is just that these cannot so readily be connected with the chronology of the treatises. So if these apparent inconsistencies reflect changes of mind, we would have to suppose that Plotinus changed his mind on some topics rather often. This may occasionally be the case, but I suspect that by and large the apparent inconsistencies are to be explained in a different way.

The passages of the *Enneads* dealing with the topics that are my main concern here constitute no exception from what has just been said. Let me give a few examples. Plotinus sometimes speaks as if it is quite natural to attribute a kind of activity (*energeia*) to the One (V.4.2; VI.8.20), at other times he seems to reject the legitimacy of such an attribution (VI.7.17; VI.8.16). Sometimes he writes in such a way that one wonders whether there can be any distinction between subject and object of thought in Intellect (cf. V.3.5). At other times, usually in fact, he speaks of such a distinction as a matter of course. Sometimes he emphatically denies that Intellect undertakes any kind of search (*zêtêsis*) (V.3.5, 22; V.9.7, 10–11), it possesses its object; on occasion, however, he attributes search to it (V.3.10, 50–1). He sometimes speaks without any reservations as if Intellect's thoughts can be rendered by sentences. Admittedly, these sentences don't constitute any ordinary shop-talk, they are rather philosophical and abstract, but ordinary sentences nevertheless (V.3.10; 13); at other times he suggests that these thoughts are of a kind that our discursive reason employing its ordinary sentences is incapable of expressing (V.8.6). He sometimes suggests that the One and Intellect, in proceeding, give something of themselves to what follows upon them; at other times he says that they do not. And so forth.

The problems such apparent inconsistencies give rise to must of course be tackled one by one in context. It turns out that the inconsistency can often be explained away as purely superficial. There is, however, a certain pattern in Plotinus that is not to be overlooked. On many delicate issues it is as if he wishes to say both 'yes' and 'no', or in a way 'yes', in another way 'no'. Sometimes he says both 'yes' and 'no' virtually in the same breath. Occasionally this may be a matter of style more than anything else. When he for instance says of a principle that it 'gives itself and doesn't give itself'

(IV.9.5), he might have explicated himself, as he often does elsewhere, by saying that the product arising from the principle is to some degree similar to it and that the principle must to that extent have given something of itself to the product. On the other hand, he also believes that the principle is not in the least affected by this act of image-making and that it loses nothing of itself by it; in this sense it doesn't give itself. In this case, I believe, the air of contradiction can easily have been eradicated—even if the doctrine behind it may remain something of a puzzle.

In some other cases, however, I suspect that the apparent contradiction lies deeper: Plotinus is trying to say things that he thinks cannot be properly expressed in ordinary language. This is surely the case, for instance, with his statements about the internal activity of the One. Strictly speaking neither activity nor anything else can be ascribed to the One. Nevertheless, he thinks that if one were *per impossibile* to describe the One as it is in itself, it would be natural to attribute activity to it. More or less the same goes for the apparent contradiction mentioned above about Intellect speaking discursively: intellect thinks but it doesn't use words or sentences in its thinking (on the issue of talking and writing about the non-discursive, see Rappe 2000). Plotinus, however, when accounting for Intellect's thought not only uses words to describe it (that goes without saying), he also attributes words and sentences to it. He even says that Intellect 'says' certain things. Here he is expressing in language thought that, according to him, is essentially independent of language: linguistic expression of it is at best an inferior image of what it really is (cf. V.8.6). In any case, Intellect is supposed to be atemporal and non-spatial. The vocabulary of our language is adapted to describe the sensible world which is crucially different in these and other respects (cf. VI.5.2, 1 ff.). This means that in his accounts of the supra-discursive sphere, i.e. Intellect and the One, Plotinus often uses words metaphorically as a hint and they cannot be taken at face value. But at which value then are they to be taken? Obviously none that can be rendered by alternative words.

I mention all this not only because it is interesting and relevant in itself, as indeed it is, but also because just like Plotinus himself a significant bulk of whose writings are an attempt to say discursively in words something that avowedly cannot be said, much of what I will be discussing, discursively in language, of course, deals with matters for which that kind of treatment, according to the author we are dealing with, is not fit. This situation not only raises the question of whether what I have to say can be taken as an adequate account of what Plotinus means. It also sometimes raises the question of consistency for me. I have found myself in one chapter taking a Plotinian 'no' quite seriously and sought to expound the reasons for it, while in a different chapter, or elsewhere in the same chapter, focusing on his 'yes', which I have tried to give the same sort of fair treatment. A case in point is the way in which the thinker and the object thought in Intellect are both the same and different. This is a central theme in Chapters 2 and 3. On this subject Plotinus apparently wishes to maintain a position that allows for some distinction between thinker and thought while at the same time insisting that they are more unified than e.g. the different parts of a bicycle: they amount to one thing in a stronger sense than that. With adequate provisos and cross-references, I hope to have avoided attributing blatantly contradictory views to Plotinus on this and other such topics. Whether I have left him intact with a discursively intelligible position, I leave to the reader to judge.

V

As is to be expected, the book contains quite a few quotations from the *Enneads*. I quote rather fully, i.e. rather than citing a sentence or two that may contain the bare point at issue in each case, I seek to provide some of the context of the passages I discuss. The readers are then in a better position to form an opinion of the claims made. Often the lengthier quotations also serve as a kind of basis to which I repeatedly return. For the translation of the quoted passages I use A. H. Armstrong's translations in the Loeb Classical Library as my basis. This is no doubt the best English translation. A number of times, however, Armstrong's translation appears modified, in some cases significantly, though there may be no special note of that. For the Greek-reading readers' convenience I have supplied the Greek text for all passages I am seriously engaged with in the footnotes. Though based on Henry–Schwyzer's *editio maior* (H-S[1]) of the Thesaurus Linguae Graecae electronic publication, I have changed this text so that it for the most part complies with their *editio minor* (H-S[2]).

In the references to the *Enneads*, 'V.3.10, 18–19', for example, means 'the fifth *Ennead*, third treatise, tenth chapter, lines eighteen and nineteen'. References such as 'V.3.10–11' and 'V.3.10; 13', on the other hand, mean 'the fifth *Ennead*, third treatise, chapters ten and eleven' and 'the fifth

Ennead, third treatise, chapter ten and chapter thirteen, respectively. A thin reference such as '3.10' or '10, 13–15' presupposes a previous reference and may mean, depending on context, 'V.3.10' (if V.3 is the previous reference) or, in the latter case, 'V.3.10, 13–15'. Only occasionally, when I find this relevant, do I give Porphyry's chronological number of a Plotinian treatise in brackets after the treatise number.

1

Emanation and Activity

This is, if we may say so, the first act of generation: the One, perfect because it seeks nothing, has nothing, and needs nothing, overflows, as it were, and its superabundance makes something other than itself. This, when it has come into being, turns back upon the One and is filled, and becomes Intellect by looking towards it. Its halt and turning towards that other [the One] constitutes Being, its gaze upon it, Intellect.[1]

(V.2.1, 7–12)

These lines from *Ennead* V.2.1 are an account by Plotinus himself of the generation of Intellect and being from the One. Even if this is a quite concise account, many of the central ideas are present. Let me begin by giving a somewhat fuller outline. Intellect, we see here, is derived from the One, as is everything else. To the One pertain two kinds of activities or acts (*energeiai*) that are not mentioned by that name here: an internal activity and an external one.[2] The external act is usually described with the aid of emanative metaphors as some kind of efflux or illumination from the One itself ('overflow' here) or, which may come to the same thing, as an image of the internal act. The One's external activity is the first step in the

---

[1] V.2.1, 7–12: καὶ πρώτη οἷον γέννησις αὕτη· ὂν γὰρ τέλειον τῷ μηδὲν ζητεῖν μηδὲ ἔχειν μηδὲ δεῖσθαι οἷον ὑπερερρύη καὶ τὸ ὑπερπλῆρες αὐτοῦ πεποίηκεν ἄλλο· τὸ δὲ γενόμενον εἰς αὐτὸ ἐπεστράφη καὶ ἐπληρώθη καὶ ἐγένετο πρὸς αὐτὸ βλέπον καὶ νοῦς οὗτος. Καὶ ἡ μὲν πρὸς ἐκεῖνο στάσις αὐτοῦ τὸ ὂν ἐποίησεν, ἡ δὲ πρὸς αὐτὸ θέα τὸν νοῦν.

[2] For the internal activity of the One see e.g. V.4.2, 27 ff; V.6.6, 8–11; VI.8.20. Plotinus sometimes also says, however, that the One is beyond activity: I.7.1, 17–20; V.3.12, 22 ff. At least one reason for denying internal activity to the One emerges from I.7.1: because the One is beyond being, it transcends activity. This argument evidently presupposes that activity implies being. In VI.8.20, 9–10, however, he explicitly says that activity may be without Being (*ousia*). In any case, Plotinus evidently believed that the One has an internal 'character' that can be likened to activity and which is responsible for the external act of the One. See Bussanich 1988, esp. ad V.6.6, 1 ff. and VI.8.16, 15–18, and Gerson 1994: 26 and 235, n. 28.

generation of Intellect. It is sometimes identified as inchoate Intellect or potential intellect and likened to 'sight not yet seeing'. The fully-fledged Intellect comes about by a conversion (*epistrophê*) of the inchoate intellect towards the One as a result of which the former becomes informed. This conversion is commonly described, as here, by means of visual metaphors: The inchoate Intellect 'looks' back to the One and 'is filled' by it. The potential, inchoate intellect is then no longer merely potential, and by this stage we have an actual Intellect identifiable as the sphere of being and, which is the same thing, the sphere of Platonic Ideas.

This account leaves of course much to be explained. There arise for instance fundamental questions of the following sort: Given that everything else is derived from the One, could we start with just what we know about the One and tell a logically compelling or even just a reasonable story about how the fully-fledged Intellect comes to be? Or would we have to add a number of premisses, perhaps quite arbitrary ones, in order to arrive at Intellect? Or is the idea of deriving the rest from the One in a more or less logical manner somehow misconceived? More specifically, we can distinguish two questions here: First, granting that the One is some kind of internal activity, why does it have an external one in addition? What precisely is the relationship between internal and external activity? Secondly, taking the idea of the One's double activity for granted, we may ask how conversion enters the story. Is the conversion an entirely new moment or is it something we should have been able to foresee from the beginning?

Double activity and conversion are terms of art in Plotinus. His accounts of the processes these terms refer to, however, are highly metaphorical. The question stated above, whether one could give a cogent account of the generation of Intellect, boils down to the question to what extent it is possible to fit the metaphors into a single account. For the metaphors Plotinus uses here are quite diverse: the One's having an external activity at all is most frequently described in terms of the pregnancy and generative nature of what is perfect;[3] this may be mingled with emanative metaphors of overflow (see e.g. V.1.6, 7; V.2.1, 8) or illumination (V.1.6, 28–30; V.3.12, 39–44). The informing

---

[3] Cf. V.1.6, 37–8; V.2.1, 7–9; V.4.1, 23–31. Plotinus' view that what is *teleion* produces something like itself no doubt claims Platonic authority in *Timaeus* 29e, the celebrated passage about the god's ungrudging nature (cf. V.4.1, 34–6). Plotinus may also draw on Aristotle here, who says that a living being that is *teleion* reproduces (*De an.* II, 415a 26–8). The sense of *teleion* here, however, is presumably 'mature' rather than 'perfect'.

of the inchoate Intellect is, as we already noted, most frequently described by means of visual metaphors often in combination with desiderative ones. This diversity is a serious obstacle to giving a rationally cogent account: there is no smooth passage from talk of efflux or begetting to talk of vision. Another source of difficulty is the fact that Plotinus' language in his accounts of the genesis of Intellect suggests a process with a beginning and an end. For instance, the conversion appears as subsequent to the constitution of the inchoate Intellect. However, this takes place 'prior' to the emergence of time. What 'happens' at the levels of the One and Intellect is outside time so that there can be no question of temporal process here. Nevertheless, the language Plotinus uses to describe the genesis of Intellect from the One is unmistakably the language of events and it is not clear how we are to think about this at all without the terms suggesting a process in time. But if we are bound to use the language of events, it seems that we are entangled in a net of notions which fail to capture the intended nature of the case.

These are pervasive and difficult questions. In the course of this book something will be said about most of them, though it should be confessed that the last question about the application of temporal notions to the atemporal remains unaddressed and unresolved. In Chapter 2 in particular I shall have something to say about the conversion part of the story. In this first chapter, however, I shall focus on one aspect of what has just been told: the nature of double activity. How is it supposed to work? What is the relationship between the internal and the external act? These and related questions will be our main concern on the following pages. In the final section of the chapter, I shall also offer some suggestions about the sources of Plotinus' notion of double activity.

1. Internal and External Activity

In the treatise 'How that which is after the first comes from the first, and on the One' (V.4) we find what is probably Plotinus' fullest account of internal and external activity.[4] In the context of explaining the generation of Intellect from the One, he writes:

---

[4] See also e.g. II.9.8, 23–4; IV.5.7, 13–23 (on light); V.1.6, 28–53; V.3.7, 13–34; V.9.8, 11–19; VI.2.22, 26–9, VI.7.21, 4–6. The phenomenon of the two acts is alluded to in many other passages, though not explicitly mentioned.

When, therefore, the intelligible[5] abides 'in its own proper way of life' [*Tim.* 42 e] that which comes into being does come into being from it, but from it as it abides unchanged.... But how, when that abides unchanged, does Intellect come into being? In each and every thing there is an activity which belongs to the Being[6] (*ousia*) and one which goes out from the Being; and that which belongs to Being is the activity which is each particular thing, and the other activity derives from that first one, and necessarily follows it in every respect, being different from the thing itself: as in fire there is a heat which constitutes its Being, and another which comes into being from that primary heat when fire exercises the activity which is native to its Being in abiding unchanged as fire. So it is also in the intelligible; and much more so, since while it [the first principle] abides 'in its proper way of life', the activity generated from its perfection and its coexistent activity acquires substantial existence, since it comes from a great power, the greatest of all, and arrives at being and Being: for that other is beyond Being.[7] (V.4.2, 21–37)

The first modern study which focuses on the notions of internal and external acts (or 'activities', I use both terms) is Rutten (1956).[8] He claims (1956: 101) that this distinction 'plays a central role in Plotinus' philosophy'.

---

[5] What is called 'the intelligible' (*to noêton*) in the early treatise V.4—the seventh on Porphyry's chronological list—is what normally is called the One or the Good. Plotinus does not use these terms for his first principle in this treatise.

[6] Not entirely happily I have chosen to render *ousia* as Being (with an initial capital) in translations of Plotinus' text. What makes me unhappy about it is that it is not conventional. Both the conventional terms, however, 'substance' or 'essence', strike me as potentially misleading. The question may be raised whether it is not important to keep *on* (being) and *ousia* distinct. Plotinus himself after all explicitly mentions a distinction between the two in II.6.1, 1 ff.: being (*on*) is along with motion, rest, identity, and difference one of the constituents of Being (*ousia*) which is the totality of these. It is not clear, however, that he endorses this proposal, since he continues to say e.g. that motion in the intelligible world is *ousia*. As Corrigan (1996: 106) notes, *on* and *ousia* are generally coterminous. In a private conversation Donald Morrison once expressed the opinion concerning Aristotle that *ousia* was merely an honorific word for being, *on*. I suspect there is something to his view, also with respect to Plotinus. Hence, I capitalize in order to keep some distinction and to pay due respect.

[7] V.4.2, 21–37: Μένοντος οὖν αὐτοῦ ἐν τῷ οἰκείῳ ἤθει ἐξ αὐτοῦ μὲν τὸ γινόμενον γίνεται, μένοντος δὲ γίνεται. Ἐπεὶ οὖν ἐκεῖνο μένει νοητόν, τὸ γινόμενον γίνεται νόησις· νόησις δὲ οὖσα καὶ νοοῦσα ἀφ' οὗ ἐγένετο—ἄλλο γὰρ οὐκ ἔχει—νοῦς γίγνεται, ἄλλο οἷον νοητὸν καὶ οἷον ἐκεῖνο καὶ μίμημα καὶ εἴδωλον ἐκείνου. Ἀλλὰ πῶς μένοντος ἐκείνου γίνεται; Ἐνέργεια ἡ μέν ἐστι τῆς οὐσίας, ἡ δ' ἐκ τῆς οὐσίας ἑκάστου· καὶ ἡ μὲν τῆς οὐσίας αὐτό ἐστιν ἐνέργεια ἕκαστον, ἡ δὲ ἀπ' ἐκείνης, ἣν δεῖ παντὶ ἕπεσθαι ἐξ ἀνάγκης ἑτέραν οὖσαν αὐτοῦ· οἷον καὶ ἐπὶ τοῦ πυρὸς ἡ μέν τίς ἐστι συμπληροῦσα τὴν οὐσίαν θερμότης, ἡ δὲ ἀπ' ἐκείνης ἤδη γινομένη ἐνεργοῦντος ἐκείνου τὴν σύμφυτον τῇ οὐσίᾳ ἐν τῷ μένειν πῦρ. Οὕτω δὴ κἀκεῖ· καὶ πολὺ πρότερον ἐκεῖ μένοντος αὐτοῦ ἐν τῷ οἰκείῳ ἤθει ἐκ τῆς ἐν αὐτῷ τελειότητος καὶ συνούσης ἐνεργείας ἡ γεννηθεῖσα ἐνέργεια ὑπόστασιν λαβοῦσα, ἅτε ἐκ μεγάλης δυνάμεως, μεγίστης μὲν οὖν ἁπασῶν, εἰς τὸ εἶναι καὶ οὐσίαν ἦλθεν· ἐκεῖνο γὰρ ἐπέκεινα οὐσίας ἦν.

[8] Valuable treatments of double activity may be found in Smith 1974: 1–19; Lloyd 1990: 98–105, 1987: 167–70; Gerson 1994: 23–37; and Narbonne 2001: 61–79.

Others, e.g. Smith (1974: 7), Lloyd (1990: 98), and Narbonne (2001: 62), have since followed suit with similar evaluations. It is certainly right that the doctrine of the two acts crops up frequently and in central contexts. To my knowledge, however, there is to date no detailed study of it.

The doctrine is phrased in what may appear as properly philosophical terms and may therefore carry a certain promise of enabling us to detect a philosophically manageable pattern in Plotinus' unbridled metaphors of image-making and emanation. Yet, the doctrine of the two acts cannot be said to be altogether lucid itself. Nor is it clear that it can, after all, stand by itself unaided by the metaphors that typically surround it: we may have to appeal to the metaphors for determining the exact sense of the doctrine. But let us in any case see what we can extract about each of the two kinds of activity and their relationship by focusing on the passage just cited from V.4.2 and some other passages.

(1) We see here that double activity applies all over in Plotinus' universe. We find an internal activity (*energeia tês ousias*) and an external activity (*energeia ek tês ousias*) 'in each and every thing,' he says. Thus, every distinct stage in the ontology, and it seems every natural substance, has an internal activity accompanied by an external one (cf. also IV.3.7, 17). Note further that Plotinus does not merely say that *in* each thing there is an internal activity, he goes on to say that this activity constitutes each thing, and a few lines below he says that it 'completes the Being'. By this he means that it constitutes the full essence of each thing. So the internal activity of each thing defines it. This internal activity is, in turn, accompanied by an external activity. I deliberately use the vague expression 'accompanied by' in order not to prejudge the issue of the nature of the relationship. Plotinus says that the external activity 'is derived from' and 'follows' the internal one. The external activity becomes a kind of matter for the next stage below, which is brought to completion by a conversion towards its source, the internal activity. This conversion, I take it, constitutes the internal activity of the next stage, which in turn is accompanied by a new external activity. Processes of this kind are repeated until we reach matter itself which, on account of the increasing weakness the further down one goes, is quite impotent and thus has no external act. Or, to put it somewhat differently, there is reason to believe that when the low level of mere bodies is reached, plurality is so advanced that theoretically there is no room for greater dispersion. Hence, the ultimate forms in matter are impotent and do

not make anything below themselves. So it is not quite true that absolutely everything has an external act even if most things do: matter surely doesn't. But then matter is hardly anything according to Plotinus. We may gather from this that internal and external activities are somehow the backbone of Plotinus' grand view of things.

(2) The external act is caused by or derived from the internal one. Furthermore, according to our passage above, it is a necessary consequence of it. In the lines before the quotation Plotinus says that the Intellect is a representation (*mimêma*) and image (*eidôlon*) of the One, and some other passages state explicitly that the external act is an image of the internal one (IV.5.7, 16–18; V.1.6, 33; V.2.1, 15–21; V.3.7, 23–4). This is significant. I mentioned above that the doctrine of the two acts tends to come mingled with several metaphors in Plotinus. One such metaphor, which perhaps by Plotinus' time no longer counts as a genuine metaphor in Platonist circles, is that of an image, implying a corresponding paradigm. In any event the doctrine of the two acts is interlocked with the Platonistic expressions for a paradigm and its image. We shall see later on that Plotinus presumably thought that the Aristotle-inspired doctrine of double act could be used to underpin the Platonic relationship between a paradigm and its image.

(3) We see here a typical emanation analogy, that of fire, which the context shows to be just that, an analogy or illustration through something similar and familiar: the internal act is supposed to correspond to the native heat in the fire itself, whereas the external act corresponds to the heat surrounding the fire (cf. II.6.3, 16 ff.; V.1.3, 9–10; 6, 34; V.3.7, 23–4). Elsewhere there are similar analogies in terms of cold, smell, and light (V.1.6, 34–7; IV.5.7). However, even if the physical phenomena are used as analogies or metaphors for causation at the intelligible level, double activity as such is not to be taken as a mere analogy or metaphor. As Lloyd (1987: 167–70; 1990: 100–1) notes, Plotinus undoubtedly held that double activity applies to the ordinary physical phenomena induced to illustrate it. This seems indeed to be confirmed by his saying that it can be found in 'each and every thing'. However, as Gerson (1994: 235, n. 29) remarks, double activity will nevertheless not apply in quite the same way to intelligible and sensible entities.

(4) Plotinus frequently says, though not here in V.4.2, that the external act is not 'cut off from' (I.7.1, 27; V.2.1, 13–22; V.3.12, 44; VI.2.22, 33–5; VI.4.3, 8–10; cf. VI.4.9–10) the internal one or that the external act

'depends on' the internal one.[9] By this he wishes to make the point that in spite of being 'in something else', the external act still depends on the internal one: should the internal one cease to be, so would the external one, just as a mirror image depends on the mirrored object and is not 'cut off' from it (cf. VI.4.9, 36–10, 30). The expression 'not cut off from' comes from Aristotle who uses it to make the same or a similar point: even if the activity of an agent is in the patient that is different from the agent, the activity is not 'cut off from the agent'; it is a case of one thing acting in another.[10]

(5) In connection with double activity, Plotinus frequently notes that the cause, the internal activity, is not changed by acting. He typically expresses this by saying that the cause 'remains' or 'abides' (*menei*), as we see here. Philosophically speaking, Armstrong is quite right in translating *menei* in such contexts by 'remains unchanged'. Plotinus has at his resources also other means of expressing what seems to be more or less the same thought. Thus, he may for instance say of a principle much to the same effect that it does not leave itself (*apoleipein*) (cf. V.1.2, 9; VI.4.2, 15; 8, 28; 11, 5–6) or that it in no way is diminished (*elattousthai*) (VI.9.5, 37). He even paradoxically asserts that a cause, in this case the soul, gives itself and does not give itself (IV.9.5, 3–5). By saying that the soul gives itself, he is doubtless referring to the soul's external act by which it produces an image of itself. When he says that it doesn't give itself, he is referring to the view we are considering, i.e. that in producing an image it loses nothing and remains totally unchanged.

A complement to the point about the cause's abiding unchanged is the view of the internal act as self-contained. This is not explicit in our passage above but can be seen e.g. in the following passage:

But peace and quiet (*hesychia*) for Intellect is not going out of Intellect, but the peace and quiet of Intellect is an activity taking its rest from all other activities, since for other beings also, which are left in peace and quiet by other things, there remains their own proper activity, above all for those whose being is not potential but actual. The being [of Intellect], therefore, is activity, and there is nothing to

---

[9] The most common word that is used to express the dependence of the external act on the internal one is probably *anartan*, 'to depend'. Cf. I.7.1, 26; I.8.2, 3 etc. Cf. *exartan* IV.5.7, 40; V.3.8, 14.

[10] Aristotle uses the same expression, *ouk apotetmēmenē*, in *Phys.* III, 202b 8 in explaining how the actualization/activity of an agent such as a teacher takes place in the patient, in this case the pupil: the learning which takes place in the pupil is not cut off from the activity of the teacher.

which the activity is directed; so it is self-directed.... For it had to be first in itself, then also directed to something else, or with something else coming from it made like itself, just as in the case of fire it is because it is previously fire in itself and has the activity of fire that it is able to produce a trace of itself in another.[11] (V.3.7, 13–25)

What is said here about 'peace and quiet' in Intellect and 'taking rest from all other activities' implies that the internal activity of Intellect, and no doubt internal activities generally, are self-contained. He sometimes couples this idea of 'peace and quiet' with a phrase borrowed from *Timaeus* 42e (said of the Demiurge): the principles 'abide in their proper way of life', which we saw in the passage from V.4.2 above and which presumably is alluded to in the passage just quoted (cf. also V.2.2, 2; V.3.12, 34). As the passage makes clear, 'peace and quiet' does not mean inactivity, only that the activity is self-contained. The external act, by contrast, is other-directed, and hence not confined to the agent.[12]

Nothing in the passage just cited indicates that the sense of self-containment involved here is such that what is self-contained cannot have effects outside itself. On the contrary, the passage says that what is to have external acts must first be 'in itself', the implication obviously being that what is self-contained can have external acts. So the internal act isn't self-contained in the sense that it has no effects outside itself. This, however, we knew all along. The remark that the internal act 'takes leave of all other activities', however, still leaves me puzzled as to the internal act's relation to the external one. How can what 'takes leave of all other activities' have effects outside itself?

(6) We should finally note that Plotinus' internal activities are also liable to be called powers (*dynameis*). This fact is perhaps not rightly described as an integral part of the doctrine of the two acts itself but it is nevertheless

---

[11] V.3.7, 13–25: Ἀλλὰ νῷ ἡσυχία οὐ νοῦ ἐστιν ἔκστασις, ἀλλ' ἔστιν ἡσυχία τοῦ νοῦ σχολὴν ἄγουσα ἀπὸ τῶν ἄλλων ἐνέργεια· ἐπεὶ καὶ τοῖς ἄλλοις, οἷς ἐστιν ἡσυχία ἑτέρων, καταλείπεται ἡ αὐτῶν οἰκεία ἐνέργεια καὶ μάλιστα, οἷς τὸ εἶναι οὐ δυνάμει ἐστίν, ἀλλὰ ἐνεργείᾳ. Τὸ εἶναι οὖν ἐνέργεια, καὶ οὐδέν, πρὸς ὃ ἡ ἐνέργεια· πρὸς αὑτῷ ἄρα. Ἑαυτὸν ἄρα νοῶν οὕτω πρὸς αὑτῷ καὶ εἰς ἑαυτὸν τὴν ἐνέργειαν ἴσχει. Καὶ γὰρ εἴ τι ἐξ αὐτοῦ, τῷ εἰς αὐτὸν ἐν ἑαυτῷ. Ἔδει γὰρ πρῶτον ἐν ἑαυτῷ, εἶτα καὶ εἰς ἄλλο, ἢ ἄλλο τι ἥκειν ἀπ' αὐτοῦ ὁμοιούμενον αὐτῷ, οἷον καὶ πυρὶ ἐν αὐτῷ πρότερον ὄντι πυρὶ καὶ τὴν ἐνέργειαν ἔχοντι πυρὸς οὕτω τοι καὶ ἴχνος αὐτοῦ δυνηθῆναι ποιῆσαι ἐν ἄλλῳ.

[12] Cf. II.9.8, 22–3: Εἶναι γὰρ αὐτοῦ ἐνέργειαν ἔδει διττήν, τὴν μὲν ἐν ἑαυτῷ, τὴν δὲ εἰς ἄλλο (['Intellect's] activity must be double, one in itself, the other towards another'). Cf. IV.3.10, 37; I.2.6, 16; II.6.3, 13–20; V.3.7, 23–5.

telling about it. Plotinus wishes to distinguish sharply between active and passive powers, between the power of something and being potentially something (II.5.1, 21–37; cf. VI.8.1, 11–13). He suggests in II.5.1 that in referring to the latter kind of power one should stick to the adverbial dative, *dynamei* (potentially), and reserve the nominative *dynamis* to the active kind. As Tornau (1998: 99, n. 63) observes, Plotinus, however, does not consistently stick to this proposal. So *dynamei*, potentially, at least when used of the intelligible realm, usually implies power in the sense of power to act. It is this sense of *dynamis*, the power to do something, which also is an activity. Or conversely, any genuine activity is also a power to do something. This latter formula is equivalent with the claim that anything perfect begets (cf. p. 23 above). What the power in such cases is a power to do is its external act. The power so described, however, is not the external act itself. It is the internal act but referred to as the productive cause of the external one. The power wouldn't be a power to do anything of the sort unless it at the same time was an internal activity in its own right. This aspect of the double act doctrine will be of relevance in Chapter 4.

An instance of this sort of use is to be found in Plotinus' description of the One as the *dynamis pantôn*, the power of all things, i.e. the power to make all things (V.1.7, 9; V.3.15, 31–2; V.4.2, 38). The idea behind this phrase is of course not that the One is potentially everything in the sense in which matter may be said to be potentially everything, nor is he saying that the One is first actualized when it makes the things of which it is the power, as if it first then would have made itself complete. The idea is rather that the One is a kind of activity in its own right in virtue of which it is the power of producing all things, properly so called.

2. One or Two Acts?

Our task now is to see if we can capture a concept that satisfies all these conditions. A difficulty immediately presents itself: it is evident from (2), and strongly suggested by (3) and (4), that the agent of the internal act is the same as the agent of the external act: in the one case it acts internally, in the other externally. Combining this with the feature mentioned in (1) about the identity of agent and activity in the case of internal acts, we may even say that the internal act is the agent of the external one. Plotinus is obviously not suggesting that one and the same agent accomplishes two unrelated acts. Rather, the point must be that in accomplishing or, we might say, in being the first act, it accomplishes the second. This does not, however, square well with the views expressed in (5), according to which the internal act is self-contained. For how could anything that 'takes leave of' everything outside itself be the cause of anything outside itself? To describe the internal act as a cause having its effect elsewhere seems to be to misconstrue the internal act, for this amounts to saying that it is no longer in itself and 'taking leave' of other activities. In short, this is like saying that an activity which by definition is totally self-contained is in fact the agent of an act that reaches out of this same agent! Plotinus, it will seem, cannot have it both ways.

But perhaps we need not interpret Plotinus in a way that makes him inconsistent in this way. We have been proceeding as if the inner and the outer acts are two different episodes (or rather quasi-episodes, for the stages above Soul are atemporal) in the sense that first (in some logical rather than temporal sense of 'first') the internal act is established and then the external act issues from it as a new and different episode. The inconsistency arises if we say that the internal act is a cause of the external one, while defining the internal one in such a way that it cannot be a cause of anything external. Do we have to take the two acts to be different in this way?

There are indeed texts saying quite explicitly that the two acts differ, for instance the passage from V.4.2 that served as our main source for the double act doctrine above: the external act 'necessarily follows [the internal one] in every respect, *being different from the thing itself*'. And there are further aspects of the doctrine that may be taken to indicate that the two acts are different. For instance, designating the internal act as a paradigmatic cause and the external one as imitative effect, as Plotinus regularly does (V.1.3, 5–10; V.4.2, 25–6; VI.7.18, 2–8), shows that the two acts have different ranks. When trying to visualize Plotinus' emanative metaphors, of flowing water or the emanation of light, heat, cold, or smell, we see before us two separate phenomena: the source and what issues from it. None of this, however, needs to be taken to imply that the inner and the outer act are in reality two separate acts in the intuitive sense that first one thing is accomplished, the inner act, and then as if through an extra effort that thing accomplishes a second, new act. There are textual considerations that may count against taking the internal and the external acts as two ontologically different items. Consider the following passage: 'The intelligible could not be the last, for its activity had to be double (*dittos*), one in itself, and one directed towards something else' (II.9.8, 21–3).[13] The fact that Plotinus uses the form 'the activity (singular) of *x* is double' suggests that there is just one activity in each case which happens to be somehow two-sided.[14]

That there is some important distinction to be drawn between the 'two acts' was of course clear from the start. The question is what exactly it amounts to. The foregoing shows that some other account than one which posits two different exertions is needed.

Let us proceed on the assumption that there is just one exertion but it is two-sided in that there is on the one hand the activity in itself, on the other that activity in relation to something external. This does not by itself solve the dilemma raised above about the internal act being self-contained and at the same time being the agent of the external one. It now takes the form of asking how one and the same act can be said to be both self-contained and other-directed. Obviously, just saying that there are two sides of the activity is not much of an answer. I do think, however, that a reasonably satisfactory answer is available if we follow the present track of positing just one exertion. If the number of activities follows the number of exertions, there is in this sense at least only one activity. It will be our principal task on the following pages to try to work out this answer. As we shall see, however, trying to come to grips with it will involve us with several other subsidiary questions.

The double act is described in the language of events and actions. So it might seem promising to look into the topic of events for a clarification. The identity and differentiation of events in general, however, is an extremely complex and controversial matter. One kind of consideration can lead us to classify two descriptions as different descriptions of one and the same event, while another takes them to refer to two distinct events. Is

[13] Cf. also VI.2.22, 26–9: 'For when [Intellect] acts in itself, the results of its activity (*ta energoumena*) are the other intellects, but when it acts outside itself, the result is soul. And since Soul acts as genus or specific form, the other souls act as specific forms. Also the activities of these are double.' There is presumably an underlying singular here: the activity of *each soul* is twofold. Plotinus is not suggesting that each soul has two activities, each of which is twofold.

[14] This reasoning may however not be conclusive, since Plotinus sometimes uses the word *dittos* simply in the sense 'of two kinds' (cf. VI.1.21, 31) in which case he would simply be saying that the activity of *x* is of two kinds, which would be perfectly compatible with there being two different activities in the sense of two different exertions.

for instance, a walker's walking on the beach the same act as his making a trace in the sand?

Contemporary philosophers of action take radically different stands on such cases. Davidson (1980: 179), who gives an extensional, non-essentialistic account of events (of which actions are a subclass), would say that this is just one event, since the walking and the making of a trace have identical causes and effects. Goldman (1970: 1–19), on the other hand, who sees as many actions and events as there are non-synonymous predicates describing actions, would say they are different because 'walking' and 'making a trace' are not synonymous. Aristotle's position on the identity of motions and actions is carefully discussed and evaluated in the light of contemporary theories by Charles (1984: 5–56). According to Charles—and this seems plausible indeed—Aristotle's position turns out to be somewhere in between the extremes of Goldman and Davidson. It departs from Goldman in refusing to make the identity of an action depend on the language in which it is described and in allowing, with Davidson, that actions described in semantically different terms may well be one and the same action. Aristotle, however, thinks that events and actions do have an essence of a kind. That essence is determined by the nature of the being that initiates them. That is to say, beings have certain essential capacities that may be actualized; events and actions are the actualizations of such capacities. Two descriptions describe one and the same event (action), if they are true descriptions of the same actualization of the same capacity. The essence of the event (action) is given by the description of it that best captures the capacity involved, which in turn is determined by the theory which best fits the being which is the agent.[15]

Now, as we shall see, Aristotle's views on these matters are actually relevant to the issues in Plotinus we are addressing. For the time being, however, let us leave them aside and just keep in mind that the fact that people have come to very different conclusions about the identity of events and actions shows that it is not particularly surprising that Plotinus on occasion speaks of the inner and outer activities as two, on other occasions as one, but double. For as we have seen, the external and the internal acts have the same agent. We have come to the conclusion that the internal and the external acts are at least not two in the sense that they involve two

---

[15] For the details, see Charles 1984, especially 30–44; 60–7.

different exertions of this agent. The external act, however, is according to our main passage some kind of consequence of the internal one. Cases of this sort, where the question is whether an immediate consequence constitutes a new event or is the same event as the act that caused it, are among the cases about which our intuitions about the identity of events and actions are not firmly settled. They may not have been firmly settled for Plotinus either.

3. Motion and Activity in VI.1 and VI.3

In his treatises VI.1 and VI.3 on Aristotle's *Categories,* which he takes to be about 'kinds of being', Plotinus discusses the notions of making (*poiein*), undergoing (*paschein,* suffering, being affected), motion (*kinêsis*) and activity, and their interrelations (VI.1.15–22; cf. also 3.21–8). He is not directly concerned with his own doctrine of double activity here, and the examples he discusses are mostly ordinary sensible rather than intelligible activities, makings, undergoings, and motions. Yet these passages constitute the fullest and in a sense the most scholarly treatments we find in the *Enneads* of the relevant notions. There is every reason to suppose that what he has to say about them here is relevant to the understanding of his double act doctrine. I shall now consider what we may gather about the latter doctrine from these passages, keeping particularly in mind the puzzle about it we have raised. First, however, I shall make a few remarks about Plotinus' views on motions and activities and his differences with Aristotle on that issue.

Aristotle distinguishes between complete and incomplete activities (*energeiai*) and identifies motions with the latter (*Phys.* III, 201b 31–2; *Meta.* XI, 1066a 20–1; *De an.* III, 431a 6–7; *E.N.* X, 1174a 14–23).[16] Building a house is an example of a motion that is not a complete activity: This is a process that is incomplete till the house has been built after which time, however, the motion exists no more. Seeing and understanding are examples of activities in the strict sense: if one is at

---

[16] *Metaphysics* IX, 6, 1048b 18–35 is also one of the main sources for this sort of distinction in Aristotle. Here, however, he suggests that *kinêseis* are not to be counted as *energeiai* at all, not even incomplete. Plotinus seems to be drawing on the other Aristotelian passages that count *kinêseis* as incomplete *energeiai*, cf. VI.1.16, 1–5.

all seeing or understanding, one is already in the state of having seen or understood.[17]

Plotinus is not quite happy with this distinction and he attacks it on two fronts (VI.1.16; 18, 1–3; 19, 1–8). On the one hand, he argues that the so-called *motions* aren't really incomplete in the way Aristotle maintains; on the other hand, he argues that some of the Aristotelians' prime instances of activities such as seeing and living are just as much in time as Aristotelian motions are in time (VI.1.16, 17–19; 19, 1–6).[18]

As to the first point, Plotinus notes that so-called motions such as walking or cutting are not incomplete when considered in themselves but only when qualified by a certain quantity or extent (*posê kinêsis*): walking *across the racecourse*, for instance (cf. VI.1.16, 8–13).[19] It is first when such an extent is specified that motions such as walking appear incomplete. But this extent is something in addition to walking as such, which is complete at any moment during which it occurs. For Aristotle and his followers this specification of the extent of the motion often states the goal of the motion and thereby provides its essential feature: if I walk to the station to catch a train, the specification of this destination gives the immediate end of the walk, something that gives its 'what' and 'why'. Plotinus' approach is totally different in this respect. He entirely ignores the aspect of the Aristotelian theory which consists in seeing a given motion in terms of the goal to be reached by it.[20] The extent of the motion, he claims, is subsequent to and different from the motion itself (16, 7–9). If an extent is not specified, the motion is not incomplete during the period of its occurrence. 'I am walking' or 'I am cutting' seems indeed to imply, and certainly is compatible with,

---

[17] Much has been written on the distinction between *kinêsis* and *energeia* in Aristotle since Ackrill's seminal article, 'Aristotle's Distinction between Energeia and Kinêsis' from 1965 (here referred to as Ackrill 1997), certainly much more than I have been able to digest. What I have found most useful is Kosman (1969) and Waterlow (1982: ch. 4).

[18] For extensive discussion of Plotinus' criticism, see Natali (1999) and Chiaradonna (2002: ch. 2, 'movimento').

[19] Contrast Aristotle, *E.N.* X, 1174a 32–4.

[20] Iamblichus, who defends a traditional Platonic-Aristotelian account against Plotinus' revisionist views on *dynamis* and *energeia*, appears to adopt an Aristotelian position on this point and criticizes Plotinus for not seeing that motions are incomplete in the sense that while occurring they are on their way towards, but have not reached, their goals. It seems that Iamblichus too is taking the reference to the end (or, in Plotinian terms, the extent) of the motion to be essential to the motion (Iamblichus, *apud* Simpl. *In Cat.* 303, 36–306, 12). See the informed discussion of Iamblichus' objections to Plotinus in Chiaradonna (2002: 150–67).

'I have walked' and 'I have cut' (16, 13–14).[21] So, Plotinus suggests, when considered apart from the specification of extent, the so-called motions are like Aristotelian activities in being complete: they are fully completed in however short a period they occur (16, 12–14). In fact he says that the so-called motions are activities (16, 6–8). Thus, it seems that for him *kinêsis* and *energeia* become virtually synonyms.[22]

When Plotinus proposes to disregard the extent of the motion in relation to which motions appear incomplete so long as the specified extent is not reached, he is of course not proposing that we consider for instance the act of cutting without regard to anything that is being cut. He would not, any more than would Aristotle, consider cutting apart from any object that is being cut as a coherent notion. What he proposes to disregard is a specific extent of the cut, e.g. the cut *through this loaf*. The motion in the loaf, if the extent is disregarded, would be just as complete at any instant as any other motion (cf. VI.3.28, 2–4). Thus, to preclude a possible misunderstanding on a point where Plotinus is not too explicit, his refusal to include the extent in the specification of motion as such does not at all amount to a denial of a distinction between actions in the sense of 'acting on' (*to poiein*) and 'being acted on' (*to paschein*): the object that undergoes, say, a cut is not to be identified with the extent of the cut.

Let us now turn to Plotinus' other strategic point against the Aristotelians, that some of their supposed *energeiai* are just as temporal as any *kinêsis*. Some of the Peripatetics' allegedly complete *energeiai*, such as seeing, living, and living well, may go on continuously and in that sense they may be said to be in time (VI.1.16, 16–19).[23] He takes the Peripatetic doctrine of

---

[21] This point as well as Plotinus' other main critical point of Aristotle's distinction between *energeia* and *dynamis*, namely that some of the alleged *energeiai* indeed go on in time, are noted in Ackrill (1997). Plotinus, however, gets no credit.

[22] As has been noted by many scholars, Plotinus adopts the notion of *kinêsis* from Plato's *Sophist* and makes it, along with the other four 'highest kinds' of the *Sophist*, into the highest kinds of the intelligible realm. This intellectual *kinêsis*, however, is just the same thing as what he also calls *energeia* in connection with Intellect.

[23] As many commentators have noticed, when Aristotle says in *E.N.* X, 1174a 19 that every *kinêsis* is in time, he need not be taken to be contrasting this with an *energeia*, understood as something completely outside the realm of time, but rather, as Ackrill (1997: 150) puts it, contrasting it with something which 'did not occupy a fixed time determined by the goal to be reached'. Alexander of Aphrodisias, however, understands Aristotelian activity as something that takes no time at all (*Mantissa*, 143, 24–35; *In* De sensu, 135, 13–22). See De Groot (1983: 177–96) and Chiaradonna (2002: 182–6).

the completeness of activities to imply that activities are timeless.[24] So he argues that if the Aristotelians are saying that motions are in time and that they differ in this respect from activities, the same indeed holds for at least some of their candidates for activities. Plotinus' own position is that 'As activity is in timelessness (*en achronôi*), there is nothing in the way for motion to originate in timelessness; time came to it by its having become of a certain length' (16, 31–3). This seems to mean that so far as the agent of a motion is concerned, there is an activity of the agent which is 'in timelessness' but this activity may be reflected by an extended measured motion. I shall return to this admittedly murky view in a little while.

One easily gets the impression from Plotinus' criticisms of Aristotle's distinction between *kinêsis* and *energeia* that *kinêsis* on his account simply boils down to an Aristotelian *energeia*: if we leave out the reference to the extent of a motion and focus just on the motion as such, we seem to be left with something which Plotinus regards as complete at any instant as an Aristotelian *energeia* narrowly construed is supposed to be. This may, however, not be quite so simple. For as Chiaradonna (2002: 189) notes, even if Plotinus emphasizes that a *kinêsis* is complete in the sense that once it is enacted it does not require (more) time to be complete, he also makes the point that it is characterized by the feature of 'recurrence' (*to palin kai palin*).[25] This feature of recurrence belongs to motions as such, not to the motion of a certain extent. For the latter is presented as what results from the recursive character of motion as such but different from it. That is to say, to have walked half a mile is the result of recurring motion which brought the walker from the one place to the other.

It would take us too far afield to inquire into the details of all of this, which, it must be admitted, are in several respects obscure. But let me state in mere outline what I take Plotinus' position to be. When he asserts of sensible activities that they are in timelessness and that sensible motions originate in timelessness (VI.1.16, 31–2), he need not be taken to be asserting anything more than that, at any moment they are admitted

---

[24] This is an understanding which Plotinus seems to inherit from Alexander of Aphrodisias, cf. the previous note and VI.1.16, 16–17.

[25] For a conjecture and references that this aspect of Plotinus' views on motion reflects a Stoic position, see Chiaradonna (2002: 189–90), especially 190 n.65. This relates especially to the feature of recurrence, *to palin kai palin*.

to occur, they do not need more time to be complete.[26] There is no time during which they are in their making, taking place without being completed. The feature of recurrence, however, keeps the motion going, as it were. In VI.3.22, where he returns to the theme of motion, Plotinus says that common to all motion is that 'each thing is not in the same in which it formerly was, ... but, in so far as motion is present, is always being led away to something else and its being other is not abiding in the same; for motion perishes where there is no other' (VI.3.22, 37–41). The 'perpetual otherness' referred to here as a characteristic of motion is presumably the same feature as the recurrence, 'the over and over again', in the earlier passage. Plotinus identifies the motion of walking with an activity: 'One must not think that the things which are being moved are movement: for walking is not the feet but the activity in the feet which comes from a power' (VI.3.23, 5–7). As such, the activity of walking is not extended in time but it has the character of 'again and again' which results in a change in what is being moved.

So Plotinus ends up with a rather different picture of this whole sphere than Aristotle, both in terminology and in substance. The generic term for him is *kinêsis*, which is divided into makings (*poiêseis*), passions, and absolute (*apolytoi*) motions (VI.3.28, 1–3, cf. VI.1.22, 1–5 and VI.1.19, 6 ff.). We shall turn to the last mentioned class shortly. It appears that all three subclasses, however, resemble Aristotelian activities as opposed to motions in that when considered generally they are complete in the way Aristotelian activities are supposed to be. That is to say they appear to be fully achieved at each instance at which they occur and hence to need no more time to be completed.

4. Absolute Motions

In the discussion of motion and activity in VI.1 and 3 Plotinus appeals to a phenomenon he calls 'absolute (*apolytoi*) makings (*poiêseis*)' or 'absolute motions (*kinêseis*)'. He says that making (*poiein*) 'is either to have in oneself

---

[26] This is the sense of *achronôs* in Alexander of Aphrodisias, *Mantissa*, 143, 29–33: 'what doesn't need time to be fullended and brought to completion, that happens timelessly' (ἃ δὲ μὴ δεῖται χρόνου πρὸς τὸ συμπληρωθῆναί τε καὶ τελειωθῆναι, ταῦτα ἀχρόνως γίνεται). Cf. *In* De sensu 135, 15–17.

absolute motion which comes from oneself or a motion which starts in oneself and ends in another' (VI.1.22, 3–5). By 'absolute makings' he clearly has in mind 'intransitive' doings in contrast to transitive ones such as cutting, which by their very nature imply an external object on which the action is exercised. (By 'intransitive' I intend not strictly the grammatical sense of the word but a sense derived from it: an intransitive action is one that implies no object outside the agent onto which the action is done; a transitive action is one that does.) Examples he mentions of absolute makings are 'walking' and 'talking', and what he says about 'dancing' (VI.3.22, 9–12) and 'writing' (VI.1.19, 27–9) implies that he thinks of these too as absolute. Later he restricts the term 'making' to 'transitive makings' and prefers to speak about 'absolute motions'.[27]

The term *apolytos* does not occur in Aristotle and one may wonder whether his scheme allows for such a notion applied to motions. For all motions are according to Aristotle either affections originated by something other than what is affected or are the effects of an agent who acts on something else.[28] Aristotle certainly classifies 'walking' and 'talking' as *motions*[29]—but of what kind? Are they actions or passions? Presumably, the typical instances of walking and talking and other Plotinian absolute motions are instances of what Aristotle labels as self-motion—a class Aristotle certainly makes use of[30] but which is problematic for him exactly because the penchant of his thought about motion is that any motion involves both an agent and a patient and that these are distinct. Thus, it remains in a sense true that anything that is moved is moved by something else. The notion of moving oneself, without distinguishing between parts or aspects of oneself that fill the role of agent and patient,

---

[27] The word *apolytos* is of course a verbal adjective of *apolyein*, 'to set free'. It is a fairly common term in second century grammarians such as Apollonius Dyscolus and Aelius Herodianus, where it appears to mean '(grammatically) independent' in the sense in which certain words may be grammatically independent of other words in a sentence. There are also instances in philosophical authors where the term is used in the general sense of 'independent', 'free' (cf. Plutarch, *De defectu oraculorum* 29). Sextus Empiricus contrasts what is *apolytos* with what is relative, what is *apolytos* being what can be conceived without bringing in anything else (cf. *Adv. math.* VIII, 162). This seems to come close to Plotinus' specific use. No doubt *apolytos* becomes 'absolutus' in Latin. Thus, here in Sextus and Plotinus we have an early instance of 'the absolute' as a philosophical notion.

[28] This is convincingly argued by Waterlow (1982: ch. 4, see especially 159–79).

[29] 'To walk' is one of Aristotle's stock examples of *kinêsis*, cf. *Meta.* IX, 1048b 29 and *E.N.* X, 1174a 31 ff.

[30] Self-motion is discussed extensively in *Phys.* VIII. For helpful discussions of this notion, the problems involved, and attempts to solve them see e.g. Waterlow (1982: ch. 5) and Gill (1991).

appears self-contradictory. So it turns out that even in what he calls self-motion there is a distinction between the agent and the patient: one moves oneself in the sense that one part which remains unmoved moves a different part (cf. *Phys.* VIII, 258a 1–b 9).

For Plotinus absolute doings are not completed in something else outside the agent, nor are they the completion of an action by a different agent. But what exactly counts as the agent in the case of absolute doings of the sort Plotinus has in mind in VI.1 and VI.3? For Aristotle it becomes something of a problem to explain how the bodily movements of animate things initiated by their souls don't constitute a case of one thing moving another: the soul, being one sort of thing, acting on the body which is quite a different thing. It would seem that Plotinus faces the same problem on this score. It may well be that intuitively speaking, walking or dancing are not cases of being moved by another nor are they in themselves cases of moving something else. But as we can gather from the quotation from VI.3.23 above, walking on Plotinus' account is a case of the soul moving the feet: walking is an 'activity in the feet which comes from a power' (7–8). As O'Meara (1985: 257) notes, the power in question is without doubt a power of soul. But we have seen that walking is an absolute activity, neither a passion nor a transitive action. Plotinus never even raises the question how this is supposed to be compatible with holding that the soul acts on the body in walking.[31]

My guess is that sensible activities/motions are absolute only relatively speaking. That is to say, in classifying walking, talking, and dancing as absolute motions, Plotinus takes the composite of soul and body as a unit and considers the relationship between this unit and other things.[32] This

---

[31] For an illuminating discussion of the topic of how soul acts on body in Plotinus, including a treatment of the passages considered here, see O'Meara (1985); see also the thorough discussion in Chiaradonna (2002: 188–225).

[32] How can the classification of walking as absolute be compatible with analysing walking in terms of the soul's action on the body? I shall not attempt to give a full and detailed discussion of this question, but here are some considerations. Plotinus might insist that the activity/motion which is the walking (cf. VI.3.23, 6–7) belongs to the 'life of the body', which he mentions as a kind of definition of (sensible) *kinêsis* in the same discussion (VI.3.22, 17). This would entail that the activity/motion in question is a common undertaking of body and soul. So the question of who is the agent would not arise: they are both together parties to it. This answer, however, would only postpone the question. For the activity in the feet was 'from a power' (VI.3.23, 7–8). On what did this power act? Not the body *per se*, if that which is in motion is the composite of soul and body. If the power belongs to a higher form of soul, which acts on the compound of embodied soul and body, we are still left with one thing acting on another rather than an absolute motion. Thus, this answer is not promising. So it seems

indeed reflects the grammar of the verbs in everyday language: to walk is not to 'walk the legs' (as one may walk the dog) but a certain kind of motion of the legs, and hence of the whole compound of soul and body. In calling these absolute, he is disregarding the fact that when we, so to speak, look inside these activities, we see agency and patiency at work.

However this question may be resolved, what has just been said about absolute doings inevitably calls to mind what was said earlier about internal activities: neither absolute motions nor internal activities imply a relation to other things, at least not to things that stand below them in the order of things. So it would seem plausible to suggest that internal acts are kinds of absolute motion. Plotinus makes little use of the term *apolytos* outside this discussion in VI.1 and 3. The term does occur once, however, in a rather interesting passage in VI.8.20 ('On the Voluntary and on the Will of the One'). In discussing problems involved in holding that the One makes itself, Plotinus considers the difficulty that '[I]f [the One] makes (*poiei*) itself, it *is* not yet, in so far as it is the object of the making; but in being the maker, it *is* already before itself, since itself is the product' (2–4). To this he responds:

Against this it must be said that [the One] is not to be ranked as product but as agent; we hold that its making is absolute (*apolytos*), not so that something else should be accomplished from its making, as its activity does not aim at accomplishing a product, but it is entirely it.[33] (VI.8.20, 4–8)

Plotinus speaks here of an activity of the One. The activity in question is evidently the One's internal activity, and not surprisingly, it is said to be *apolytos*, absolute. We also know that the One has an external activity which derives from its internal one, but nothing is said about the latter here. Plotinus, however, cannot be supposed to have forgotten about the fundamental tenet of his philosophy that something comes from the One. So it follows that the One's internal activity may well be absolute,

to me that Plotinus is not particularly better off than Aristotle, who insists on there being self-motion in the sense of a thing moving itself, while actually accounting for this in terms of one unmoved part or aspect of it moving another.

[33] VI.8.20, 4–8: Πρὸς ὃ δὴ λεκτέον, ὡς ὅλως οὐ τακτέον κατὰ τὸν ποιούμενον, ἀλλὰ κατὰ τὸν ποιοῦντα, ἀπόλυτον τὴν ποίησιν αὐτοῦ τιθεμένοις, καὶ οὐχ ἵνα ἄλλο ἀποτελεσθῇ ἐξ αὐτοῦ τῆς ποιήσεως, ἄλλου τῆς ἐνεργείας αὐτοῦ οὐκ ἀποτελεστικῆς, ἀλλ᾽ ὅλου τούτου ὄντος.

even if there is an external activity accompanying it. There is clearly no incompatibility between positing the internal activity of the One as absolute and supposing that there is an external activity in its wake. Let us generalize from this and propose that internal activities generally speaking are absolute. This must, however, be tested against what else is said about absolute doings in VI.1 and 3.

5. The Case of Walking and its Trace

After presenting his criticisms of the Aristotelian distinction between activities and motions in chapter 16 of VI.1, Plotinus turns to actions and passions in chapters 17–22. Though he raises a number of very interesting questions about this topic, his treatment is disappointing in that many of the questions are hardly dealt with and it is often difficult to tell when he is working out what he takes to be the consequences of Aristotle's view and when he is speaking his own mind. But at any rate, when we come to chapter 22, Plotinus is unquestionably speaking for himself. Here he divides motion into two kinds: agency or making (*poiein*) and patiency (*paschein*). The former is in turn divided into the kind of agency that has patiency as a correlate, and absolute makings. After discussing agency and patiency, he turns to absolute makings (which he now refuses to call 'makings'), taking walking and thinking as examples:

And thought is not a making either—for it is not directed at the object of thought itself, but is about it: it is not any kind of making (*poiêsis*). And one should not call all activities makings or say that they make something. Making is incidental. Well, if someone walking leaves a trace, do we not say he has made it? But he did it out of being something else. Or [we may say] he makes incidentally and the activity does it incidentally, because he didn't have this in view. For we also speak of making in the case of lifeless things, that fire heats, for instance, or 'the drug acted (*enêrgêse*)'.[34] (VI.1.22, 26–34)

---

[34] VI.1.22, 26–34: Ἡ οὐδὲ τὸ νοεῖν ποιεῖν—οὐ γὰρ εἰς αὐτὸ τὸ νοούμενον, ἀλλὰ περὶ αὐτοῦ—οὐδὲ ποίησις ὅλως· οὐδὲ δεῖ πάσας ἐνεργείας ποιήσεις λέγειν οὐδὲ ποιεῖν τι· κατὰ συμβεβηκὸς δὲ ἡ ποίησις. Τί οὖν; Εἰ βαδίζων ἴχνη εἰργάσατο, οὐ λέγομεν πεποιηκέναι; Ἀλλ' ἐκ τοῦ εἶναι αὐτὸν ἄλλο τι. Ἡ ποιεῖν κατὰ συμβεβηκὸς καὶ τὴν ἐνέργειαν κατὰ συμβεβηκός, ὅτι μὴ πρὸς τοῦτο ἑώρα· ἐπεὶ καὶ ἐπὶ τῶν ἀψύχων ποιεῖν λέγομεν, οἷον τὸ πῦρ θερμαίνειν καὶ ἐνήργησε τὸ φάρμακον.

This passage is of course rather elliptical. Plotinus is here raising the question whether activities are necessarily makings, i.e. whether all activities produce or affect something else. He is evidently using 'activity' synonymously with 'motion', which is the term he set out from (cf. note 32). Previously he has spoken of absolute makings (*apolytoi poiêseis*), where 'makings' refers to the absolute motion itself, i.e. walking and talking are considered as a kind of making of the walk or the talk themselves. Now, however, he seems to be restricting 'making' to transitive actions and denying that what he previously has called 'absolute makings' are properly called 'makings' at all. He is eager to maintain that no activities are makings, implying that absolute ones such as walking are not. This is, in content, the same point as the one we saw in the passage from VI.8.20 about the 'self-making' of the One, which is not an ulterior product, but whose 'making' is identical with the One itself. Plotinus clearly thinks that this holds for absolute activities generally: the original activity and what it does or makes is one and the same thing.

The question then arises whether such effects of absolute activities as leaving a trace in the case of walking should not count as makings in the strict sense according to which making means making something else, some product different from the activity. Plotinus first responds that in this case the walker did this 'out of being something else', the meaning presumably being that the making of the trace has nothing to do with the walker as a walker, i.e. the making of a trace is not a part of what walking is as such. So if the walker did make a trace, it was not out of being a walker. Then he adds that we may say that the making of the trace is incidental, since the walker did not have this in view. This suggests that the intention may determine what sort of activity it is a question of: it counts as walking because walking is the intention and the making of a trace is not at all aimed at; in another situation one may walk in order to make a trace, in which case the action would presumably count as the transitive action of trace-making. So the making of a trace is incidental in the sense that this effect forms no part of the activity itself, which is not defined or understood in terms of what it does or produces outside itself. Nevertheless, absolute activities, albeit intransitive in themselves, may produce something.

The meaning and role of the last sentence of the passage quoted is somewhat obscure. It looks as if what it says about the effects of fire and drugs is somehow supposed to explain why the leaving of a trace may be called 'making'. Here is my best guess about what Plotinus may mean: we do call the effects of soulless things such as the heating done by fire or the healing effects of drugs, makings (*poiêseis*), even if these effects are by-products of the primary (internal) activities of the beings in question and are not at all aimed at. So we may also call unintended effects of intentional actions such as leaving a trace when walking incidental makings as well.[35]

Now it is of course to be admitted that Plotinus does not say explicitly here that the making of a trace is an external act of walking. Even if it is granted that walking, being absolute, is or is similar to an internal activity, it does not follow that Plotinus regarded the making of the trace as its external activity. For two quite independent reasons, however, it seems to me certain that he did so regard it. First, the *Enneads* abound in uses of the word 'trace' (*ichnos*) to describe the external acts of the hypostases. Thus, Intellect is or contains a trace of the One (III.8.11, 19; V.5.5, 13–14; VI.7.17, 13–14; VI.8.18, 15), Soul is a trace of Intellect (V.1.7, 44; VI.7.20, 12), the sensible form is a trace of the intelligible form (I.6.8, 7; II.6.3, 18), and so forth. This is of course an instance of the feature mentioned above that the external act is some kind of image of the internal one, *ichnos* being one of several words used to convey the Platonic notion of image. If 'leaving a trace' in a metaphorical sense is apt to describe external acts in the intelligible sphere, one would expect 'leaving a trace' in the original concrete sense to have the relevant structure of external acts generally. So, leaving a trace in a concrete, physical sense ought to count as an external act of that of which it is the trace just like the heat from a fire counts as an external act.

The other reason for taking the leaving of a trace as a kind of external act has to do with the examples of 'lifeless activities' Plotinus compares this with at the end of the passage. The heating of fire is of course a standard model for an external act, but in an interesting passage in V.4.1, 31–3 he mentions the effects of drugs as examples of external acts along with the

---

[35] This seems to be confirmed by an interesting passage describing double activity (emanation) in V.4.1, 27–32: 'Now when anything else comes to perfection, we see that it produces (*gennan*) ... and makes (*poiein*) something else. This is true not only of things that have choice (*proairesis*), but also of things that make by growing without choice and even of soulless things that impart themselves on others as far as they can: as fire warms, snow cools, and drugs act on something else in a way corresponding to their own nature ...' Not only are the effects of drugs presented as parallel to fire imparting heat as in VI.3.22, 32, Plotinus also makes the point that making may apply to soulless things that do not aim at their making by choice.

effects of fire and of snow (see note 35). The fact that the leaving of a trace is put into the same class as these other well-known examples of external acts strongly suggests that Plotinus regarded it too as a kind of external act. In any case, I shall proceed on the assumption that the making of trace is an external activity of walking.

Even if Plotinus, as we have seen, describes the leaving of a trace as an incidental making of walking, and supposing that the leaving of a trace is in fact a case of external activity that is suitable to shed light on the notion, it does of course not follow that every incidental effect of something counts in Plotinus' view as the external activity of the cause of the effect. Collecting a debt incidentally when going to the marketplace, to use Aristotle's example, will certainly not count as an external activity of going to the marketplace (cf. *Phys.* II, 196b 35–6). This is so for at least two reasons: first, collecting a debt incidentally in this way is, as it were, 'too incidental'. It wouldn't accompany its internal counterpart of going to the marketplace universally and necessarily, as Plotinus expects his external acts to do (cf. (1) in Section 1). Secondly, the Plotinian external acts are always some sort of images of the internal ones. The marketplace example fails in this respect too.

This last point may make us wonder about the appropriateness of calling the external act 'incidental' in relation to the internal one at all: if the former necessarily accompanies the latter like a shadow, how can it be said to be an incidental product? The best I can do to respond to this is to repeat: trace-making is no part of what walking essentially is; it is not needed in order to understand what walking is nor for walking to be what it is. So it is incidental in relation to walking.

The two last passages cited seem to indicate that if the aim of an act is an external result, the act is not absolute. In the former passage Plotinus remarked that the activity of the One is not *apotelestikê*, i.e. aiming at a product, and in the second one he said that the agent of walking 'didn't have [the making of a trace] in view'. Compare this with the case of teaching for Aristotle in *Physics* III, 202b 3–9. Teaching is according to Aristotle a transitive action, like cutting or burning. Even if there may be a way of describing an intransitive aspect of teaching in terms of e.g. the teacher's talking and pointing, the talking and pointing is done for the sake of the result, namely the skill or understanding that is to arise in the pupil. The logic of the very name for the act, teaching, implies an external object.

By contrast, in the cases of double activity, the name of the act in question doesn't imply an external object acted on. The act is absolute, independent. So ordinary teaching at least would not count as an internal activity.

The foregoing raises the question whether the teacher's talking and pointing, considered in themselves, may be both absolute and transitive, depending on how they are described.[36] Or would Plotinus say that since in the case of teaching the aim of the talking and pointing is an external effect, the talking and pointing is not absolute, though it would be, if the intention that somebody learns were not present?[37] Or would he say that because of the intention the activity in question is not that of talking and pointing but that of teaching, that the latter predicate captures the nature of the action in question? I cannot see that the texts provide any clear answers to these questions, but it seems to me that it would be most plausible for Plotinus to adopt the last-mentioned alternative. This amounts to holding that an activity is indeed essentially either absolute or transitive, and that in the human case the intention determines into which class it falls.[38] At the same time it may be admitted that there are different ways of describing the same action so that actions or activities that are essentially absolute may also be said to be incidentally transitive. And similarly, actions that are essentially transitive may have non-transitive predicates true of them. This would suggest that we uphold what was suggested above that the difference

[36] It is worth mentioning, though this is not relevant to the point at issue here, that Plotinus expresses some doubt about whether learning is a genuine case of being affected, noting that it involves an activity on the part of the learner (VI.1.19, 26–32). His view on the teaching and learning, though not developed in detail, is presumably close to that of St Augustine in De magistro, according to which nobody ever teaches anyone else in the sense of making someone know something; learning essentially involves awakening knowledge the learner already has (cf. De magistro 12, 40). However this may be, the same considerations as presented here about the relationship between teaching and the teacher's talking and pointing could be raised about any transitive action, e.g. cutting and moving one's hand with a knife.

[37] In the context of 'teaching' versus mere 'pointing and talking', it may be appropriate to relate an anecdote that still is being told around the University of Oslo about the noted Norwegian mathematician and logician Thoralf Skolem, who was professor there from 1938 to 1957. It is alleged that somebody came into Skolem's classroom in the middle of a lecture and saw him engagingly presenting his mathematical theme of the day. But alas, there was no audience in the room! Had Professor Skolem been teaching?

[38] Some doubts about the claim that the intention determines whether an action is absolute or transitive may be raised by an obscure passage in VI.1.19, 39–44. Plotinus seems here to imply that the presence of the wish to hurt someone does not change the nature of an action. The pain caused is a subsequent result of the action, e.g. burning, which is just the same whether or not the intention to hurt is present. I must confess that I do not quite know what to make of this. Part of my problem has to do with the fact that I find Plotinus' reasoning in this chapter in general difficult to follow.

between an absolute action that incidentally is a making and a plain making may be determined by the intention: if the external effect is not the point of the action, the action is absolute, yet perhaps incidentally a making.[39] In the inanimate case we will, analogously, have an absolute activity with 'incidental' external acts if there is an absolute account that captures what the agent is essentially doing, however what it is doing may be reflected outside itself. Thus, a fire is essentially engaged in burning, not in the sense of burning something else, but burning; as a result some other things may be burnt or heated or illuminated.

So absolute motions are not done for the sake of an external result. Does this mean that absolute motions or internal activities are accomplished for the sake of an internal goal or result? In general, teleology does not play a very significant role in the *Enneads*, the account of the internal workings of the hypostases included.[40] It is noteworthy that in neither one of the two last quotations, where we saw Plotinus making the point that absolute activities are not done for the sake of an ulterior result, does he say or imply that they are *done for the sake of themselves* or for an internal motive. Plotinus tends to avoid attributing aims or goals to self-contained activities except in so far as they aim at their own source—this is a point I shall take up explicitly in the next chapter in connection with Intellect's relation to the One.

Which incidental effects should count as external acts? It is instructive that Plotinus describes the internal activity as the activity of the Being (*tês ousias*) and contrasts it with the external one which is said to be 'from the Being' (*apo tês ousias*). This, I take it, indicates that the external act, even if it may be called an incidental effect, nevertheless expresses the nature of the agent, perhaps together with a certain type of matter, such as we have in the case of walking: leaving a trace is incidental to a walker's action, it is no part of what walking is in its essence; yet, given what walking is, and the presence of a suitable material to walk on, leaving a trace is something that we are bound to do when we walk.

---

[39] The question arises here whether the view that the intention may determine the nature of an action may be in conflict with Plotinus' position noted earlier that the end to be achieved is irrelevant to the action's status as *kinêsis* or *energeia*, that only the action as such is to be considered and its end disregarded (see pp. 35–6). It seems to me to be too little to go on, however, to give a definite answer to this question.

[40] See O'Meara (1993: 75–7), who comments on Plotinus' non-artisanal view of how nature and the other levels of the hierarchy work. 'Non-artisanal' implies, among other things, that the workings of nature are not teleologically conceived.

It seems reasonable to relate the characterization of the external act as being 'from the Being' to the external act as an image of the internal one. For we know that in general the external act is an image of the internal one. Its being an activity 'from the Being' indicates that it is an activity which is caused by the Being and bears its mark, leaves its trace.

As we noted in connection with point (1) in Section 1, Plotinus says that the external activity follows the internal one necessarily. More recently we have been saying, primarily on the basis of VI.1.22, 30–4, that the external act is a kind of incidental effect, a by-product. Can Plotinus have it both ways? It is of course true that an effect such as a trace is dependent on there being a suitable matter onto which a trace can be made. The trace might be described as incidental on account of the contingent presence of such suitable matter. I do not think, however, that this is the point of Plotinus' claim that making a trace is an incidental effect, cf. his remark that it is not out of being a walker that the walker makes a trace. The point is rather that the internal act is self-contained and the external act follows from this without being a part of what the internal act essentially is. It nevertheless follows necessarily.

6. Emanation and Internal and External Acts Again

Perhaps it is time to consider where we stand and see how far, if at all, we have advanced towards solving the problems we faced initially. Taking walking as our model, we find that there is just one exertion: in making the trace, our walker doesn't exert himself in addition to what he does when he walks. So in this sense there is only one activity. That activity is the activity of walking. Walking is what it is quite apart from the trace it leaves. It doesn't depend on the trace in order to be there. Nor do we need the trace in order to understand and account for the walking. (We might, however, learn about the walking, initially, by studying the trace). In this sense walking is self-contained with respect to the trace. Furthermore, the walk is the cause of the trace, and moreover the trace is the kind of effect that reflects its cause: it tells us where the walk went and even further details about the walk and its agent. It seems to be quite in place to say that the trace 'necessarily follows [the walk] in every respect' inasmuch as distinctive features of the trace can be traced back to the walk and its agent. If the relationship between internal and external acts is like that between walking and the trace, we can also see why a certain ambivalence as to the identity and number of acts involved would be natural. There is just one exertion all right, just one activity that the agent so far as it is concerned is engaged in. Still, we may feel that walking and making a trace are 'different', that the making of the trace is something in addition to walking, a different accomplishment (cf. V.4.2, cited on p. 25 above).

As asserted several times already, there is only one exertion, only one thing that a principle engaged in an activity does. This exertion is the inner activity. If we count the acts by the exertions, we would have to say that there is only one act and that the so-called external act is a different way of describing the original exertion, the internal act, or we would have to say that the external act is not really an act in its own right at all, but rather a different episode, a consequence, externally expressed, of the internal act. Plotinus may not be altogether clear about which of these alternatives he adopts. It appears, however, that he rather tends to go for the latter alternative. Here the remark in V.4.2 that the external act is different from and a consequence of the internal one must weigh heavily.[41] We cannot easily accommodate this claim with a view postulating one act with two descriptions. However, even if we adopted the former kind of interpretation, the internal act and the external one would not be on an equal footing for Plotinus, as they would be for example for Davidson. Referring to the internal act by means of the external one would be missing the 'essence' of it, describing it by means of a lower manifestation, like describing somebody's walk in terms of footprint-making.

So, to return directly to the problem stated at the outset of this discussion, the internal activity's self-containment, its 'taking leave of all other activities', amounts to its being something in itself without any reference to anything outside it. So far as it is concerned, it 'takes leave' of other things. This means that both ontologically and epistemically the internal act is absolute, independent. It so happens, however, that just in virtue of being what it is in itself it has external effects—or alternatively, if we insist on only one act, works externally—that resemble itself. In any

---

[41] I am grateful to Øystein Galaaen for making me realize this, obvious though the point is once realized.

case, nothing in addition to the internal act is done in order to bring about the external one.

We have seen that the walking-trace model serves reasonably well for illustrating the relationship between the internal and the external act. We might have taken other models, such as the fire and its emitted light or heat that Plotinus commonly uses to illustrate double activity. These might have served us just as well. There are two reasons why I chose the walking and the trace, however. First, the fact that in the passage from VI.1.22 we have considered Plotinus has instructive things to say about just that case. Secondly, his views on fire and emitted light, interesting as they are, involve a physical theory that may be rather alien to us and which Plotinus never explains in detail, while the workings of walking and leaving a trace are reasonably uncontroversial.

The model of walking and trace may nevertheless fail in some ways to capture everything Plotinus wishes to say about the relationship between internal and external activities. For instance as we noticed in (4) in section 1 above, the external act is not supposed to be 'cut off from' the internal one, implying that it is constantly dependent on the internal one like a mirror image constantly depends on the mirrored object (cf. VI.4.9, 36–10, 30; VI.2.22, 34–5; VI.4.10, 11–15). The trace isn't quite like that, for it will stay at least for a while until it is withered away by wind and rain. Constant dependence may be true of the hypostatic external acts, and thus the trace or, for that matter, the heat in warmed objects would not exactly fit as illustrations. Plotinus' views on the nature of external acts in the sensible world are however slightly more complicated. For he notes about the trace (*ichnos*) of soul in the body, which must be a kind of external act of the soul itself, that it is more like the heat in warmed bodies (IV.4.14, 6), which stays on for a while after the source has departed, than the emitted light that disappears instantly when the source of light is blocked or removed (cf. IV.5.7). The trace in the sand is not so different from the heat of the heated object: both stay for a while and then gradually fade because they lack their own source of activity to stay in existence.

Someone might object to using the relationship between walking and leaving a trace as a model or metaphor for expressing the generation of the hypostases, on the grounds that the former presupposes some matter on which the trace is made. Leaving a trace when walking presupposes sand or some other pliable matter onto which the trace is made. In the case of metaphysical generation there is no antecedent matter or recipient on which to leave a trace. The same with fire heating or light that illuminates. When the One, superbly self-sufficient, nevertheless has an external act, there is absolutely nothing onto which it can act. Such considerations may well play a part in Plotinus' preference of emanative metaphors and analogies. For on the face of them, emanative metaphors of emitted heat or light, or of overflow of liquids, may seem to fare better than leaving a trace on the ground inasmuch as they do not presuppose a pre-existing receptacle onto which the source acts.

I quite agree that the emanative metaphors may indeed be more apt than talk of traces for capturing just this aspect of the metaphysical causation. This is not to say, however, that the emanative metaphors manage to do full justice to the case. For just like any other physical metaphors these metaphors presuppose a notion of space: we are asked to see the cause as a limited physical object which emits something of itself into its surroundings. We cannot conceptualize this without picturing the source along with its surroundings. This, however, is already too much: not only is the One not an item in space, it cannot be anything like that at all. Might it be an item which by its 'emanation' creates 'intellectual space', as space itself is said to have been created by the Big Bang according to recent cosmological theories?[42] So it is not the case that the One is as if located at some point in space from where it emanates something into this space; rather, in emanating it makes the space at the centre of which we tend to picture it. Well, something like that may well be the right picture. If so, however, none of the physical metaphors, including the emanative ones, is quite apt to capture the nature of the case.

All this raises deep and intricate questions about the very meaning of Plotinus' language. Given the supposed non-physical, non-spatial, and non-temporal nature of the One (or for that matter of Intellect), what can it mean to say, for instance, that it 'overflows'? It is not just that this is a metaphor, which in itself is perfectly fine. The problem is that we are at a loss in relating the metaphor to the object it is applied to. I shall not attempt to solve these puzzles. Let me say, however, on a more positive note, that the metaphors do after all suggest a certain structure, namely the

---

[42] For the expanding universe and space, see e.g. April Holladay at **www.wonderquest.com/ ExpandingUniverse.htm**

basic structure of double activity that we have been considering. That may not be a whole lot but it is not nothing either.

7. The Sources of the Double Act Doctrine I: Aristotle

There has been some scholarly discussion about the historical roots of Plotinus' notion of double activity. Various hypotheses have seen the light, in particular Plato, Aristotle, and the Stoics have been proposed as sources. In what follows I shall first briefly consider Plotinus' immediate predecessors and the Stoics, and then turn to Aristotle and Plato. As will soon become clear, I do not believe that the Stoics are a significant source for Plotinus' views here, whereas both Plato and Aristotle have had a hand in shaping them. As we shall see, Plato's role in this reveals interesting aspects of Plotinus' manner of interpreting and using Plato.

To my knowledge nobody has systematically considered Plotinus' immediate predecessors as a possible source of the double act doctrine. I have myself not carried out any extensive systematic search of the kind, but it seems to me that the central features of double activity are at least not present in any obvious way in Plotinus' predecessors such as Numenius and Alcinous. And Alexander of Aphrodisias does not strike me as developing Aristotle's views here in Plotinus' direction.[43]

Among the Hermetic excerpts preserved by Stobaeus, however, there is at least one text that contains ideas that resemble Plotinian double activity (Festugière and Nock [1946], III, 19 = Stob.1, 4, 8).[44] The context is

[43] Two passages in Alexander of Aphrodisias have been pointed out to me as providing possible parallels to Plotinus' two acts doctrine: *Mantissa*, 142,10–13 (Bruuns) and *On Providence*, 139 (Fazzo). The Greek text of the latter work is lost, but it is preserved in an Arabic translation. While seeing the point of drawing parallels to Plotinus here, I do not find the content of these passages so strikingly close to Plotinus' double act doctrine that I would venture to suggest them as real precursors, not to say sources. In the former case, the doctrine is significantly different, in the latter the characteristic language is missing and Alexander's view in fact somewhat unclear: see the interesting discussion in Sharples (1982).

[44] Here is the whole relevant passage in Greek (Festugière and Nock [1946], III, 19, 1–5): Ψυχὴ τοίνυν ἐστὶν ἀίδιος νοητικὴ οὐσία νόημα ἔχουσα τὸν ἑαυτῆς λόγον, συνοῦσα δὲ διάνοιαν τῆς ἁρμονίας ἐπισπᾶται, ἀπαλλαγεῖσα δὲ τοῦ φυσικοῦ σώματος αὐτὴ καθ' αὐτὴν μένει, αὐτὴ ἑαυτῆς οὖσα ἐν τῷ νοητῷ κόσμῳ. Ἄρχει δὲ τοῦ ἑαυτῆς λόγου, φέρουσα ὁμοίαν κίνησιν τῷ ἑαυτῆς νοήματι, ὀνόματι ζωήν, τῷ εἰς ζωὴν ἐρχομένῳ. Τοῦτο γὰρ ἴδιον ψυχῆς, τὸ παρέχειν ἑτέροις ὅμοιόν τι τῇ ἰδιότητι αὐτῆς. Δύο τοίνυν εἰσὶ ζωαὶ καὶ δύο

the relationship between soul and body. The soul is described here as an intelligible Being. It is in its nature to bestow something of its own character (*idiotês*) on others. So it has two kinds of motions (*kinêseis*) of life, one 'by its Being' (*kat'ousian*), another 'by the nature of body' (*kata physin sômatos*). The first is free (*autexousios*), the second necessary. There are indeed certain similarities to Plotinus' double act doctrine, though the author here speaks of *kinêseis* rather than *energeiai* and most of Plotinus' typical vocabulary about the two acts is missing. I find the evidence of this passage too vague to assert an affinity with Plotinus' views, still less to propose it as a possible source. We do not know who the Hermetic author of this text is or when exactly he lived. He might be a contemporary of or possibly even later than Plotinus. Moreover, the passage leaves unclear exactly how the two soul movements are related. The conception need not be like that of internal and external activity at all.

The hypothesis that the double act doctrine is of Stoic origin or relevantly influenced by a Stoic position has been advanced by at least two eminent scholars, Armstrong (1937: 61–6; 1967: 240) and Hadot (1968: 229), though they cite different aspects of Stoic doctrine in support of their view. Recently, Hadot's proposal has been renewed and defended at some length by Narbonne (2001: 61–79), although he, as indeed to a certain extent Hadot himself, also recognizes Plotinus' debt to Aristotle in this regard.

Armstrong cites the 'late Stoic' view that the ruling principle in human beings is an emanation from the Sun which leaves the Sun undiminished (cf. Plutarch, *De facie in orbe lunae* 943 A). That the external act doesn't diminish its source is of course a feature of the double act doctrine (cf. (5) in Section 1). As we shall see, however, there are other more probable sources of this aspect of Plotinus' doctrine than this Stoic view which, moreover, is stated in terms quite remote from those of Plotinus.

Hadot and Narbonne cite the Stoic doctrines of tenors (*hexeis*) consisting of tensional motions (*tonikai kinêseis*) (see Long and Sedley 1987: 47 I, J, K) as a kind of model for the internal and external acts from which Plotinus' doctrine is to have developed. In Stoicism tensional motions go both out from a thing's centre to the periphery and backwards towards the centre:

κινήσεις, μία μὲν ἡ κατ᾽ οὐσίαν, ἑτέρα δὲ ἡ κατὰ φύσιν σώματος. Καὶ ἡ μὲν γενικωτέρα, ἡ δὲ μερικωτέρα· καὶ ἡ κατ᾽ οὐσίαν ἐστὶν αὐτεξούσιος, ἡ δὲ ἀναγκαστική· πᾶν γὰρ τὸ κινούμενον τῇ τοῦ κινοῦντος ἀνάγκῃ ὑποτέτακται. I am grateful to Paulos Kalligas, who pointed out to me the resemblance between the ideas presented in this text to the Plotinian two acts.

the former are identified with the thing's qualities and the latter with its Being (cf. Nem. 70–1 = Long and Sedley 47 J). I shall not dwell on this hypothesis. I simply fail to see the plausibility of it. Not that I wish to deny that Plotinus was in certain respects under Stoic influence. As Graeser (1972) and others have shown, there can be no question about that. In this case, however, the evidence for significant Stoic influence simply strikes me as inadequately supported and somewhat far-fetched. This is so because the main features mentioned in support of the Stoic relevance such as the identity of a thing's *hexis* with the being of the thing, which, I take it, is supposed to correspond to Plotinus' identification of each level, each 'thing', with its internal act, is equally, in fact better, explained by the Aristotelian identity of form and activity/actuality. The same holds for the point that a *hexis* does what it does of itself or according to itself. This too is the case for Aristotelian or Platonic natures. In favour of the latter's greater relevance must count Plotinus' vocabulary, which is thoroughly Platonic and Aristotelian, not to mention what we know about his doctrinal sympathies.

Let us then turn to Aristotle. Rutten (1956) and, in his footsteps, Lloyd (1987: 167–70; 1990: 98–101) have made a case for the view that Plotinus' internal and external acts derive from Aristotle's doctrines of potentiality and actuality and that Plotinus' view is to be seen as a modification of Aristotle's.[45] It is incontestable that a significant part of the terminology of the double activity doctrine is Aristotelian. Not only is the central term for activity, *energeia*, thoroughly Aristotelian, but also certain other details as we shall see. Thus, it is a very likely bet that Aristotle has quite a bit to do with this doctrine.

Rutten and Lloyd hold that the Plotinian internal act corresponds to an Aristotelian active power, such as fire's capacity to heat or a teacher's capacity to teach, whereas the external act corresponds to the actualization of these capacities in something else. That is to say, the internal act corresponds to the capacity to burn or to teach, identified with a first activity = second power, while the external act is the actual heating or teaching which is realized in something else which as a result becomes hot or learns.

---

[45] In Rutten's (1956: 101) words, 'cette théorie n'est rien qu'une habile transposition et un subtil gauchissement de la théorie aristotelicienne de l'efficience'. And Lloyd (1990: 99) remarks that the theory 'takes over Aristotle's model of physical causation, transposing it, of course, to non-physical causation'.

Lloyd makes two interesting comparative points in addition. The necessity of emanation, i.e. of the external act, corresponds to 'the absence of need (according to Aristotle) for an additional cause of this second actualization' (1990: 100). That is to say, according to Aristotle for what is potentially F to become actually F, it suffices to be in the presence of what is actually F: in order for a cold object to become hot, nothing more than the presence of fire is needed, if nothing prevents (cf. *Phys.* VIII, 255b 1–13). Secondly, he mentions, as an element common to Aristotle and Plotinus, the metaphor of 'not being cut off from'. Aristotle says: 'Teaching is the activity of a person who can teach, yet the operation is performed on some patient—it is not cut off from a subject, but is of A on B' (*Phys.* III, 202b 7–8). He uses this phrase to emphasize that though the motion incurred is in the patient, it is still an actualization of the agent. Plotinus too uses the phrase 'not being cut off from' to make the point that the external act is a case of one thing acting in or on another (or at least outside itself). In the metaphysical contexts, it appears to be used to suggest that the act and its result last only as long as the agent acts (for references see pp. 27–8 above): were the external act to be cut off from the agent, it would altogether disappear (cf. VI.4.9, 36–10, 30). In Aristotle's example of teaching and learning we may suppose that though the learner ceases to learn when the teacher stops teaching, what he already has learnt nevertheless stays: he has become an actual knower (cf. *Phys.* VIII. 4, 255a 34 ff.).

It seems to me that in identifying Plotinus' internal act with Aristotelian capacities, Rutten and Lloyd's accounts leave some important features out. As Tornau (1998: 98) rightly notes, for Aristotle the exercise (actualization) of capacities is prior to the capacities themselves (*Meta.* IX, 8 1049b 4 ff.). This is so because a capacity is defined in terms of what it is the capacity of, i.e. its exercise. For Plotinus, on the other hand, the capacity is prior to its exercise. The capacity, however, is not a mere capacity, but something active and actual in its own right (cf. (6), Section 1). That is to say, what in Plotinus corresponds to the Aristotelian capacities is an activity/actuality (*energeia*) of the whole sphere of which a particular exercise is an instance or specification. This prior activity is what we in previous sections have referred to as the self-contained aspect of the internal act.

Let us compare this with Aristotle's account of such acts as teaching or building. A builder has a capacity (*dynamis*) to build; this capacity is actualized in the act of building; this actualization is a motion or process (*kinêsis*) as opposed to a complete activity (*energeia*), since it is incomplete until the house is built. The house that is being built has as its moving cause the art of building which the builder possesses. In this case there is no obvious candidate for a prior activity/actuality corresponding to the Plotinian internal act from which the act of building arises. True enough, the act of building itself is the *energeia* of the builder as a builder, but this *energeia* is already one that is other-directed: it is completed in the materials of the house. In the view of Rutten and Lloyd, this is what corresponds to the external act.

Considerations of Aristotle's views about cases such as building may, however, lead one to wonder whether, within his account, there isn't a ground for distinguishing between the actualization of the builder and the actualization/process that takes place in the materials and turns them into a house. As Waterlow (1982: 187) and others have argued, it may indeed be reasonable to make such a conceptual distinction. Think of a builder who is building a house; of course, what he is doing is something that is completed in the materials and isn't finished until the house has been built; nevertheless, from a certain point of view, he is just exercising his capacity of building; he may continue to do so indefinitely, starting on a new house when the first one is finished; in a sense he *has built* ever since this exercise started (though he has not built the whole house). Seen thus, the activity of a builder, i.e. what the builder does when building a house, is or resembles an *energeia* narrowly construed that may be contrasted with a *kinêsis*. The point is that if one conceptually separates the activity of house-building from the particular extent of the act (cf. on *posê kinêsis*, in Section 3), house-building would be complete in the sense that one can continue to engage in it indefinitely; it doesn't have a limit, and thus in this respect it becomes like seeing or living. Considering the transitive activity of building in this way may help us see why the agent, according to Aristotle, is not changed by acting: 'It is wrong to say that the thinker, when he thinks, is altered (*alloiousthai*), any more than a builder when he builds.' The reason for this is, as Waterlow (1982: 187) puts it: '[The activity of building] is not a process of acquiring a new property' (*De an.* II, 5, 417b 8–9). The builder may go on and on building. In doing so he does not acquire any new properties (though his materials do), except perhaps incidentally. Aristotle, however, never explicitly makes such a distinction within transitive acts, still less does he say that building or other such processes can be seen as *energeiai* in the narrow sense of *Metaphysics* IX, 6 in which *energeiai* are different from *kinêseis*.

A conception of agency such as the one sketched in the previous paragraph with a distinction between the activity/actualization of the agent and the processes brought about through this outside the agent would bring Aristotle considerably closer to Plotinus' doctrine of internal and external activities—or Plotinus closer to Aristotle, depending on how we choose to see it. The agency of the builder begins to look like the Plotinian internal activity, which, as we have seen, behaves like an Aristotelian *energeia* in the narrow sense. Moreover, the conceptual separation of the act from its particular extent Waterlow proposes to make within an Aristotelian agency is close to what Plotinus himself suggests, where he argues against the *kinêsis/energeia* distinction. And the lesson he wishes to draw from this is also similar: if the extent of the transitive action is disregarded, the Aristotelian incomplete *energeiai*, i.e. *kinêseis*, acquire completeness.

In comparing the double act doctrine with Aristotle on actuality, Lloyd, however, has not only in mind capacities such as that of teaching or building and their exercise. Aristotle is untiring in insisting that actuality is prior to potentiality, his favourite example of this being that Man begets Man, an example that runs through the corpus (cf. e.g. *De gen. anim.* 735a 21; *Meta.* 1070b 34; *De part. anim.* 640a 25). In general terms the view Aristotle wishes to express here is that what is potentially F becomes F by the reception of a form from something which is actually F: Man begets Man; fire generates fire, and so forth. This is sometimes referred to as the Principle of Prior Actuality. Lloyd is also appealing to this general principle in his comparison. Indeed, this principle resembles Plotinus' doctrine of double activity: the latter too essentially involves something making something else similar to itself.

It is not quite clear how the Aristotelian Principle of Prior Actuality relates to the equally Aristotelian claim we have been considering that the activity/actualization of a capacity takes place in the patient. In *Metaphysics* IX, 8 1050a 30–5 Aristotle says:

Where, then, the result is something apart from the exercise, the actuality is in the thing that is being made, e.g. the act of building is in the thing that is being built … and similarly in all other cases, and in general the movement is in the thing that is being moved; but when there is no product apart from the actuality, the actuality is in the agents, …

How does this fit the claim that an actual fire generates fire or that an actual human being begets another human being? One would presume that the fire and the human being are already actually such before, and independently of, generating anything; this is indeed what the principle asserts. Nevertheless, they are entities whose activities/actualities have products outside themselves. The passage just cited would seem to suggest that the fire and the human being become fully actual only in their external act of generation, and moreover, in their offspring. Aristotle, however, cannot and surely does not mean to suggest that. It is beyond the scope of this work to attempt to resolve these and other related questions that are internal to Aristotle's theory of actuality. I bring this up in order to show that it is not obvious what Aristotle's position is with regard to the very points Plotinus is supposed to have depended on him for. Thus, supposing that he did depend on Aristotle here, we still have to face the question which aspects of Aristotle's doctrine in particular he did pick up and which interpretation of Aristotle he adopted: it is not evident what Aristotle really meant.

Among the points Aristotle adduces in support of his Principle of Prior Actuality is the fact that one acquires the capacity for building by building, one becomes a musician by practising music, and so on (*Meta.* IX, 8 1049b 28–1050a 2). This, however, is not the sense in which Plotinian external activities depend on a prior actuality/activity. The latter presume an agent whose actuality/activity embraces the external act but of which the latter is an inferior and more particular instance,[46] whereas Aristotle's statement here seems to aim at explaining how the possession of a capacity presupposes some prior actualization of the capacity. In accounting for how actuality is prior to potentiality also with respect to time (*Meta.* IX, 8 1048b 17 ff.), Aristotle notes that prior to musical or building capacities there are actual musicians and music, actual builders and houses. I doubt, however, that this sense of prior actuality would have served as a model for Plotinus' double act doctrine, which seems to be differently conceived: in the latter case it is crucial that the agent of the external act is itself a self-contained activity which explains the external act.

As applied to things such as fires and human beings, however, the Principle of Prior Actuality is in content close to the double act doctrine.

---

[46] For Greekless readers it may be noted that what, depending on context and taste, are variously called 'actuality', 'activity', 'actualization', 'act', 'actually', 'in act', here and in the secondary literature on and translations of Aristotle and others who use his terminology, are all forms of one Greek word, *energeia*.

An actual hot fire makes other things surrounding it hot. Moreover, as I have argued for in Plotinus' case, for Aristotle too the activity of fire by which it heats its surroundings is nothing other than the activity/actuality in virtue of which it is a fire. In other words, the heating is not a result of any additional exertion besides managing to be a fire. So Aristotle and Plotinus agree that the causal act is not an extra effort on the part of the cause in addition to what the cause is doing anyway by virtue of being what it is. The same, presumably, holds for Man as a begetter of Man. I believe that such instances of the Principle of Prior Actuality must indeed be very important sources of the Plotinian double act.

The analogy, however, is not perfect, not even in such cases as that of the fire generating fire or Man begetting Man. As Lloyd (1990: 100) notes, while for Aristotle there is in general no implication about a lower status of the product than of the maker, this is a crucial aspect of the Plotinian external act. Although fire and the heat it emits is one of Plotinus' favourite examples to illustrate double activity, this example may not capture well this aspect of the doctrine: for fire tends not merely to heat but to generate another fire, which is fire in just as full a sense as the generator. Fire as an illustration would be better if fire merely produced heat. And humans in fact beget humans rather than some inferior humanoids.

There are still other parts of Aristotle's philosophy that may have inspired Plotinus' double activity doctrine. There is, for instance, Aristotle's doctrine of the unmoved mover as a pure *energeia* of self-contained thought that somehow causes the everlasting rotary motion of the outermost sphere (cf. *Meta.* XII, 8 1073a 26 ff.; *De caelo* I, 2; II, 3–6; *Phys.* VIII, 8–9). In Aristotle's view the prime mover is the ultimate cause of all motion. Moreover, it seems that Aristotle considers the uniform rotary motion of the *primum mobile* as an effect that retains important characteristics of its cause but involves a loss nevertheless. This motion resembles its cause in being uniform and eternal. It is as perfect as anything changing can be. Being motion, however, it involves a loss in comparison with the agent. Similarly, the endless cycles of generation are the best approximation of the perfection of God that the sublunary beings are capable of and an imitation of it.[47] The notion of *energeia* of course plays a crucial role in the account of the prime

---

[47] For Aristotle's view that the eternal motions of the heavens are the cause of the eternal cycles of generation and corruption, see *Meta.* XII, 6 1072a 9–18; *De caelo* II, 3, 286a 31; *De gen. et corr.* II, 11, 336b 25 ff. In the last-mentioned passage Aristotle makes it clear that he conceives of continuous cycles

mover, but it is otherwise not systematically relied on in these parts of Aristotle's teaching. The general pattern nevertheless is strikingly close to Plotinus' double act doctrine, so much so indeed that I venture to propose these features in Aristotle as a background for the cycles of double activity in Plotinus. But then again, as seems to be commonly acknowledged, these aspects of Aristotle bring us to Plato, cf. Solmsen (1960).

Let us summarize the conclusions from this comparison between Plotinus and Aristotle. Not only the language, but many of the crucial ingredients of the double activity scheme have antecedents in Aristotle's account of agency. Double activity may indeed be seen as an application of the Principle of Prior Actuality, which certainly is Aristotelian—though, as we shall see, also Platonic (cf. Sedley 1998). There are interesting deviations, however. It is not only that the external act involves a loss. Unlike for Aristotle, the *kinêsis/energeia* distinction doesn't play a role for Plotinus: he makes no point of insisting that the external act is a motion as opposed to a complete activity. After all he is, as we have seen, critical of Aristotle's use of this distinction. Nor do we see in Aristotle, despite his commitment to the Priority of Actuality Principle, the same sort of emphasis on the self-containment of the prior *energeia* as there is in Plotinus on the self-containment of the internal act: the Plotinian agents, the internal activities, tend to be presented as not essentially agents, i.e. their acts on other things, as we have seen, are necessary but incidental in the sense that they do not enter into the account of what their causes are. To conclude this, even if Aristotle surely plays an important role for the development of the double act doctrine, there are interesting differences. The one we have just considered, the lower status of the external act, together with claims about a certain transcendence of the cause, cf. (5), already point in the direction of Plato, to whom we shall now turn.

8. The Sources of the Double Act Doctrine II: Plato

Let us then turn to Plato. Several suggestions have been put forth about individual passages in Plato that may have inspired Plotinus' notion of

---

of generation as as close an approximation perishable things can come to eternal being and as imitation of the *eternal* uniform circular motion of the heavens.

double act: Gerson (1994: 23−4) mentions three such. First, there is the famous passage about the Idea of the Good in *Republic* VII, 508e−509b. Whatever the Idea of the Good is doing privately, as it were, and the truth it infuses on the other Ideas, correspond, according to Gerson, to the internal and the external acts, respectively. Secondly, there is *Timaeus* 29e, the celebrated passage about the Demiurge's ungrudging nature, which may be interpreted as an everlasting overflow of benevolence and was so interpreted by the tradition in the doctrine that 'bonum est diffusivum sui'. Thirdly, Gerson mentions Diotima's speech in the *Symposium* (see especially 212a−b), where the possession of the Beautiful itself is said to result in the production of beauty. The idea is that the possession of the Beautiful in itself brings about beauty in other things.

I do not wish to take issue with these suggestions at all. On the contrary, I find them all quite plausible. It seems to me, however, as Gerson's proposal of *three* different Platonic passages as sources indeed may suggest, that it may be worthwhile to consider the different aspects of the double act doctrine and see if they have antecedents or parallels in Plato. So I shall summarize the features of the double activity we set out with and see if in the wording of each of the features some particular Platonic teachings may be reflected. Then I shall raise the question in a more general way whether there is something in Plotinus' adherence to Plato that may explain his adoption of this doctrine.

Some six characteristics of double activity were listed at the outset. For the readers' convenience I repeat them here in a short version—for details see Section 1 above: (1) Double activity is pervasive; it is instantiated at every stage from the One down to the level of the sensible form. (2) The internal and the external act are equated with a paradigm and its image, respectively. (3) The internal act and the external act are described in terms of emanative metaphors. (4) The external act constantly depends on the internal one; the former is not 'cut off from' the latter. (5) The internal act itself remains unaffected, in spite of issuing in the external act. (6) The internal act is also a power.

Not all of these features have any clear antecedents in Plato, but most of them do in a significant way. As to the first characteristic, the pervasiveness of double activity, we shall note in connection with the discussion of feature (5) below that Plotinus indeed sees double activity in quite a wide range of Platonic passages covering different levels of reality as it is according to

Plato. It is not at all confined to the relationship between Ideas and sensibles. Feature (2) describes the internal act in its capacity of paradigmatic cause of its own images. It is needless to say that this too is Platonic. The Ideas of course have such a function, but also other principles in Plato such as the Demiurge in the *Timaeus* and souls. For, as *Timaeus* 29e referred to by Gerson makes clear, the Demiurge, being good, makes the world as good as the latter will allow for. So the Demiurge makes the world like himself. And we find that both the World-Soul and individual souls impart their own features on that which they act. There is evidence suggesting that Plotinus took both the *Phaedrus* 245c–d about the soul's self-motion and the account of virtue and virtuous action in *Republic* IV, 443c to exhibit this aspect of the double act. I shall return to these passages below.

Emanation comes third on the list. While there may not be fully-fledged emanation metaphors in Plato, there surely are some passages Plotinus cites that may have led him to such ideas. As already mentioned, there is the Analogy of the Sun in *Republic* VI 509b, which clearly suggests that something comes from the Good to the objects of knowledge like light from the Sun which shines on sensible objects. This is not all, however. In *Phaedrus* 245c–d Plato describes the soul's self-motion as 'the spring (*pêgê*) and beginning (*archê*)' of all other motion. The phrase 'spring and beginning' is cited several times in the *Enneads* and not only in connection with the soul but especially in connection with the One's productive activity (cf. I.9.1, 41; I.7.1, 15; VI.7.23, 21). In III.8.10, 2–5 we find the following passage: 'But what is above life is the cause of life; for the activity (*energeia*) of life, which is all things, is not the first, but itself flows out, as it were, as if from a spring (*ek pêgês*).' The use of the word *pêgê* in such a context is no doubt an allusion to the *Phaedrus* passage, which Plotinus here and in the lines that follow develops into a full-blown emanation or flow metaphor. Moreover, what 'flows' from the 'source' is the external *energeia* of the One. So in this way this *Phaedrus* passage is clearly linked to the double act doctrine. If we take into consideration that *Phaedrus* 245c–d also contains the fifth feature on our list, the self-containment of the cause (see below), it becomes tempting to regard this passage as quite important as a background for the double act doctrine.

The fourth item on our list had to do with the constant dependence of the image (external act) on its model (internal act). We noted that Plotinus is liable to express this in Aristotelian terms, by saying that the image is 'not cut off from' the model and that this is a case of one thing acting in another. However, even if Plato may not say in so many words that images constantly depend on their models, at least as regards the relationship between the Ideas and their sensible images, this is no doubt the case. Plato surely never suggests that the Ideas are merely responsible for the coming to be of sensible items which thereafter sustain themselves without any further involvement of the Ideas. On the contrary, it is fairly evident that so long as a sensible item has a certain feature, F, it participates in the Idea of F; this latter relation is naturally taken to imply that the sensible item is not cut off from its model.

We mentioned as the fifth item on the list of the characteristics of double activity that the cause, the internal act, 'remains', i.e. it is itself unaffected by performing the external act. Now, as we saw in the main passage from V.4.2, one of the phrases Plotinus uses to talk about this, '[It] remains in [its] own proper way of life,' is a quotation from the *Timaeus* 42e, 5–6, an inexact quotation to be sure, as Platonic phrases in Plotinus tend to be, but clearly a quotation nevertheless.[48] In the context in the *Timaeus*, the Demiurge has assigned tasks to the lesser gods, his children, having to do with the management of the sensible world. It is after he has given them these tasks that he retires to his own abode. Plotinus does not interpret the *Timaeus* historically, as a story which relates events in a chronological order. Rather he interprets it as a myth that has to be given a philosophical interpretation. This means that he regards as timeless or synchronous events that the myth relates as a temporal sequence. In this particular context this means that as the Demiurge rests in his proper place, he is still, through his orders and his children, busy with management. That is to say, what the myth relates as consecutive events, first the Demiurge's issuing of orders, and then his leave, which is synchronous with the execution of the orders by his children, is in Plotinus' version just one activity, as if the Demiurge at the same time remained in his proper abode and in so doing also gave orders to the lesser gods.

Plotinus' use of this phrase from the *Timaeus* is not limited to his account of Intellect or the soul, the items that in Plotinus correspond to the functions of the Demiurge in the *Timaeus*.[49] He takes the phrase to apply to

---

[48] Plato says about the Demiurge in *Timaeus* 42e: ἔμενεν ἐν τῷ ἑαυτοῦ κατὰ τρόπον ἤθει ('he remained in his customary way of life'); Plotinus says in V.4.2, 21 about the internal activity: μένοντος οὖν αὐτοῦ ἐν τῷ οἰκείῳ ἤθει ('As he remained in his proper way of life').

[49] Cf. Charrue (1978: 137–9). That the functions of the Demiurge in Plotinus belong both to Intellect and the World-Soul is noted already by Proclus (*In* Tim., I, 305, 16–19).

causes quite generally. Thus he says for instance in V.2.2, 1–3: 'So it goes on from the beginning to the last and lowest, each [cause] ever remaining in its own abode.'[50] This means, I take it, that for Plotinus what Plato says about the Demiurge is a lesson to be learnt about all genuine causes: even if they act on other things, they remain. Apart from those passages in Plotinus that obviously reflect this *Timaeus* passage, the *Enneads* abound in talk of remaining (*menein*) or synonyms such 'not leaving' in contexts having to do with causes (see Section 1 (5) above). All these passages, I suspect, would claim this *Timaeus* passage as their authority.

In the *Timaeus* too there is a passage about time as an image of eternity (37d). The Demiurge would like his creation to be as similar to his model as possible, but 'it isn't possible to bestow eternity fully upon anything that is begotten'. Hence, he reasoned that he would make a moving image of eternity. So 'at the same time as he brought order to the universe, he would make an eternal image, moving according to number, of eternity *remaining* in unity'.[51] Again we see here the idea of remaining. Plotinus uses the phrase 'remaining in one' several times, but not exclusively in connection with the Intellect and the generation of time.[52] Even if in the former passage it is the Demiurge himself who is said to remain, while in this one it is his intelligible model, for Plotinus it is natural to interpret the two passages as carrying more or less the same message, since for him the Demiurge and his model make up one thing, Intellect.

That the cause remains is further confirmed by another Platonic passage which contains the same message but stated in terms closer to Aristotle in that the cause is said not to be affected (*paschein*). In *Symposium* 211b Socrates (Diotima) says about Beauty itself: 'But itself by itself with itself, it is always one in form; and all the other beautiful things share in that, in such a way that when those others come to be or pass away, *this does not become the least bit smaller or greater nor is it affected at all*.'[53] Beauty itself is responsible for whatever beauty there is in others, but it is not in the least affected by this. This passage may well be a direct Platonic source for

---

[50] This is the phrase from *Timaeus* 42e in disguise, *hedrai* ('abode' replacing *êthei* 'way of life').

[51] *Timaeus* 37d: μένοντος αἰῶνος ἐν ἑνί, cf. III.7.2, 35; 6, 6. I am indebted to Laszlo Bene for pointing out the relevance of these lines to me.

[52] Cf. V.8.4, 27, where stronger things in general are said to 'remain more in one' than weaker things, and V.9.2, 27, where the phrase is used of the One.

[53] *Symposium* 211b: ... μηδὲν ἐκεῖνο μήτε τι πλέον μήτε ἔλαττον γίγνεσθαι μηδὲ πάσχειν μηδέν.

Plotinus, not only as regards the cause not being affected, but also about its not becoming less by being a cause. It may of course be said that if the cause is not affected at all, it can't become less. However, since Plotinus is wont to portray his causes by means of emanative metaphors, the question of whether the causes are reduced by acting becomes quite pertinent (cf. e.g. VI.9.5, 38).

Another expression relating to this same aspect of the double act doctrine is the claim that a principle does 'not leave itself' (*ouk apoleipei heauto*) (cf. Section 1 (5)). This phrase is to be found in *Phaedrus* 245c—its Platonic source is recognized by Henry–Schwyzer, cf. their *index fontium*—where Plato is describing the soul's self-motion. So the soul, any soul, moves itself, and it does so without leaving itself, *ouk apoleipon heauto*. Thus, this *Phaedrus* passage contains both the idea of remaining and, as we saw above, the idea of a source that might suggest some kind of emanation. If we further take into account that for Plotinus *kinêsis* in the intelligible realm is a synonym for *energeia* (cf. n.22 p. 36 above), the account of the soul here in the *Phaedrus* as self-moving and ever-moving while imparting secondary motion onto other things, may be seen to involve the distinction between the internal and external activities.

I mentioned in the comparison with Aristotle above that Plotinus' talk about the remaining of the cause could be seen as a version of Aristotle's claim that agents are unaffected by acting. Plotinus' use of the Platonic passages we have just brought up, however, shows that he has Platonic authority for this view. Thus, for Plotinus this aspect of the doctrine can be seen as primarily Platonic, although, as is his regular practice, he develops what he takes to be Plato's view with the aid of Aristotelian vocabulary and insights.

Interestingly, Plotinus also interprets Plato's views on virtue in terms of the double act doctrine. In the *Republic* 443c–d Plato says about true justice that it consists in doing one's own 'not as regards one's own external action (*peri tên exô praxin*) but as regards the internal one since it truly concerns oneself and what belongs to oneself'. Plotinus obviously has this passage in mind where he says in connection with autonomy that 'so that also that which is autonomous (*autexousion*) and depends on us (*eph'hêmin*) in actions is not referred to the acting (*to prattein*) or the external activity but to the internal one (*eis tên entos energeian*) and the thought and contemplation of the virtue itself' (VI.8.6, 20–2). Plato is of course not discussing autonomy in this passage of the *Republic*. Plotinus may, however, have taken the phrase 'concerns oneself and belongs to oneself' to refer to what 'depends on us', as he understands the latter. In any case, external virtuous action is here described as an external act of the internal activity of virtue itself. Plotinus evidently thought that the virtue itself is there as a condition of the soul quite independently of any overt actions (cf. VI.8.5).

I find it likely that this list of Platonic passages that may be seen as containing some elements of Plotinus' double act scheme could be lengthened considerably. I shall, however, not pursue such source-hunting any further. Instead, I would like to raise some questions about the topic in general. Is Plotinus reading back into Plato something that he basically has from elsewhere, Aristotle and Alexander for instance, and believes in on independent grounds? Or is his fundamental motivation Platonic (by his lights)? Secondly, if it is fundamentally Platonic, how is it so?

The literature on the sources of the double act doctrine mostly proceeds on the assumption that there must be a passage or two somewhere in Plato, Aristotle, the Stoics, or someone else, which gave Plotinus an idea that he then generalized or blew up, one might even say. I don't think this need be the case at all. We have noted that Plotinus sees salient features of his double activity doctrine in several Platonic passages that are, at least superficially, quite different. Not that he sees all the features in every such passage, but each passage gives Platonic authority to some of the features. It must be admitted that this is compatible with his mostly having the doctrine from elsewhere but finding it appropriate to decorate it with some Platonic flavour. The case does not, however, strike me as if Plotinus had come up with the double act doctrine independently of Plato, and then sought to give it a Platonic justification afterwards. I venture to suggest that he saw the double act doctrine as an interpretation of Plato on causality or 'how intelligible principles work'. Let me explain what I have in mind. Plato describes the relation between his primary causes, the Ideas, and what depends on them in terms of participation or imitation. Plotinus and the other Neoplatonists also employ these concepts, though in Plotinus, at least, participation cannot be said to play a prominent role. Both participation and imitation are notions which, so to speak, see the matter from below, from the viewpoint of the caused: it is the lower, caused item that formally is the agent in participation or imitation. It is clear, however, that for Plato the participants or imitators play a passive role in the sense that it is the participated or the imitated which has the main responsibility for the outcome: in participating or imitating, the lower is or becomes such and such because of the higher item, though the nature of the recipient also plays a role. In Plato there is, however, very little to be found about how this happens from the viewpoint of the cause. In a famous passage in *Phaedo* 100a–e the Ideas are said to be 'causes' in which other things participate and in virtue of which they come to have certain features, but nothing is said about what, if anything, the Ideas do in order to bring this about. Passages such as the analogy of the Sun in the *Republic* or the account of demiurgic activity in the *Timaeus* may give us certain clues here, but considerable interpretative work is required to elicit the message. The so-called doctrine of double activity and emanation is meant as an attempt to do just this, i.e. to account for Platonic causes from the viewpoint of the causes themselves rather than the effects. Thus, I do not take it that what is described in terms of emanation is meant to be anything different from participation or imitation. Rather, what from the viewpoint of the subordinate items is called participation or imitation may be described in emanative language from above.

Secondly, even if Plato is brief about the causality of his causes, Plotinus is able to note certain hints. For instance, by being causes of other things Platonic causes do not lose anything nor are they affected in any way. In fact Platonic causes are something in their own right without regard to the effects they may have. Nevertheless, they have certain effects. The doctrine of the double activity is intended as an explanation of how this happens. So I take it that the doctrine is an interpretation of Plato's views on causality. It is as if Plotinus had put to himself the question: What is the manner of metaphysical causation in Plato, what glimpses do we have of Plato's views on this in the dialogues? And the general answer he comes up with is the so-called doctrine of double activity. This way of looking at the matter seems to me to be supported by the fact that Plotinus' use of the Platonic passages mentioned above is in general not restricted to the kinds of things at stake in the original Platonic passages. As we have seen, a Platonic passage about the soul and its manner of causation may be used to account for the One's manner of causation. Plotinus indeed generalizes from the Platonic passages.

If this is so, the question which particular Platonic passage gave Plotinus the idea of double activity seems to me a fairly pointless question: Plotinus sees evidence of this all over the place, of different pieces in different contexts. The interpretation, however, actively makes use of Aristotle's views on activity. It provides the doctrine with some its key terms and notions. The modifications of Aristotle it involves, however, are all in the direction of what one might justly suppose was Plato's general account of causation, if he had one.

It may be worthwhile to pause here and comment on the notion of cause involved. We noted above that Plato is fairly silent about the causal agency of the intelligible realm. There may be a simple explanation of this. Even if Plato occasionally calls the Ideas 'causes' (*aitiai*) and frequently implies that they have the status of principles, it does not follow that they are causes in the sense that they do something, that they exert themselves in any way. In fact it has been plausibly argued by Frede (1987) that the notion of cause in Plato and Aristotle is rather different from ours especially in that their notion does not imply agency. Thus, when Plato's Ideas or Aristotle's end, form, matter, and mover are called causes it does not imply that these are items that do something or other in order to bring about that of which they are said to be causes. Rather, according to the same source, they are called causes because they figure in explanations of the features of which they are said to be causes (cf. Frede 1992).

In the light of this, one may wonder whether the search for the agency of the Ideas or an account of it such as I have just attributed to Plotinus is not quite mistaken, at least in so far as his account is taken as an interpretation of Plato. Let us note in response to this that whatever the facts about Plato's notion of a cause may be, the notion of paradigm/imitation is quite naturally interpreted as involving some activity on the part of the paradigm. Of course the paradigm is not supposed to do something extraordinary in order to bring about its effects. Quite the contrary, one would suppose that simply by minding its own business in 'its own way of life,' a paradigmatic cause at the same time moulds, impresses, or influences (or whatever causal verb may be appropriate) the imitator. Given the significant role of paradigms in Plato, it is not at all surprising that his late ancient interpreters and followers should attempt to give some account of how they work.

2
The Genesis of Intellect

In the previous chapter we have seen how the stages in Plotinus' hierarchy, including the One itself, produce or 'emanate' something inferior out of themselves. In the passage from V.2.1, cited at the beginning of that chapter, Plotinus asserts that the inchoate intellect, the One's first product, 'when it has come into being, turns back upon the One and is filled, and becomes Intellect by looking towards it.' This means that by now we have a second agent in place in addition to the One, i.e. the One's product becomes an agent in its own right. In this chapter I shall deal with the topic of this first product, the inchoate intellect, its so-called conversion, and the ensuing genesis of the actual Intellect.

In the first section I raise and seek to answer the question why the incho-ate intellect looks back to the One at all, why it converts. I then proceed to give an outline of the subsequent story which relates what the intellect sees in its conversion. In dealing with these topics, I make no claims to do full justice to everything Plotinus says which has a bearing on the matter. All those who have tried to work through the relevant texts, which are several, know how complex and bewildering the material is. In this first section my aim is to consider if there is a roughly coherent and comprehensible story (no claims made about full logical cogency) to be told about both the pro-cession and the conversion phase. The story I tell is not based on any single text. Usually, the texts I refer to in support of my claims contain only parts of the account and often some other trains of thought as well, which for my purposes I shall ignore. So the first section is a kind of general exposition of the issues, aspects of which are to be elaborated in detail in later sections.

In Section 2 I address a particular question that arises in connection with Plotinus' account of the genesis of Intellect: how are the two kinds of plurality that come about 'early' in the 'history' of Intellect, the duality of thinker and thought, and the necessary plurality of the object of thought, related, if at all?

This is the main question of this chapter. Its full solution, as I see it, only comes in the last section and it involves a certain interpretation of what Plotinus means by self-thinking, which in this last section becomes a topic in its own right. The intermediate sections all discuss particular topics pertinent to this central question. The issues dealt with here may now and then seem to take us in other directions. These other directions are, however, relevant to our main topic whose solution, or so it seems to me, we wouldn't be in a position to fully appreciate without these roadside stops and excursions into neighbouring areas.

1. The Inchoate Intellect and its Conversion

So why does the inchoate intellect convert at all? In this connection it is worth noting that the metaphors of emanation, so prominent in the account of the One's external act, the inchoate intellect, entirely fail to explain the conversion. There is certainly nothing in the emission of light or heat, or the flowing of liquids, that provides a reason for a conversion of the efflux. However adequately such metaphors may capture the constant dependence of the external act on the internal one, there is nothing in such dependence to suggest a conversion of the external act towards the internal one. And, turning to metaphors of parenthood, even if offspring may have some tendency to love their parents, and depend on them, the notion of begetting is not much better off in this respect. Moreover, the conversion is mostly described in psychological terms as involving a desire for the One and a vision of it. So from the perspective of the physical metaphors in the procession, the conversion may appear as a new event, unexplained by, and even conceptually alien to, anything that precedes it. It is this gap between the procession and the conversion that I shall focus on in the following paragraphs.

We should not let the physical metaphors of emanation mislead us into forgetting that we are, after all, dealing with psychological (= mental?) phenomena in some broad but still legitimate sense of the term. Not only is the efflux from the One an intellect, even if an inchoate or potential one, 'not yet seeing'. The One itself is in some sense a psychological entity too, even if Plotinus is wary of ascribing ordinary human psychological attributes to it, because they tend to be incompatible with its utter simplicity. In VI.8.16, 32 he attributes to the One some kind of 'thought transcending thought' (hypernoêsis). In the same context he ascribes to the One both activity (energeia) and a kind of will (boulêsis, thelêsis), though he has included a warning that such positive attributes do not strictly apply (13, 1–5). He also says that the One

… is not like something senseless; all things belong to it and are in it and with it, it being completely able to discern itself. It contains life in itself and all things in itself, and its comprehension of itself is itself in a kind of self-consciousness in everlasting rest and in a manner of thinking different from the thinking of Intellect.[1] (V.4.2, 15–19)

I take it that this shows that the One is not at all void of mental life but its way of possessing it (= being it?) is such that if we ascribe our human, mental vocabulary to it we tend to be misled into thinking that the One possesses the attributes in question in the same way we do. Our mental attributes for the most part contain elements that suggest incompleteness and diversity. Not so in the case of the One. Even Intellect, though its kind of thought differs from ours, is not free from this. The One is evidently something 'of the mental kind' whose 'life' is free from such implications. It is no accident that the next stage after the One is Intellect, and this fact may actually give us an inkling about what sort of thing the One is: the One, were it to give up its unity in the smallest possible degree, would degenerate into an entity of the kind of the divine Intellect.

So as a very first step towards answering our question, we may affirm that, despite the physical metaphors, the psychological vocabulary of desire and vision (the latter of course to be understood metaphorically) is in itself not out of place in talking about the inchoate intellect and its relation to the One.

Plotinus identifies the One with the Good. This is not a gratuitous identification. In VI.9.6 he discusses in what sense we apply the word 'one'

---

[1] V.4.2, 15–19: … οὐκ ἔστιν οἷον ἀναίσθητον, ἀλλ' ἔστιν αὐτοῦ πάντα ἐν αὐτῷ καὶ σὺν αὐτῷ, πάντη διακριτικὸν ἑαυτοῦ, ζωὴ ἐν αὐτῷ καὶ πάντα ἐν αὐτῷ, καὶ ἡ κατανόησις αὐτοῦ αὐτὸ οἱονεὶ συναισθήσει οὖσα ἐν στάσει ἀιδίῳ καὶ νοήσει ἑτέρως ἢ κατὰ τὴν νοῦ νόησιν. It is true that the subject of this sentence is to noêton, not 'the One' or 'the Good', the usual designations of the principle above Intellect, which do not appear in this treatise (cf. note 2 to Chapter I). In general 'the intelligible' plays the role of the One in V.4. Because V.4. is an early treatise (number 7 on Porphyry's chronological list), the failure to use the usual terms for the principle above Intellect as well as Plotinus' willingness here to ascribe a kind of thought to this principle (though it is clearly said to be of a different kind than the thought of Intellect), may be taken to show that the full doctrine of the One has not yet been developed. In a much later treatise, VI.8 (39), however, such language is also employed, though this is thoroughly qualified by 'as if' qualifications. In any case, my point is not that Plotinus after all means to say that the One thinks. It is rather that whatever it does, it is so close to thinking that it is very tempting to apply the vocabulary of thought to it.

to the One. In the course of considering this he makes a conceptual move from the One not being many to the One being totally self-sufficient: 'But everything which is many is also in need, unless it becomes one from the many' (VI.9.6, 18–19). So not being one, i.e. being many, signifies incompleteness, a lack and a need. At the lower levels of the Plotinian hierarchy plurality takes the form of dispersion in time and in space. This too is a sign of incompleteness, I presume an incompleteness ultimately to be explained in psychological terms (cf. III.7.11–12 on the genesis of time). At the first stage of the unfolding of reality, however, where our focus now lies, the lack of unity at stake is straightforwardly a psychological lack. That is to say, what has departed from the One is not totally one in the sense that it needs something, is not totally self-sufficient. Not being totally self-sufficient psychologically speaking is not to be whole and hence in a sense to be many: such a being contains internally a reference to something which is not it and which it does not possess.

This explains why the One is also the Good: it is the Good in the sense of being totally self-sufficient[2] and in the sense of being the completeness other things aspire to. So everything desires the Good which is the ultimate final cause. Plotinus states this final causality of the Good in an interesting way. He says that in desiring the Good each being wants rather to be it than what it is (VI.8.13, 12–13). This means, I take it, that every being that desires the Good desires to be in the state of self-sufficiency the Good is in. But if it were in that state, it would be the Good itself, for there cannot be more than one thing of that nature.[3]

Beings that are not by their very nature self-sufficient, however, beings for whom their well-being is incidental (see VI.9.6, 29–30; cf. VI.8.13, 41–3), are in a general state of need, even when they are satisfied: their satisfaction is not, so to speak, built into them and it depends on something outside themselves. Thus, even when fulfilled, such beings are not self-sufficient and are still needy. The self-sufficiency of the Good itself is still

---

[2] Plotinus often remarks or implies that the One is self-sufficient: V.3.13, 17–18; V.4.1, 10–12, V.6.2, 15–16, VI.7.38, 23–4, VI.9.6, 17–18. He also often says that Intellect is self-sufficient, implying that it is self-sufficient after its kind, as a thinker. In V.3.17 he says that the One is beyond *autarkeia* because it is the cause of *autarkeia* in Intellect. The reasons for this are no doubt parallel to the reasons why the One as a cause of Ideas or Forms is itself formless and in general Plotinian causes do not possess the multiple features of which they are causes in the same way as the effects possess them. So Beauty, for instance, does not possess the particular beautiful form it causes (cf. VI.7.32, 34–9 and D'Ancona Costa's 1996 illuminating discussion of Plotinian causality).

[3] For a discussion of the unicity of the One and references, see Gerson (1994: 10–12).

an end for them which they seek to achieve as best they can, though, not being the Good, they are doomed to fail in achieving it completely.

The Good is the *telos* of everything but pre-eminently it is the *telos* of its first product, the inchoate intellect. To the degree that this intellect has departed from simplicity and perfection, it will lack these features. Being an intellect, it naturally desires its end and seeks to attain it. This is the ground for the conversion. It seeks to do this according to its own nature, i.e. it will seek to attain its end in intellection, possess the Good by knowing it (cf. V.6.4, 5–6; V.6.5, 10). That knowing something is a way of possessing it is a perfectly natural and understandable thought, at least given the premises of Plotinus' philosophical tradition. Plotinus' story is beginning to look more coherent in that the very fact of departure from the One is seen to contain in itself a reason for the conversion.

Yet, we can perhaps do better still. We may describe the constitution of the inchoate intellect as the constitution of a subject-stance. By this I do not mean that the inchoate intellect in itself constitutes a full-blown subject of thought. As will become evident as we proceed, a full-blown subject/object distinction only comes about when the intellect converts and becomes a fully actual thinking intellect, i.e. Intellect. The inchoate intellect, however, is not only different from the One, it is in some sense aware of this difference in that it needs and longs for the One. In this sense it constitutes a subject-stance. Thus, the distancing from the One amounts to the constitution of a rudimentary subject of need and desire. The conversion, on the other hand, is this subject's intentional stance or directedness towards its object, and its actual sight is its intentional object. In what follows I shall refer to the external object aimed at, as the One is in this case, as the 'intended object', and the object as it appears I shall refer to as the intentional object. These are not at all equivalent.

One may wonder whether attributing a desire to the inchoate intellect isn't already granting too much to it: for mustn't there be not only a subject/object distinction in that which desires, but also a mastery of the concept of the object of the desire and thereby, no doubt, of several other concepts? Plotinus himself does not raise this question and I do not know for sure how he would have responded to it. He might, however, have insisted that the desire in question is not a desire that involves a clearly demarcated intentional object, and hence not conceptualization. He says in fact that the inchoate intellect desires the One in a vague or indeterminate way (*aoristôs*), which may suggest that the desire is less than fully articulated.[4] It seems natural to compare it with some inarticulate feeling of loss of, and longing for, unity and perfection, the sort of feeling small infants presumably have when they long for their mother's breasts without being able to conceptualize this yearning.

It is tempting to describe the affair as the One's distancing itself from itself, in order to become an object of its own view. But of course, this cannot be so strictly speaking, for the One 'abides in its proper way of life' and does not leave itself. It has no need to see itself. What distanced itself was something from the One but not the One itself. At any rate, the mere fact that something in need has arisen, in particular something in need of the One, implies that we are no longer dealing with the One: for the One needs nothing.

The emergence of the inchoate intellect is thus of itself the emergence of something which has an end different from itself. That end is the One (the Good), the intended object of the subject. We should not be misled, however, into thinking that this difference is constituted in a temporal process in such a way that there are temporally distinct episodes of procession and conversion. One implication of this would be that there exists at some point a distinct 'pure subject of desire' without an object which would first be constituted when this pure subject converts. Plotinus warns his readers of such interpretations, however difficult it may be to talk about this matter without using language implying time (cf. V.1.6, 19–22). Intellect is at every stage directed towards the One, which means that it always has an object:

The Good, therefore, has given the trace of itself on Intellect to Intellect to have by seeing, so that in Intellect there is desire, and it is always desiring and always attaining, but the Good is not desiring—for what could it desire?—or attaining, for it did not desire.[5] (III.8.11, 22–4)

It follows that there is no such thing as a pure inchoate intellect which is not already 'converted'. It follows also that the end of what has distanced

---

[4] V.3.11, 6–7: 'So that it desired one thing, having vaguely in itself a kind of image of it' (ὥστε ἄλλου μὲν ἐπεθύμησεν ἀορίστως ἔχουσα ἐπ' αὐτῇ φάντασμά τι). For translating thus, see Bussanich (1988: 222, cf. commentary 224) and Lloyd (1987: 163) who have *aoristôs* ('vaguely') qualify *epethumesn*, 'desired', rather than *echousa* as Armstrong and most other translators take it. The full passage in which these lines occur is discussed in Section 4, pp. 92–5.

[5] III.8.11, 22–4: Τὸ μὲν οὖν ἐπ' αὐτοῦ ἴχνος αὐτοῦ τῷ νῷ ὁρῶντι ἔδωκεν ἔχειν· ὥστε ἐν μὲν τῷ νῷ ἡ ἔφεσις καὶ ἐφιέμενος ἀεὶ καὶ ἀεὶ τυγχάνων, ἐκεῖνος δὲ οὔτε ἐφιέμενος—τίνος γάρ; οὔτε τυγχάνων· οὐδὲ γὰρ ἐφίετο. The text shown here contains an emendation suggested by Theiler and accepted by H-S[2] of the manuscripts' ἐκεῖ to ἐκεῖνος.

itself is in one way always attained: the One is always given as its intended object and there is no other object for it: '[Intellect] thinks that from which it came, for it has nothing else' (V.4.2, 24–5). The inchoate intellect, if I may indulge in mythological talk, proceeds from the One facing it; the intellect, as it were, backs out (cf. III.8.9, 29–31).

There has been an interesting scholarly disagreement between Lloyd and Bussanich on the question of the role of the One in Intellect's vision. Lloyd (1987: *passim*) has maintained, quite rightly, that the inchoate intellect sees an image of the One. In addition, he holds (ibid.: 175 ff.) that the inchoate intellect already contains an indefinite image of the One and that this latter image is 'the One as an object of thought'. According to Lloyd, this, rather than the One itself, is the agent which activates the inchoate intellect into actual thought whose object is 'existence', which is Lloyd's rendering of *ousia* (Being). So Lloyd explicitly denies the direct involvement of the One in the generation of being. Bussanich (1988: 14), on the other hand, argues that 'The One … continues to act as primary cause on the inchoate Intellect; it is not the case that the efflux from the One is left to itself.'[6]

There are many texts that, contra Lloyd, clearly present the One as the agent of the imbuing of the inchoate intellect. And though Plotinus does not always clearly say this in the kind of contexts where one might think it is relevant, he to my knowledge nowhere denies or says anything incompatible with its being so. I agree, therefore, with Bussanich that this must be taken as Plotinus' considered view. This point, however, is quite independent of the question whether what the inchoate intellect apprehends, when so imbued, is the One or merely an image of the One.

There are, however, certain additional difficulties here, not addressed by Lloyd or Bussanich. Given what has been established in the previous chapter about the nature of the distinction between internal and external activity, we can firmly assert that not only the inchoate intellect but also the imbuing is an external act of the One: it is a clear case of the One acting in or on another, namely in or on the inchoate intellect. The latter is of course, as we have seen, also an external act of the One and as such other than it.

---

[6] For Bussanich's (1988) discussion of Lloyd's interpretation see also 13–14, 59–60, 117, and 227–31. Bussanich (1996: 51–5) modifies his view suggesting that Plotinus has two independent accounts of the genesis of Intellect that cannot be collated: one from the point of view of the One itself, in which the One's active role is explicit, another account from the viewpoint of Intellect in which the One as it is in itself does not appear because it is out of Intellect's reach. For a discussion of this modified view, see pp. 96–7 below.

The question then arises whether the One has two different external acts, one by which the inchoate intellect as a recipient is constituted, another one by which this inchoate intellect is informed.[7] It seems that Bussanich's position lays itself open to this question: is the One, on the one hand, externally doing two different things, i.e. first constituting a recipient and then filling up that recipient? I don't think this is what Plotinus wishes to maintain. I believe Lloyd has a point when he insists that what the inchoate intellect apprehends is somehow contained in itself and, hence, right in holding that the actualization of Intellect is a kind of self-determination. I shall return to this question in Section 4 of this chapter.

Plotinus evidently believed that that which has distanced itself from the One, and hence needs it, has no hope of fully getting it. That is to say, what it can get is a substitute, an appearance of the One, but not the One itself. For the mere fact that that which is seeking the One and the One itself are different implies an unbridgeable difference between the intended *telos* and the one attained, Intellect's intentional object. This is brought out by the passage from III.8.11 quoted above: what the intellect actually sees is a trace of the One, not the One itself. Thus, so long as there is a subject different from the One seeking to apprehend it, there is a difference between the intended object and the intentional object. It is important to observe here that a subject identical with the One is not a possible case either: the One is utterly beyond the subject/object distinction, even the rudimentary one we have been envisaging for the inchoate intellect. So the fact that something which is not the One seeks to relate to it suffices to conclude that what this seeker attains isn't the One as it is in itself. For, as Plotinus says, in order to grasp the One, Intellect must surpass itself and cease to be an intellect (III.8.9, 32; VI.7.35).

Why does Plotinus then often simply say that the inchoate intellect sees the One (V.1.6, 41–2; V.3.10), if he means that it really sees an image of it? As we shall see in greater detail in Chapter 3, Section 2, in ordinary vision too, seeing is ontologically speaking of an image of the object, even if Plotinus usually talks about seeing the object without qualification and only occasionally sees a need to point out that the object of vision is an image. The sensible object is an external act of an intelligible item, and hence an image of it. In the case of the inchoate intellect, as in that of

---

[7] The idea of 'imbuing' or 'informing' (*plêrôsis*) by the One is not present in all of Plotinus' account of the genesis of Intellect. It is strikingly present, however, in one of the fullest accounts in VI.7.15–16. Cf. also III.8.11, 6–8.

ordinary vision, it would be normal usage to call seeing such an image 'seeing the thing'. However, any cognition of another is a cognition of an image, of that thing's external act. As a cognition of the One, the inchoate intellect's vision is a cognition of another, for the external act of the One is an image of it and the One in itself remains outside the intellect's reach.

Interestingly, in the context of Intellect's awareness of the One, Plotinus uses visual metaphors without modifying the notion of vision in the sense that he retains the polarity of subject and object. For Intellect vision of the One is vision of another. By contrast, when he uses visual metaphors to describe the mystical, hyperintellectual 'vision' of the One, he has to modify the ordinary notion to the effect that it doesn't imply a polarity of subject and object (VI.9.10).[8] So I suggest that the contrast between 'seeing the One' and 'seeing an image of the One' is a false one: what one sees when one sees the One is really only an image or appearance of the One. It is true that he employs the language of vision also in connection with the mystical union with the One in which case the One is 'seen' as it is in itself. But as already noted, this is a modified notion of seeing.

If asked why the image that Intellect has of the One couldn't constitute knowledge of the One in itself, Plotinus might answer that the One is unknowable; so if you have some object of knowledge that you think may be the One, rest assured that it isn't!

This reasoning as it stands, however, will appear question-begging: 'Why is the One unknowable? I have got a clear and accurate image of it, so I must know it!' it might be retorted. In replying to such an objection Plotinus will appeal to the more general argument which I have made use of in the previous paragraphs: the inchoate intellect is other than the One; hence, the apprehension of the One is an apprehension of another, of something imposed on a different thing, just as in vision and sense-perception generally. No apprehension of one thing by another is an apprehension of the object as it is in itself.

Behind this model lies an important but mostly only implicit assumption: knowing anything as it is in itself is assumed to be knowing it as it is from an

---

[8] Even here in VI.9.10, where Plotinus starts by talking about something that has become simple as seeing itself (which implies that the subject/object distinction is superseded), he qualifies this statement right afterwards by noting that it would be better to say 'has seen', because seeing seems to imply the distinction between seer and seen and hence, strictly speaking, there can be no question of 'seeing the One' in the present tense, even if one afterwards may be tempted to report the experience by saying 'I have seen it'. The implication seems to be that the memory of the experience of the One is like a memory of something seen, which fact need not imply that anything has literally been seen.

internal point of view, knowing it from the point of view of its own internal activity (= being it?). So knowing something in this way means being or becoming identical with it. This is presupposed by the argument above offered in response to the claim that having an accurate image of the One must be good enough for knowing it: however good an impression Intellect had of the One, it would not count as knowing the One as it is in itself, for this wouldn't be knowing it through its internal activity. The One in itself, as we have noted, has a sort of 'mental' life. But this activity or 'quasi-activity' is not that of thought or knowledge. So no thought of anything would capture that activity as it is in itself, for it would fail to be such an activity. Thus, the argument makes a tacit appeal to the fact that the internal activity of the One is not an activity of thought; knowing the One itself would be knowing it through this internal activity. But that is impossible, because this internal activity is not of the order of thought or knowing.

This pattern of reasoning is not at all peculiar to the relation between the One and Intellect, but holds quite generally, e.g. for a soul's apprehension of Intellect: so long as it remains soul, the soul's mode of cognition is an apprehension of another and of an image. To a soul which remains a soul, Intellect in itself is as unknown and unknowable as, and for parallel reasons, the One is to Intellect.[9] The difference is that Intellect is not unknowable *tout court*: by becoming Intellect, one will know the intellect; becoming the One, by contrast, will not make one know the One, for knowing is not the sort of thing that goes on there.

This difference that we have been expounding, between the intended and the intentional object of apprehension, provides the dynamics of the stages in Plotinus' world: it ensures a difference between what a giver has and what is received, a difference which gets the unfolding of reality going.

2. Kinds of Plurality or Otherness

In the previous section we touched upon Plotinus' distinction between subject and object in Intellect. There is, I claimed, a rudimentary distinction

---

[9] The soul may know that Intellect is there above it, that it depends on it and that it has its rational capacities from it; this is however not to know Intellect from the internal point of view (cf. V.3.4, 15). In an entirely parallel way Intellect is aware of the One as its principle, knowing it through its works (V.3.7, 1–9).

between subject and object in the very nature of the inchoate intellect as an entity in need of and longing for the One. The full-blown distinction, however, comes about in the intellect's conversion towards the One, which at the same time is Intellect's apprehension of itself. The difference between the subject of this apprehension and whatever it apprehends is one way in which plurality is introduced (V.4.2, 11–12; V.3.10, 14–16). Plotinus frequently says or implies that this duality between subject and object in Intellect is the first duality (V.4.2, 11–12; III.8.9, 5–12; V.6.1, 7; 5, 10). This is, however, not the only kind of plurality in Intellect, for Intellect also contains many intelligibles or Ideas. So in Intellect the unity of the One is lost, because a subject aiming at something outside itself has emerged and because what this subject apprehends is multiple. Plotinus frequently notes that Intellect falls short of the unity of the One and that it is in fact many. It varies, however, which one of these two kinds of plurality he brings up in support of this claim, and sometimes he mentions both in the same passage (V.3.10, 24–46; VI.7.39, 4–13). Intellect is many on both scores.

The question I now wish to address, a question Plotinus never takes up directly but which I find puzzling, is how these two kinds of plurality are related. Does the differentiation between intelligibles somehow follow upon the subject/object distinction or are there two independent sources of plurality? They certainly appear to be rather different sorts of otherness: the one amounts to the difference between a thinker and its object of thought and the other to the internal differences within the object of thought. It seems to be one thing to assert that there are many different intelligibles and quite another thing to assert that a thinker is different from what he thinks about.

There is a presumption, however, against taking the two kinds as radically independent. Plotinus, as we know, starts with the absolute unity of the One. We know too that this perfect state of affairs is not all there is: from the One, plurality, otherness, somehow arises. However, there is reason to believe that Plotinus wishes Intellect to be so unified that if it were to become more so, it would collapse into the simplicity of the One. The different hypostases and stages in the Plotinian hierarchy of being are identified by a charactistic degree of unity. It is clearly Plotinus' intention not to leave out any possible degree of unity that marks out an entity. Hence, one would not expect him to introduce two different sorts of plurality there without good reason. If the two kinds were entirely unrelated, why wouldn't just one of them do to mark out the second most unified level? But this is not what he proposes. So, presumably, the two kinds are connected.

In fact, alluding to otherness and sameness in Plato's *Sophist*, Plotinus seems to treat otherness as a unitary notion without commenting on its apparently radically different roles. The following passage provides a clear example:

For one must always understand Intellect as otherness and sameness, if it is going to think. For [otherwise] it will not distinguish itself from the intelligible by its relation of otherness to itself, and it will not contemplate all things if no otherness has occurred to make all things exist: for [without otherness] there would not even be two.[10] (VI.7.39, 5–9)

We have here both the difference between subject and object ('the relation of otherness to itself') and within the object (otherness 'makes all things exist'). It would be extremely odd, if Plotinus believed that once the unity of the One is lost, plurality came about in two radically independent ways. We should presume, at least until the contrary is forced upon us, that the two kinds of plurality are connected. There are also passages, e.g. V.3.10, which I am going to consider in some detail, where the distinction between the two roles of otherness seems to be more or less blurred. So the question I now shall address is how the two types of otherness are related if at all.

This question is in itself interesting. It turns out, however, that a satisfactory answer to it requires that we address other fundamental questions about the nature of the intellect and its relationship to the One. Some of these questions were raised but not fully dealt with in the previous section, others will emerge as we proceed.

3. Analysis of V.3.10

Some insight into Plotinus' views on otherness can be extracted from his account of the generation of Intellect from the One given in V.3. I shall now change perspective from the bird's eye view of the *Enneads* that has

---

[10] VI.7.39, 5–9: Δεῖ γὰρ τὸν νοῦν ἀεὶ ἑτερότητα καὶ ταὐτότητα λαμβάνειν, εἴπερ νοήσει. Ἑαυτόν τε γὰρ οὐ διακρινεῖ ἀπὸ τοῦ νοητοῦ τῇ πρὸς αὐτό ἑτέρου σχέσει τά τε πάντα οὐ θεωρήσει, μηδεμιᾶς ἑτερότητος γενομένης εἰς τὸ πάντα εἶναι· οὐδὲ γὰρ ἂν οὐδὲ δύο.

been the mode of inquiry so far in this chapter and consider in some detail a given passage, V.3. 10, 8–11, 16. I take this passage to be quite informative about our question, but there certainly are several other relevant passages as well, many of which I shall turn to in due course.

Chapter V.3.10 begins with considerations of the relationship between the One and Intellect: Plotinus first asserts that the primary principle and the making principle must be one and the same. He then proceeds to consider whether this principle is the One or Intellect. He indicates that indeed the One is needed but the discussion ends in rather inarticulate and general questions and answers (6–8). He promises to resume these questions later. I take it that this is what he does towards the end of the chapter (47–52): the discourse on the One that rather abruptly starts there is not comprehensible in the context, unless it is to be considered as resuming the questions raised in the beginning of the chapter.[11]

In any case, Plotinus proceeds in line 9 to claim that:

Again, it should be said that the intellect needs to see itself or rather possess the seeing of itself, first because it is multiple, and then because it belongs to another, and must necessarily be a seer and a seer of that other, and its seeing is its Being.[12] (V.3.10, 9–13)

It is not immediately clear what is the reference of 'intellect' here. Is it the inchoate intellect, which is not yet seeing, or is it the actualized Intellect? It seems to me that it is both, or rather that Plotinus speaks of the two indiscriminately here: what has a need to see itself is most naturally taken to be

---

[11] In V.3.10, 44–8 Plotinus says: Δεῖ δὲ τὸ νοοῦν μηδὲ αὐτὸ μένειν ἁπλοῦν, καὶ ὅσῳ ἂν μάλιστα αὐτὸ νοῇ· διχάσει γὰρ αὐτὸ ἑαυτό, κἂν σύνεσιν δῷ τὴν σιωπῶσαν. Εἶτα οὐδὲ δεήσεται οἷον πολυπραγμονεῖν ἑαυτό· τί γὰρ καὶ μαθήσεται νοῆσαν; ('But the thinker itself must not remain simple either, especially in so far as it thinks itself: for it will duplicate itself, even if it gives an understanding which is silent. Then it [the One] will not need to make a kind of fuss about itself: for what will it learn by thinking itself?') There is a problem with the text here; I follow Armstrong, who against H-S² emends *siôpên* to *siôpôsan*. Two other points about this passage are beyond doubt: the subject of the first part is *to nooun* in line 44 (which cannot refer to the One) and the implied subject to which *neauto* refers is the One (as Armstrong's translation indicates). The latter point emerges from the content of what is asserted, even if no substantive reference to the One appears in what precedes it. So this is a strange and abrupt shift. What Plotinus goes on to say about the One, however, does indeed respond to some of the questions about it that he raised in the beginning of the chapter, where he says 'Does it not see itself? This one has no need of seeing. But this we will deal with later' (5–7). It appears that this topic is picked up in line 46. So it looks as if these last lines of the chapter are a kind of addition unrelated to what immediately precedes them.

[12] V.3.10, 9–13: ... τοῦτον τὸν νοῦν δεηθῆναι τοῦ ὁρᾶν ἑαυτόν, μᾶλλον δὲ ἔχειν τὸ ὁρᾶν ἑαυτόν, πρῶτον μὲν τῷ πολὺν εἶναι, εἶτα καὶ τῷ ἑτέρου εἶναι, καὶ ἐξ ἀνάγκης ὁρατικὸν εἶναι, καὶ ὁρατικὸν ἐκείνου, καὶ τὴν οὐσίαν αὐτοῦ ὅρασιν εἶναι.

the inchoate intellect, while that whose vision is Being is the fully-fledged Intellect. Interestingly, the passage speaks of the intellect as both a self-seer and as a seer of the One.[13] There is no indication that there are two different visions, that the seeing of the One is different from vision of self. On the contrary. Thus, the passage provides an example of what was noted in the previous section that what is called the self-vision of the Intellect and Intellect's vision of the One may well be the same thing. As we shall see, the first lines of the following chapter of V.3 and several other passages also make it clear that an attempt to see the One results in Intellect's self-vision. In a sense the intellect is exposed to the One but doesn't see it; what it actually sees instead is itself. More on this later.

Nor is it evident why Intellect needs to see itself because it is multiple, or how its seeing itself is connected to its seeing the One. The last point, however, is no doubt to be explained by the fact that though the One is the intended external object of this intellect's vision, which doesn't reach out to this object and must make do with an image of it, it is, nevertheless, the cognition of this image that constitutes Intellect's self-thinking. That this is so is again fairly explicit in the beginning of chapter 11, which we shall come to, and several other passages.[14] Thus, self-thinking is nothing other than the thinking of the One, or perhaps better, the self-thinking of Intellect is the form the attempt to think the One takes.

The question why Intellect needs to see itself because it is multiple (*tôi polyn einai*), is complicated by the fact that it is not immediately clear what Plotinus means by calling this intellect 'multiple'.[15] Is it the

---

[13] Ham (2000: 189) takes the two genitives, *heterou* and *ekeinou*, to refer not to the One but to the internal object of the intellect's vision. This is possible, though, if this were the case, *heterou*, as an internal object of thought, would be very abruptly introduced and *ekeinou* would be a highly unusual way to refer to an internal object of thought. The One, however, has been referred to in the context (*houtos* in line 6) so that a reference to it here by the two genitives would not be so abrupt. For these reasons I prefer to see here a reference to the One as the object of the intellect's vision. This is, however, not to deny that what the intellect in fact sees when it 'sees' the One is an internal object, cf. the next note.

[14] A passage that very explicitly asserts that the vision of the One and self-thinking are the same is V.6.5, 16–17 (cf. also VI.9.2, 33–43): '[I]n thinking the Good it [Intellect] thinks itself incidentally; for in looking towards the Good it thinks itself.' It may seem rather odd that Plotinus says that Intellect thinks itself incidentally. The meaning is no doubt that what the intellect primarily intended to do was to grasp the One, but what it in fact ended up doing was thinking itself. See Bussanich's (1988) commentary on these passages *ad loc.*

[15] It should be noted that Plotinus uses here in V.3.10, 10 a singular form of *polys* ('many'). It is not clear to me what the significance of this is, if any. One might suppose that the singular form by itself would exclude multiplicity in the sense of 'many intelligible objects', i.e. the first option of

multiplicity within the object of thought, i.e. the plurality of intelligibles that he has in mind? Or is it the fact that the inchoate intellect is indefinite or unlimited (*aoristos, apeiros*) but potentially any and everything, that lies behind Plotinus' calling it 'multiple'? There surely are passages where Plotinus describes the inchoate intellect's great potency in terms of its being multiple and its *plêthos*.[16] Thirdly, may the intellect Plotinus speaks of here be called multiple because it involves a kind of distinction between a subject of need and an object this subject is directed to?

The first option is hardly a genuine possibility, even if the plurality of the objects of thought is at stake later in V.3.10 and even if we disregard the question whether we are dealing with the inchoate intellect or the full-blown Intellect. For the multiplicity on the object side is something that comes about in or through Intellect's vision of itself. It would be implausible to suppose that this plurality of objects, which first appears in the intellect's vision, explains the intellect's *need* to see itself. It is first in the vision that a multiplicity of objects arises. Hence, the explanation of the need cannot appeal to the multiplicity of the object as if this was something already established. The sentence is surely most naturally understood as implying that the intellect is already multiple 'prior' to the vision, and that this multiplicity somehow explains its need to see itself.

As to the second alternative, even if it may make some sense if we look at the sentence in isolation, it doesn't seem to be the case that the sort of plurality proposed here, the inchoate intellect's potential plurality, its pregnancy, if we may call it that, is explicitly at stake in the context at all. So I would not venture to suggest this as a real option. It wouldn't help explain anything of what follows.

One might argue for the third option as follows: by the very fact of having departed from the One, the intellect spoken of here is other than the One. What has departed from the One and become other than it no longer has the utter simplicity and perfection of the One. What has departed from such unity and perfection lacks it, and, in this case at least, needs it. In virtue of being in this state of incompleteness and ensuing need and desire,

interpretation discussed in the main text here. There are, however, two occurrences in chapter 11 of V.3 (lines 7 and 9), where the singular is used to convey the plurality of intelligibles. As a matter of fact, Plotinus quite often uses *polys* in the singular to qualify *nous*. Cf. e.g. III.8.8, 33; V.1.5, 1; VI.4.4, 25; VI.7.39, 15.

[16] For a discussion of *plêthos* in such context and its possible relation to the indefinite dyad, see Szlezák (1979: 65) and Bussanich (1988: 15–17; 167).

the inchoate intellect is multiple: need is a relational stance implying a difference between what is in need and that which it needs. So that which has a need is not one, hence it is a complex, i.e. a multiple thing. As I explained in the previous section, this need is a kind of longing for the unity and perfection of the One. The One itself, because it lacks nothing, has no such need (III.8.11, 10–16; V.3.10, 6; V.3.13, 17; VI.7.38, 1–2) but the first thing posterior to it, the inchoate intellect, does (cf. e.g. III.8.11, 15; V.3.13, 11–12; VI.9.6, 18–19). Hence, the latter is in this respect incomplete and not self-sufficient. This lack of self-sufficiency cannot be fully overcome by anything which is not the One itself. However, the intellect may achieve the highest degree of unity and perfection that falls short of the One itself. This is the unity and perfection that pertain to seeing the One in an intellectual vision. That vision is at the same time Intellect's vision of itself. It is this third option that I go for. The plurality at stake here is of course the plurality we explained in the previous section that is involved in the rudimentary subject/object distinction implied by the inchoate intellect's need for the One. This is a subject/object distinction in a way but it is not yet the articulate distinction between thinker and object of thought.

Plotinus then proceeds to argue for the necessity of the full-blown subject/object distinction in Intellect. First he remarks that without an object distinct from the subject there can be no vision (V.3.10, 14–16). Then this same point is hammered through in terms of the necessity for activity (*energeia*) to have an object on which to act (16–26): activity involves the plurality between the agent and that on which the agent acts. This distinction, however, does not appear to be, or at least it is not necessarily, a distinction between an agent and a patient in an Aristotelian sense. What he has primarily in mind is the difference between a thinker and the thinker's thought. He concludes this discussion thus:

Therefore, that which is active must either be acting on something else, or must itself be a multiple thing, if it is to be active within itself. But if a thing is not going to go forth to something else, it will be immobile; but when it is altogether immobile, it will not think. That which thinks then, when it thinks, must be in two parts, and either one must be external to the other or both must be in the same, and the thinking must be in otherness, and necessarily also in sameness; and the proper objects of thought must be the same and other in relation to the intellect.[17] (V.3.10, 20–6)

[17] V.3.10, 20–6: Διὸ δεῖ τὸ ἐνεργοῦν ἢ περὶ ἄλλο ἐνεργεῖν, ἢ αὐτὸ πολύ τι εἶναι, εἰ μέλλοι ἐνεργεῖν ἐν αὐτῷ. Εἰ δὲ μή τι προελεύσεται ἐπ' ἄλλο, στήσεται· ὅταν δὲ πᾶσαν

This whole passage is about the duality of subject and object, about the necessity of such a duality if there is to be thinking. The multiple nature of the object as such is not yet explicitly at issue in the argument. It is worth noting that this passage suggests that it is the otherness of a thinking subject, a subject's taking a stance towards an object, which is the driving force of the process towards multiplicity. This seems to me to emerge from the remark in the passage above that 'if a thing is not going to go forth to something else, it will be immobile; but when it is altogether immobile, it will not think' (cf. VI.7.13, 11 ff.). That is to say, such distancing from the source is essentially involved in both the thought that arises from the original separation from the One and in the proliferation of subordinate intelligibles within Intellect (cf. VI.7.13; VI.7.39, 6–9). Such distancing is also at work in the generation of new hypostases, i.e. of Soul from Intellect, the difference no doubt being that in the latter sort of case the object aimed at is external as the One is external to Intellect's vision (see Chapter 3, Section 8 for more on the role of distancing). I take it that such externality is implied by Plotinus' view that a lower hypostasis is a mere image of and apprehends only an image of a prior hypostasis (cf. V.3.3–4).

Now, back to our text. Plotinus proceeds immediately after the last quote above to say:

And, yet again, each of the things that are being thought brings out along with itself sameness and otherness; or what will the thinker think which does not contain different things?[18] (V.3.10, 27–9)

With this he embarks on a discussion of the necessary plural nature of the object of thought. The transition from the last passage quoted to the present one is an instance of what I mentioned above about how Plotinus seems to move freely between the two kinds of otherness involved in the attempt to grasp the One and otherness within the object of thought. For at the end of the passage cited above (lines 20–6), he speaks about thinking being in otherness, clearly having in mind otherness between the thinker and its object of thought. Thus here, without any special warning, he turns

στάσιν, οὐ νοήσει. Δεῖ τοίνυν τὸ νοοῦν, ὅταν νοῇ, ἐν δυσὶν εἶναι, καὶ ἢ ἔξω θάτερον ἢ ἐν τῷ αὐτῷ ἄμφω, καὶ ἀεὶ ἐν ἑτερότητι τὴν νόησιν εἶναι καὶ ἐν ταυτότητι δὲ ἐξ ἀνάγκης· καὶ εἶναι τὰ κυρίως νοούμενα πρὸς τὸν νοῦν καὶ τὰ αὐτὰ καὶ ἕτερα.

[18] V.3.10, 27–9: καὶ πάλιν αὖ ἕκαστον τῶν νοουμένων συνεκφέρει τὴν ταυτότητα ταύτην καὶ τὴν ἑτερότητα· ἢ τί νοήσει, ὃ μὴ ἔχει ἄλλο καὶ ἄλλο.

to the diversity within the object of thought, employing again the very term *heterotês*, 'otherness'. Again, I note this at the present stage to return to the point more fully later on. After a few lines Plotinus continues:[19]

For if [that which thinks] directed its gaze to a single object without parts, it would be speechless: for what would it have to say about it, or to understand? For if the altogether partless had to speak itself, it must, first of all, say what it is not; so that in this way too it would be many in order to be one. Then when it says 'I am this', if it means something other than itself by this 'this', it will be telling a lie; but if it is speaking of an attribute of itself, it will be saying that it is many or saying 'am, am' or 'I I'. Well, then, suppose it was only two things and said 'I and this'. It would already be necessary for it to be many: for, as the two things are different and in whatever manner they differ, number is already there and many other things. Therefore, the thinker must grasp one thing different from another and the object of thought in being thought must contain variety; or there will not be a thought of it, but only a touching and a sort of contact without speech or thought, prethinking because Intellect has not yet come into being and that which touches does not think.[20] (V.3.10, 31–44).

Parts of this quotation are quite obscure in the details. Whichever way these are to be interpreted, however, the passage provides a clear example of the blurring of the distinction between otherness within the object and otherness between subject and object. For 'the partless' spoken of here is introduced as a partless object of thought, a hypothesis that is to be shown to be untenable. So the object of thought cannot be partless. However, when Plotinus turns this into the question about how the partless could 'speak itself' and argues that this would be impossible, he is addressing

---

[19] The omitted sentence καταμανθάνει τοίνυν ἑαυτὸ τῷ ποικίλον ὀφθαλμὸν εἶναι ἢ ποικίλων χρωμάτων (30–1) ('it understands itself by being a many-coloured eye or [an eye] of many colours', sounds interesting but I haven't been able to decipher its message satisfactorily. The various translators' versions differ quite widely in meaning. The one ventured here just above is only one of several possibilities. The word *poikilos* ('many-coloured', 'variegated') is in any case commonly used to indicate the plurality and variety of intelligible objects, e.g. in line 41 (rendered here by 'variety') of the present passage, quoted below. Cf. also e.g. IV.4.1, 21–3; VI.2.2, 3; VI.4.11, 15; VI.7.13, 37–8.

[20] V.3.10, 31–44: Εἰ γὰρ ἑνὶ καὶ ἀμερεῖ προσβάλλοι, ἠλογήθη· τί γὰρ ἂν ἔχοι περὶ αὐτοῦ εἰπεῖν, ἢ τί συνεῖναι; Καὶ γὰρ εἰ τὸ ἀμερὲς πάντη εἰπεῖν αὐτὸν δέοι, δεῖ πρότερον λέγειν ἃ μὴ ἔστιν· ὥστε καὶ οὕτως πολλὰ ἂν εἶναι, ἵνα ἓν εἴη. Εἶθ' ὅταν λέγῃ "εἰμὶ τόδε" τὸ "τόδε" εἰ μὲν ἕτερον τι αὐτοῦ ἐρεῖ, ψεύσεται· εἰ δὲ συμβεβηκὸς αὐτῷ, πολλὰ ἐρεῖ ἢ τοῦτο ἐρεῖ "εἰμὶ εἰμί" καὶ "ἐγὼ ἐγώ". Τί οὖν, εἰ δύο μόνα εἴη καὶ λέγοι "ἐγὼ καὶ τοῦτο"; Ἡ ἀνάγκη πόλλ' ἤδη εἶναι· καὶ γὰρ ὡς ἕτερα καὶ ὅπη ἕτερα καὶ ἀριθμὸς ἤδη καὶ πολλὰ ἄλλα· δεῖ τοίνυν τὸ νοοῦν ἕτερον καὶ ἕτερον λαβεῖν καὶ τὸ νοούμενον κατανοούμενον ὂν ποικίλον εἶναι· ἢ οὐκ ἔσται νόησις αὐτοῦ, ἀλλὰ θίξις καὶ οἷον ἐπαφὴ μόνον ἄρρητος καὶ ἀνόητος, προνοοῦσα οὔπω νοῦ γεγονότος καὶ τοῦ θιγγάνοντος οὐ νοοῦντος.

the distinction between the subject of thought and its object as well: the partless could not speak itself without separating itself from what it thinks, could not separate the 'I' from what it says about this; if it did separate it, it would no longer be partless. But the separation of the 'I' is the separation of a subject of thought from the object. So he has invoked the subject/object distinction as well as the one between internal differences within the object.

Lines 32–4 ('For if the altogether partless … to be one') are particularly difficult. Why should the partless, if it were to speak itself, first have to say what it is not? And what does Plotinus mean by saying that it would have to be many also in this way in order to be one? I am not overly confident about this, but the following interpretation seems to make some sense of the remark and helps explain the subsequent lines.

To 'speak', i.e. (here) to think, at all, involves a demarcation, setting the object of thought apart from other things; hence, to speak oneself involves demarcating what one is from what one is not; thus, the very act of thinking what one is, is also an act of thinking what one is not. Therefore, a thinker who is 'speaking itself' has a complex mind in the sense that it thinks at least two things, what it itself is and what it is not. On the presupposition that this thinker really is speaking itself and that it really is partless, the implication that it must also think what it is not shows that it nevertheless is complex and, hence, not partless after all.

This may look suspect as an argument. For why should the complexity of the thought involving a partless object and what this object is not implicate the partless object as such in complexity? Couldn't the object remain simple though the thought of it is necessarily complex? Plotinus might respond against the view behind this question by pointing out that since the thought in question is self-thinking, 'speaking oneself', as it is put here, one could argue that if the self-thought of the partless object is necessarily complex, the object itself cannot be quite simple. For if it really was itself which contained a complex thought of itself, however simple and partless it itself appeared in that thought, its thinking is complex. So if this thinking really is its thinking, it itself is complex.

But what about the other point, that a partless object would have to be many in this way in order to be one? It must be confessed that here I am somewhat at a loss. This is not so much because the sentence doesn't make sense in itself as because it is open to several interpretations and the context does not help to decide between them. But perhaps this is what

Plotinus is getting at: the unity of a thinker who thinks itself somehow consists in its subject and object aspects making up just one thing (this will be a central topic of the next chapter). In order for a subject of thought to be one with its object, it must think this object; but if it is to do so, it must also think what its object is not—this lies in the nature of thinking. And if the object is it itself, it must in order to think itself at all think what it itself is not, since this brings about the complexity involved in a thing and its negation. Thus, complexity is a presupposition of the thought which unifies the subject which thinks itself with its object, i.e. itself.

This is what I tentatively make out of these lines. If this interpretation is at all on the right track, it may help elucidate Plotinus' train of thought in the celebrated lines of our passage which relate the thought experiment of the partless which tries, and fails, on penalty of ceasing to be partless, to utter something about itself. Here Plotinus says: 'Then when it says "I am this", if it means something other than itself by this "this", it will be telling a lie; but if it is speaking of an attribute of itself, it will be saying that it is many or saying "am, am" or "I I" '. The first point may readily be granted: I assume that this a question of the 'is' of identity: the partless is saying that it is identical with a different thing, and this is evidently false. Let us then suppose that the 'this' is an attribute of the partless. But in that case the attribute the partless refers to when it says 'I am this' either introduces something at least conceptually different from the partless itself, hence a duality in the partless that is incompatible with its partlessness, or the attribute in no way differs from the partless itself; in the latter case, the partless would be reduced to uttering 'am, am', or 'I, I', which, as Ham (2000: 196) notes, would be failing to say or think anything at all, mere gibberish.[21]

Clearly the general point is that any sort of attempt on the part of the partless to describe itself compromises its partlessness. So we have a kind of *reductio ad absurdum*: if the partless succeeds in saying (thinking) something about itself, this very fact shows that it was not partless after all. Plotinus is making an intuitive and undogmatic point about the necessary plurality of the object of thought. A mental state that has something utterly undifferentiated

[21] I think Ham (2000: 196) is quite right in rejecting both that the formulas 'am, am' and 'I, I' stand for tautologies and the view of Beierwaltes (1991: 132) and Oosthout (1991: 136–7) that by the repetition in the formulae Plotinus wishes to indicate that even these formulas involve a complexity. Ham also plausibly suggests that behind this lies the doctrine of Plato's *Sophist* 262a–d that a *logos* must contain both a noun and a verb in order to say anything at all.

as its intentional object involves no understanding, no grasp of anything. The 'something' that must be involved in any 'grasp' must be differentiated from and seen against a certain context. Otherwise there is nothing to be grasped. True enough, we sometimes have our entire visual field filled with something uniform, e.g. with darkness or the white of a heavy snowstorm, or, to take an example Plotinus uses himself in a different context, of a uniform sky that fills our vision (II.8.2, 11–14). Yet such cases would not count as counter-examples here, because these objects are differentiated against other concepts and knowledge that we have: I see the snow-filled scene as white, and thereby as something that I know to be differentiated from something else, e.g. the non-white. In the case we are considering, however, the intellect doesn't enjoy the benefit of such previously acquired notions to sort out what meets it. It hasn't had any experience so far that would enable it to do so. An undifferentiated limitless totality that cannot be contrasted with anything is not a possible object of an intellectual grasp.

Perhaps Plotinus' train of thought in this chapter, including the transition from the subjective to the objective use of *heterotês*, is relatively easy to follow. We might summarize it as follows:

(1) A duality between the One and something else has arisen.
(2) This 'something else' seeks to apprehend the One in an intellectual vision.
(3) Intellectual vision must be of something composite, otherwise it fails to grasp anything at all.

Hence:

(4) What appears in the intellectual vision directed at the One is something composite.

This account would suggest that indeed there is a connection between the otherness of the subject and the otherness within the object. Each type of otherness turns out to be an essential feature of thought, though the differentiation of a subject may be said to be primary in the sense that were we to give a discursive account of what has happened, this would have to come first as a condition *sine qua non* of thought; when it is satisfied, there is a further argument needed to show that the object of the thought of this subject must be composite. Thus, provided that the subject that has differentiated itself is a subject of thought, it follows that its object is composite.

Certain difficulties, however, remain. We saw Plotinus claiming in lines 39–44 of V.3.10 that an encounter with something partless that is experienced as such would not count as thought but be a mere undifferentiated 'touch'. What exactly is this 'touch'? Why couldn't there be an experience in which there is a subject/object distinction but has something undifferentiated as its object? Such an experience would admittedly not be thought, but if it is at all possible, it would seem to constitute a case where the two kinds of plurality part: we would have the subject/object plurality without the objective one. Isn't 'the touch' just an experience of this sort?

4. The Intellect's Undifferentiated Impression of the One

Let us start the inquiry into this by considering the scope of Plotinus' claim: what is this partless kind of thing he has in mind? Though he does not in the relevant lines of our chapter explicitly speak about the One—the word he uses for that which cannot be thought and may only be touched is *to ameres*, 'the partless'—there is no doubt that what he has in mind in the context is the One. He says that the touch in question is not thinking but pre-thinking 'because Intellect has not yet come into being'. This shows that that which touches is the inchoate intellect and the touch is meant to describe its original experience of the One. Thus, the 'touch and kind of contact' here must be seen together with the impression of the One and immediate experience (*epibolê*) of it that are spoken of in the next chapter of V.3, which we shall consider shortly.

The point about the inscrutability of the partless may however be a perfectly general one: nothing that is partless can be an object of thought. Though the One is pre-eminently partless, the only thing that is so absolutely, other things may also be said to be so relatively speaking. A genus for instance, considered in itself and without consideration of its species, is then considered as partless.[22] The claim may apply to such a case as well: for any intelligible item to become a proper object of thought, it must be seen through its parts and relations to other things. This means

---

[22] I take it that 'intellect in itself' and 'the genus in itself' spoken of e.g. in VI.2.20 are examples of such unities that *per se* do not explicitly contain a reference to what falls under them. Cf. Lloyd (1990: 81 ff.)

that anything which is apprehended as undifferentiated, even if it may not be such absolutely speaking, is, so conceived, not an object of thought. There would not be thought of such an object until it is 'unfolded' into its components or seen in relation to its equals and superiors. As we shall see later on, there is reason to believe that Plotinus actually held such a view (see Chapter 3, Section 8). As Remes (forthcoming) notes, this would render his views on this matter akin to the views expressed by Socrates in the *Theaetetus* 201e–202c about the unknowability of undifferentiated elements.

I shall now turn to another question that our text gives rise to: granting Plotinus' reasonable point that for there to be thought there must be a certain otherness, variety, within the object of thought, one may still wonder, especially in the light of his explicit introduction of undifferentiated 'touch' in the context, why something of the nature of this touch should not be an intermediate stage between the One and the thinking of Intellect. That is to say, why couldn't there be a state of contact involving a differentiation of a subject that would not yet count as thinking because its object is undifferentiated? The possibility of such an intermediate stage would upset the cogency of the argument sketched at the end of the previous section, since the possibility of such a contact would be in conflict with the tacit assumption of the argument that the first stage after the One must be a stage of thought. So the step taken from (1) to (2) above, which involves the assumption that the subject that has differentiated itself from the One is a subject of thought, would appear as dubious: for the subject of the contact, which is not a subject of thinking, comes in between the subject/object distinction and thought (intellectual vision).[23] Consequently, there would be a greater gap between the differentiation of a subject and the differentiation within the object than the story told above would have us believe.

Strictly speaking, Plotinus does not commit himself to the actuality of this 'touch and sort of contact' in V.3.10. He only says that as regards the partless, 'there will not be thought of it, but only a touching and a sort of contact without speech or thought, prethinking because Intellect has not yet come into being and that which touches does not think' (V.3.10, 42–4).

---

[23] Lloyd (1987: 180) too raises this same question about the next stage after the One: '...we are entitled to ask, why thought? (Why not love or the Niagara Falls?) Certainly we can point to a tradition which gave supreme value to *Nous* and which could be taken for granted by Plotinus. But what are his *grounds*?' I fully share the presuppositions and sentiments expressed in these questions. In Section 6 I attempt to provide an answer.

The way this is phrased does not express a commitment to the reality of this 'touch and sort of contact'. There are other passages, however, that allude to a direct experience, beyond thought, that the inchoate intellect has of the One. Thus, in VI.7.16, 13–14 he says that 'it was not yet intellect when it looked at it [the One], but looked unintellectually (*anoêtôs*)'. And in the subsequent chapter of our treatise, V.3.11, there are clear references to such pre-noetic experience of the One, though it is not expressed in terms of contact. This passage is worth quoting as a whole:

Therefore this multiple intellect, when it wishes to think what is beyond, wishes to think this itself as one,[24] but in wishing to experience[25] it immediately in its simplicity it comes out continually grasping something else made many in itself. So that it moved to it not as Intellect but as sight not yet seeing, but came out possessing the multiplicity which that sight itself made; so that it vaguely [see note 4] desired one thing, having in itself a kind of image (*phantasma ti*) of it, but came out having grasped something else which it made many in itself. The sight, again, certainly has the impression (*typos*) of what it has seen: otherwise it would not have allowed it to come into being in itself. But this impression became multiple out of one, and so Intellect knew it and saw it, and then it became a seeing sight. It is already Intellect when it possesses this, and it possesses it as Intellect; but before this it was only desire and unformed sight. So this intellect had an immediate experience of the One, but by grasping it it became Intellect, perpetually in need [of the One][26] and becoming Intellect, Being and intellection when it thought.

[24] The word ἕν ('one') here is an emendation originally suggested by Dodds (1961: 708) and adopted by H–S and Armstrong. My translation follows that of Bussanich (1988: 221–2) with a slight modification.

[25] The expression 'experience immediately' here as well as 'immediate experience' in line 15 are renderings of *epiballein*. Here in line 4 *epiballein* is a controversial reading, though it gives a much better sense than the better attested *epithallein* ('to flower upon'). See Bussanich (1988: 223) and Armstrong's footnote *ad loc*. In any case, I must apologize for the rendering of *epibolê* and its cognates by means of 'immediate experience'. Plotinus resorts to the term *epiballein* when he wishes to refer to an experience that transcends thought (cf. III.8.9, 21; VI.7.35, 19–22; VI.7.39, 2), though he may also use it of acts of thought (cf. IV.4.1, 20; 2, 12). In the latter case, he wants to emphasize the non-discursive, intuitive nature of the thought in question. Alternative translations such as Armstrong's rendering of *epibale* as 'immediate apprehension' in line V.3.11, 13 seem to me not to differentiate the experience in question sufficiently from thought and understanding. For possible Epicurean origins of the term see Rist (1967: 50–2).

[26] This translation and the Greek text provided in n. 27 endorse Igal's emendation of *endiamenos* (which does not make any sense) or *endiathemenos* ('disposed') of the manuscripts to *endeomenos* ('in need'). For a discussion of the issue, see Bussanich's (1988: 207) commentary. As we have seen, Plotinus frequently remarks that Intellect is in need of the One.

For before this it was not intellection since it did not possess the intelligible object, nor Intellect since it had not yet thought.[27] (V.3.11, 1–18)

This passage indeed deserves a close and elaborate scrutiny. I shall, however, let suffice a few observations that are directly relevant to our present concerns.

The chapter starts out by saying that the inchoate intellect wishes to experience the One in its simplicity but comes out grasping something that it has multiplied in itself (1–4). From this he concludes that 'it vaguely desired one thing, having in itself a kind of image (*phantasma ti*) of it'. Next the intellect is said to receive an impression of its object of vision, which no doubt is the One itself. This impression starts out as one, i.e. as undifferentiated, but as the intellect seeks to grasp it, the impression becomes multiple and it is as such that the intellect sees and knows it. This is followed up by the statement that the intellect 'has an immediate experience' (*epebale*) (13) of the One but by grasping it (*labôn*) it became Intellect.

I take it that what is said in lines 1–4, as well as the remarks about the impression and the *epibolê* invoked in line 13 all describe the same experience of the inchoate intellect and make more or less the same point, though in different terms that gradually fill out the picture. But the question arises whether what is said about the 'sort of image' in line 7 can be taken as yet another reference to the same experience. There would be nothing wrong, semantically speaking, with taking *typos* ('impression') and *phantasma ti* ('sort of image') to refer to the same thing. If so, Plotinus would be describing the same experience in four different ways in our passage. In fact, I tentatively lean towards this way of reading the passage (apparently, so does Ham (2000: 201–9)). This is not the only possible way, however. The sort of image can be seen as something different from

---

27 V.3.11, 1–18: Διὸ καὶ ὁ νοῦς οὗτος ὁ πολύς, ὅταν τὸ ἐπέκεινα ἐθέλῃ νοεῖν, ἓν μὲν οὖν αὐτὸ ἐκεῖνο, ἀλλ᾽ ἐπιβάλλειν θέλων ὡς ἁπλῷ ἔξεισιν ἄλλο ἀεὶ λαμβάνων ἐν αὐτῷ πληθυνόμενον· ὥστε ὥρμησε μὲν ἐπ᾽ αὐτὸ οὐχ ὡς νοῦς, ἀλλ᾽ ὡς ὄψις οὔπω ἰδοῦσα, ἐξῆλθε δὲ ἔχουσα ὅπερ αὐτὴ ἐπλήθυνεν· ὥστε ἄλλου μὲν ἐπεθύμησεν ἀορίστως ἔχουσα ἐπ᾽ αὐτῇ φάντασμά τι, ἐξῆλθε δὲ ἄλλο λαβοῦσα ἐν αὐτῇ αὐτὸ πολὺ ποιήσασα. Καὶ γὰρ αὖ ἔχει τύπον τοῦ ὁράματος· ἢ οὐ παρεδέξατο ἐν αὐτῇ γενέσθαι. Οὗτος δὲ πολὺς ἐξ ἑνὸς ἐγένετο, καὶ οὕτως γνοὺς εἶδεν αὐτό, καὶ τότε ἐγένετο ἰδοῦσα ὄψις. Τοῦτο δὲ ἤδη νοῦς, ὅτε ἔχει, καὶ ὡς νοῦς ἔχει· πρὸ δὲ τούτου ἔφεσις μόνον καὶ ἀτύπωτος ὄψις. οὗτος οὖν ὁ νοῦς ἐπέβαλε μὲν ἐκείνῳ, λαβὼν δὲ ἐγένετο νοῦς, ἀεὶ δὲ ἐνδεόμενος καὶ γενόμενος καὶ νοῦς καὶ οὐσία καὶ νόησις, ὅτε ἐνόησε· πρὸ γὰρ τούτου οὐ νόησις ἦν τὸ νοητὸν οὐκ ἔχων οὐδὲ νοῦς οὔπω νοήσας.

the impression and the rest. Since each of these two interpretations is of considerable interest for our understanding of the genesis of Intellect, I shall sketch both of them in what follows.

The image is presented here as if the inchoate intellect contained it all along. So, if the image is the same thing as the impression, the intellect also contained the impression all along. The immediate experience (*epibolê*) spoken of at the beginning and the end of the passage will then presumably also involve such an innate image, though this is not explicitly mentioned. The image is presented as a reason for the intellect's longing for the One. This makes some sense: if the inchoate intellect is to have a longing for the One, it must have some inkling of it. The intellect and its notion of the One, however, must be such that it is clear to the intellect that it itself is failing with respect to that which its image presents to it: it doesn't itself possess what it senses of it; hence, it desires it. I mentioned earlier in this chapter that the inchoate intellect's need and desire for the One amounts to a rudimentary differentiation of a subject (see p. 73 above). I take it that the image and desire here is evidence for this rudimentary differentiation of a subject that senses the lack of and need for the One, though in an inarticulate way.

How could a coherent story be made out of this? Perhaps the right way to look at the matter is along the following lines. The inchoate intellect is indefinite sight or 'sight not yet seeing'. The term 'seeing' is then understood metaphorically, of course, but still according to the logic of the ordinary sense of the word, which requires that there is a distinction between seer and seen and that the object of the vision is determinate. The inchoate intellect does not *see* anything in this sense. This is, however, not to say that the inchoate intellect's sight has no content whatsoever. It does in a sense 'see' the One (or 'touch' the One) but the image it has of it is indeterminate, undifferentiated. Hence, it is not yet seeing. This image is the content of the indefinite sight. The image is, however, sufficiently articulate for its possessor to realize that it itself falls short of the source of it. Therefore it desires this source. We may suppose that, by means of the image it has got, the intellect has some feeling of a difference between this source and itself, some awareness of a lack which the possession of the One would amend. So it seeks to make out what the source of this image is but it fails to grasp it in its simplicity and its vision becomes manifold. On this account it is supposed that the inchoate intellect faces in two directions, so to speak: it turns away from the One, thereby establishing a difference between itself and it, but it does so 'facing it' so that it innately senses it in a non-intellectual way and contains an image of it. Since, however, the inchoate intellect is essentially an intellect, whose nature it is to think or to see a manifold of determinate objects, it must break up this undifferentiated image in order to grasp it.

If we adopt this interpretation, the passage quoted above from V.3.11 describes the same phenomenon four times in different terms: the immediate experience of the One that the intellect wishes for in lines 1–3, the sort of image in line 7, the impression in line 8, and the immediate experience in line 13, all describe the vision the inchoate intellect has of the One and how this vision becomes multiple when the intellect tries to think it.

This is not the only way to read the passage, however. Alternatively, we may decide to say that the sort of image the intellect has describes something different from the impression and immediate experience. We would in that case tell the same story as before about the image, feeling of incompleteness, and longing, but we would explain the impression and the immediate experience differently. Instead of assuming that the inchoate intellect has an innate impression and immediate experience of the One, we now suppose that, on account of its desire, based on the image, it turns to the One and tries to see it. In so doing the inchoate intellect receives an immediate impression of the One in its simplicity, but, being essentially a thinker or a seer, it doesn't manage to hold on to this impression and has to multiply it in order to make something out of it.

I am uncertain which of these two accounts is closer to Plotinus' intentions. Crudely put, the difference between the two accounts seems to come to this: on the former account, the intellect's attempt at seeing the One consists in its elucidating an innate image, a process that turns out to be thought rather than the grasp of the One as it is in itself. On the second account, there is first a vague kind of image of the One; this image and its ensuing longing then lead to an attempt at seeing involving a new impression which in the same way as on the former account results in thinking. Each account could be defended as an interpretation of V.3.11, and other texts, so far as I can tell, are not particularly helpful in deciding the matter. The majority of the texts that discuss the genesis of Intellect do not explicitly mention an undifferentiated experience of the One. If I was given the choice, I would, however, opt for the former account, because it is simpler and neater.

In the first section of this chapter, I mentioned the disagreement between Lloyd (1987) and Bussanich (1988, 1996) about the role of the

One in the informing of the intellect. The former account of V.3.11 adopted above is closer to Lloyd in that it proposes that the incentive to think comes from an innate image the intellect has of the One. It is not obvious where a conversion towards the One itself would fit into this story, nor is it clear how the One plays an active role in informing the intellect. I would, however, like to do justice to Bussanich's (1988: 14) sound remark that the One, according to some central passages on the topic, indeed plays such an active role. So how could we fit that into what has been said?

The best we can do is, first, to emphasize that the image of the One the inchoate intellect contains comes from the One itself. Then we should see the so-called conversion as the intellect's attempt to attain the One, i.e. its attempt, informed as it is by its feeling of the One's perfection, to become as like it as it is capable of. Thus, the content the intellect transforms into being and beings comes immediately from the One, which is also the guiding principle of these transformations. This is all that the so-called conversion amounts to. I cannot see anything in the passages that most notably speak of the inchoate intellect as being informed or imbued by the One (VI.7.16–17; III.8.11) that contradicts such an account.

On the second account, the conversion and filling would consist in the intellect's turning around (if it wasn't always faced in the direction of the One) and getting a fresh impression of it. I believe this is close to Bussanich's view (see p. 75 above). This account is straightforward enough, but it faces the problem mentioned earlier of explaining whether there are, as it were, two emanations from the One, one constituting the inchoate intellect and another one doing the filling (see pp. 75–6 above).[28] That would for various reasons complicate the matter: are we to suppose that the One is doing one thing when 'emanating' the inchoate intellect, and something quite different when it informs it? Somehow, I have a difficulty with believing that the One is so versatile in its activities.

I am not sure to what extent Bussanich's (1996: 51–5) clever suggestion that Plotinus has two incommensurable ways of describing the relationship between the One and Intellect may take care of this problem. One of the points of view he suggests is from within the Intellect. From its point of view only the One as seen enters the picture—the intellect's One is the One

---

[28] Bussanich (1988: 225) speaks of a 'double causality' of the One, which seems to commit him to the view I have described in terms of 'two emanations'.

as seen by it, the intellect. Here there is no need to postulate any activity on the part of the One beyond what is given in the establishment of the inchoate intellect with its image of the One. The other way sees the matter from the outside or from the viewpoint of the One itself. In this case the One is taken to be active not only in establishing the inchoate intellect but also in informing it. This in itself seems reasonable. The question remains, however, whether the One is doing something else when it is informing the intellect than it did when establishing it. If the answer is 'yes, it is doing something different,' I become sceptical of the proposal; if 'no, it is just doing whatever it always did and nothing in addition to it', I am not sure what to make of Bussanich's two points of view. All the One does is to make the inchoate intellect together with its innate image of the One. The so-called conversion is the intellect's attempt to think this image. It does not follow from this that the One leaves the intellect and its image to themselves: the inchoate intellect and its image may well continuously depend on the agency of the One which in this sense remains active—I mean 'continuously' in the sense that were the One to let go its causal act the intellect with the image it has got would cease to be. If we think of the matter thus, it seems to me that Bussanich's sound insistence that the One is active not only in the establishment but also in the information of the intellect is done justice to without, however, introducing a 'double causality' of the One.

In any case, neither of the two accounts of V.3.11 sketched above posits the immediate experience of the One and the image it creates as a stable moment in the life of the intellect. There is no attempt at a positive description of it, neither here nor in other passages where it is mentioned.[29] It is as if this non-intellectual vision of the One is there only to be turned into something else, i.e. actual thought. It may be worthwhile to speculate about exactly why this is so. The remaining paragraphs of this section will address this issue from several angles.

---

[29] So far as I can tell, there are only two passages outside V.3 that clearly refer to a pre-noetic kind of experience in the context of the generation of Intellect, III.8.9 and VI.7.16, 12–14. In the latter passage it is said that the inchoate intellect 'sees the One unintellectually (*anoetôs*)'. Plotinus qualifies this immediately afterwards, however, by saying that it never saw the One but 'lived towards it'. I take it that this denial of seeing is a denial of seeing in the sense that is equivalent with intellectual vision, i.e. thinking; he need not at all be understood as denying that the inchoate intellect undergoes some experience of the One. At III.8.9, 19–22 he raises the question by what sort of immediate experience (*epibolêi athroai*) one could grasp the One. The question seems to presuppose that something of the sort is possible. The account that follows, though very interesting, does not elaborate on the exact nature of this *epibolê*.

We may wonder what motivates Plotinus to make room for a pre-noetic experience of the One on the part of the inchoate intellect. For it seems rather to complicate things. However, even if it is clearly mentioned only in a few passages and absent in many that deal with this topic, it cannot be explained away as an aberration, because it is undeniably present in the three most detailed accounts of the genesis of Intellect, i.e. in V.3.10–11, VI.7.16–17, and III.8.8–11. Moreover, it seems to me that Plotinus has compelling reasons for positing such immediate experience. For, as noted earlier, it appears to be important for Plotinus to maintain that the internal vision of Intellect, when it contemplates the intelligibles, in some sense is an appearance of the One. It is the form the One takes when it is thought. The contact or immediate apprehension of the One provides the 'sensory', causal link between the Intellect and the One. To use an analogy from sense-perception: the contact plays the role of an external sensory stimulus or impression that when processed by the faculties of sense and reason is transformed into thought. Without such a contact there would be no causal representational link between the One itself and Intellect's thought. Plotinus would, in that case, not be able to present the One as the intended or aimed at object of Intellect's thought. Rather, Intellect's thought would turn out to be something that may be caused by the One but lacking the cognitive, representational links with it that are necessary for him to maintain that the One is the intended object of the vision, however inaccurate its appearance.

It could be retorted, of course, that the One might in fact be the intended object of Intellect's vision but to the Intellect it simply appears as many without any mediation of an undifferentiated contact. Plotinus however has good reasons not to adopt such a view. If the One simply appeared as many without the contact, Plotinus would risk entering into difficulties in maintaining that Intellect's thought really is of the One at all. He might have a hard time explaining how the resulting vision, which constitutes Intellect, is even a distorted vision of the One rather than, say, simply an experience somehow caused by it. What would be lacking is something that corresponds to the sensation of the object perceived in ordinary vision, something which is not merely caused by the object but presents the object to the receiver. If he took the view now suggested, he might also involve himself in the obviously vulnerable position that the One itself is directly responsible for the multiplicity of thoughts—a position which would threaten to compromise the One's simplicity. It appears that if Plotinus wishes to maintain that Intellect's vision is indeed a vision of the One, albeit not of it as it is in itself, it is plausible for him to hold that there is a causal, 'sensory' contact between the One and the intellect in which the intellect becomes 'aware of' the One in its simplicity. The One must be the agent of this contact and leave some sort of impression of itself on the intellect. That impression, even if pregnant with many, cannot be variegated since it is an impression of the One (cf. V.3.11; III.8.8, 32).

Is there a subject/object difference in this kind of experience? Plotinus does not discuss this question explicitly. It was maintained here above that the first separation from the One is in a way the emergence of a subject. But only in a way: something which is not the One has come about and that which has come about has intrinsically some kind of intentional stance of lack and longing or desire towards that which it came from. But this longing is not conceptualized and a distinction between a subject and an articulate intentional object has not yet arisen. If we adopt the former of the two accounts given above of the line of thought in V.3.11, 1–16, the experience of the One precedes or is simultaneous with the desire. If the desire does not involve an articulate subject/object distinction, the impression of the One doesn't either. If we on the other hand adopt the latter account which has the desire logically precede the image of the One that 'became multiple out of one', there is nothing which speaks for an articulate subject/object distinction either. There are, on the contrary, indications that the full-blown subject/object distinction first arises when the intellect breaks its undifferentiated image up into determinate intelligibles.

We have seen above that the intellect's impression of the One is unified. It is an impression that in some ways faithfully reflects the simplicity of the One itself at least to the extent that it cannot be a proper object of thought. Hence, it must be broken up in order to be thought. Nevertheless, the intellect, possessing this image, yearns for the One. There might seem to be a certain tension here: in so far as the image is a faithful representation of the One, preserving its simplicity, one might think that in having it the intellect has got all it might ever wish for. For wasn't it that kind of simplicity it lacked and wanted? On the other hand, Plotinus emphasizes that so far from giving the intellect satisfaction, its image of the One is its reason for desiring the One. This latter fact evidently shows that the intellect is not quite content with its image. How is this to be explained?

I think the following lines from V.3.11 (already cited on p. 92 above) may provide the clue to an answer:

[Intellect] wishes to think this itself as one, but in wishing to experience it immediately in its simplicity it comes out continually grasping something else made many in itself. So that it moved to it not as Intellect but as sight not yet seeing, but came out possessing the multiplicity which that sight itself made.

Plotinus says in these lines, as he does at many other places, that the intellect desires the One. This presupposes that the intellect in some way has an inkling of the One. Otherwise it wouldn't be the One it desired. The inkling it has of the One, however, is of something that surpasses its powers. The impression so to say comes to pieces as soon as the intellect acts on its desire to capture its object. We see this mismatch in the lines just quoted: the intellect wishes to *think* the One. This is a kind of a wish that it is impossible to fulfil. In a somewhat obscure sentence in V.6.5, 10 speaking of the inchoate intellect, Plotinus says that 'sight's desire is vision'.[30] The term 'sight's' (*opseôs*) here must, as Lloyd (1987: 164) maintains, be a possessive genitive with '*ephesis*' (desire) rather than an objective genitive, 'for the sight', as some interpreters have presumed, and it must refer to the indefinite sight which is the inchoate intellect. The meaning of the sentence must then be that the desire of the capacity of sight is to see actually. I take it then that the inchoate intellect's desire is qualified in the following way: even if it is a desire for the One, and even for the One 'in its simplicity', it is a desire to possess the One by seeing (thinking) it. So to put it crudely: the intellect in one way desires the One as it is in itself. Of this it has a certain inkling, thanks to the image it has got. But because the intellect is after all an intellect, its desire is nevertheless of such a kind that it only can be satisfied by thinking. This is because the inchoate intellect is of the nature of intellect and it will seek to satisfy its desire according to its own nature, i.e. by an intellectual vision of the One. But this is an impossible task because there can be no intellectual vision of the One as it is in itself.

It may still seem to be the case that an appeal to the fact that the One's first product is an intellect, a thinker, plays an essential role in establishing the plural nature of the object of thought (cf. p. 91 above). For haven't I just appealed

---

[30] V.6.5, 10: ἔφεσις γὰρ ὄψεως ὅρασις. As Bussanich (1988: 62) notes, Plotinus tends fairly consistently to use *opsis* and *horasis* or corresponding verbs to distinguish between the doings of the inchoate or potential intellect and those of the actual one.

to the fact that in desiring the One the One's first product desires to know it? This, it would seem, is to presume rather than to demonstrate that this first product is an intellect, a knower. I shall resume this dilemma in Section 6.

5. Pre-noetic Experience and Mystical Union with the One

Issues relating to the topic we have been discussing have been a matter of a scholarly debate. There is for Plotinus a place for a direct encounter with the One itself. A human being may elevate himself or herself above the discursive level of soul to Intellect and even beyond Intellect to the One itself in the so-called mystical union with the One.[31] When successful, this union is apparently a genuine union, i.e. the subject of it literally comes to share in the life (or 'quasi-life') of the One. The union with the One is described in terms of touch, immediate apprehension (*epibolê*), and kindred terms, but also the language of vision is used (cf. VI.9.10). So it is described in terms that recall the undifferentiated experience the inchoate intellect has of the One.

The similarity of language in the description of the mystical union with the One and the inchoate intellect's pre-noetic experience of it may suggest, and has by eminent scholars been taken to suggest, that the hypernoetic vision (or touch) in the mystical union and the pre-noetic vision the inchoate intellect has of the One are one and the same (see Trouillard 1961: 432–4; 1955: 104–9; and O'Daly 1974: 164–5). The point is well put by Hadot (1986: 243; cf. VI.7.35) who says, citing Bergson: ' "Intelligence, reabsorbing itself in its principle, will relive its own formation in reverse." In this way, thought is born from a sort of loving ecstasy in this type of drunkenness, which is produced by nonintellectual contact with the Good from which it emanates.' So the idea is that the inchoate intellect 'sees' the One in the modified sense of seeing involved in the mystical union.

This interpretation that identifies pre-noetic and hypernoetic vision is, however, forcefully resisted by Bussanich (1988: especially 231–6 *ad*

---

[31] Porphyry tells in *Life of Plotinus* 23, 17–18 that Plotinus attained a union with the One four times during the five years or so that he, Porphyry, was staying with him. The passage that most clearly describes a personal union with the One is VI.9.9–11; IV.8.1 is often cited, but as O'Meara (1993: 104–5) notes it is a 'union' with Intellect that is at stake here, not with the One.

V.3.11, 15–16), who points out that despite the similarities of language 'any suggestion that the inchoate Intellect is in a state of ecstasy or possessed by an overpowering erotic passion or that it is flooded by the light of the One' is lacking in the passages cited by the proponents of this interpretation in its support (234). He thus insists that hypernoetic vision and pre-noetic vision are quite distinct.

It seems to me that Bussanich's view is evidently right, if the idea is that the mystical experience is really reunification (cf. O'Daly 1973: ch. 4). In none of the places where the inchoate intellect's pre-noetic experience of the One is mentioned is a complete reunification with the One suggested. On the contrary, the repeated message of the lines from V.3.11, which must be the main source for the hypothesis of the identity of the two kinds of experience, is that the unification fails. Philosophically speaking, an identification of the pre-noetic and hypernoetic kinds of experience does not make much sense. We know that the inchoate intellect comes from the One. What would be achieved by having it reunite with the latter just in order to depart again? What might we suppose it gained from that which it didn't have already when it departed in the first place? It seems to me that in so far as the genesis of Intellect is concerned, the supposition of a reunific-ation with the One would be just a hoax that fails to explain anything that subsequently happens. On a more positive note about the identificationists, however, it can be said that their hypothesis has the unquestionable merit of giving the mystical union a place within the Plotinian ontological scheme: it presents the union as a return to something that the returning subject came from and which waits there for it to return to. Thus, it serves to give the union a place within the ontology which has been established. This basic intuition that the ascent to the One may go through an already trodden path in the downwards direction may be retained. But this is not to say that the inchoate intellect accomplishes such a reunion.

An alternative view of the matter is to see the mystical experience not as a real reunification, it is not a matter of becoming the One quite literally. It is rather a matter of strongly feeling its presence without entirely mixing one's identity with it. I am not sure that this is the most natural interpretation of a text such as VI.9.10, but the view makes good sense in any case. Hadot (1986) and Rist (1989: 196–7) seem to endorse such a view, and both of them see the mystical union as a kind of reliving of the past, i.e. as a return to the place of Intellect's birth. I have not made up my mind about the nature of the mystical union. But supposing Hadot and Rist are right in this, I am not sure if Bussanich's admonitions that there are indeed significant differences in language in the descriptions of the pre-noetic and the hypernoetic experiences of the One suffice to show that the two are entirely different affairs. After all, there are many similarities as well.

6. The Two Kinds of Otherness Again

Let us now return to the two kinds of otherness that we set out from in Section 2. What we have come up with so far is a notion of thought which can be described as triadic in the following way: 'Thinking X' is A's, a thinker's, thought of something differentiated, BC. So 'A thinks BC'. There is a difference ('otherness') between A and its object BC, and there is a difference ('otherness') between B and C. The latter sort of otherness follows from the former, provided that the subject in question is a subject of thought. We have also established that the situation the first product of the One finds itself in is untenable, i.e. it is in a state of need and longing that is not at all satisfied. So this situation won't last; the one in it will not remain there happily with its inkling of the One. Indeed, the very idea of an articulate subject which is not a subject of thought, because the intentional object of its thought is undifferentiated, is suspect: if such a subject is aware of itself having this undifferentiated object, it is in a sense aware of at least two things, itself and this object; alternatively, it isn't in any way aware of itself in this experience in which case it becomes dubious to talk about a subject of a mental attitude at all.

So far so good. Yet, I suspect that this is not the whole story and important corrections and additions are needed. The impression still remain that 'otherness' plays two radically different roles, and hence that there are two radically different reasons for plurality. A subject's being other than its object is a quite different thing from otherness within the object. Even if we have made a case for saying that the plurality within the object follows from the subject/object duality, it must be admitted that it is the considerations about the nature of thought which do the main job in obtaining this conclusion. We noted at the end of Section 4 that for Plotinus himself, in arguing for the necessity of breaking up the image of the One, the reason why the intellect wouldn't get hold of its image otherwise is that it is an intellect and it is the nature of intellects to think differentiated objects. So it is still the case that an appeal to the fact that the One's first product is an intellect, a thinker, plays an essential role in establishing the plural nature of the object of thought. That the first product should necessarily be an intellect rather than some other psychological entity that possesses the subject/object distinction but has an undifferentiated object, has not been argued for.

Perhaps we can settle the worry expressed in the last paragraph as follows. We need not suppose that the intellectual nature of the One's first product is arbitrarily assumed from the start. It is just as reasonable to suppose that the desire to know the One that we have seen to be the form the desire for the One takes in the case of the first product is the very desire to make up a whole consisting of an articulate subject and an articulate object that are at once the same and different (cf. V.3.13, 16–21). In other words, it is not as if the intellectual nature of the first product is an assumed given of the case; the desire to know here may just be the desire to be such a whole. Or perhaps better put: to be a whole of the sort Plotinus envisages here amounts to being a thinker, a knower. A thinker in the situation of the first product turns itself into a whole consisting of a subject and an object; that is the only way of satisfying the innate desire. It splits itself up into a plurality constituting a whole which becomes an intentional object for itself. In any case, if this is at all correct, an inference from the intellectual nature of the product to what it does plays no essential role in Plotinus' argument, even if he, and I following him, sometimes appeal to its intellectual nature as a handy way to explain what it does. Succinctly put: the first product doesn't desire to know the One because it is an intellect; it desires to be an integral whole of a certain kind, and to desire that is what it is to desire to know the One.

We haven't, however, yet explained the relationship between the two kinds of otherness. And nothing we have said so far goes anywhere towards explaining why Intellect's thought should be a self-thought, a claim Plotinus strongly and consistently emphasizes. In the remainder of this section and the next, I shall argue for a certain view of Intellect which takes care of both these questions. In fact I have already indicated the answer I am going to give, when I said in the previous paragraph that Intellect splits itself up into a plurality constituting a whole which becomes an intentional object for itself. But this is far too cryptic, of course. It remains to work this out.

In a passage from V.3.10 already quoted above (p. 86) Plotinus makes the following remark:

Well then, suppose it [the partless] was only two things and said 'I and this'. It would already be necessary for it to be many: for, as the two things are different and in whatever manner they differ, number is already there and many other things. (V.3.10, 37–40)

And later in the treatise he says, in explanation of the fact that the One itself, being totally simple, is the principle of many:

How then does the One make what it does not have? ... Now it has been said that, if anything comes from the One, it must be something different from it; and in being different, it is not one: for if it was, it would be that One. But if it isn't one, but two, it must necessarily also be many: for it is already the same and different and qualified and all the rest.[32] (V.3.15, 35–40)

I take it that in both these passages, the main point is that given the duality of subject and object, the full plurality of the intelligible realm follows. In neither case does Plotinus say in explicit terms that he means that the two in question are the thinker and the object of thought. In the former passage just quoted, however, the context makes it virtually certain that this is what he has in mind: the 'I' corresponds to the subject and the 'this' to the object. This is the most plausible interpretation of the second passage as well. For we know from several other passages that the moment of becoming an actual thinker involves a differentiation of a subject-stance of the inchoate intellect from an object-stance.[33] Somehow the original duality between the One itself and that which comes after it is transformed into the full duality of subject and object of thought.

Our question then is this: can this duality of subject and object by itself contain or imply the duality within the object of thought that we have

---

[32] V.3.15, 35–40: πῶς οὖν ποιεῖ ἃ μὴ ἔχει; Οὐ γὰρ ὡς ἔτυχε· μηδ᾽ ἐνθυμηθεὶς ὃ ποιήσει, ποιήσει ὅμως. Εἴρηται μὲν οὖν, ὅτι, εἴ τι ἐκ τοῦ ἑνός, ἄλλο δεῖ παρ᾽ αὐτό· ἄλλο δὲ ὂν οὐχ ἕν· τοῦτο γὰρ ἦν ἐκεῖνο. Εἰ δὲ μὴ ἕν, δύο δὲ, ἀνάγκη ἤδη καὶ πλῆθος εἶναι· καὶ γὰρ ἕτερον καὶ ταὐτὸν ἤδη καὶ ποιὸν καὶ τὰ ἄλλα. For a discussion of this passage, see D'Ancona Costa (1996: 370 ff.).

[33] Thus, in V.3.10, 45–6 he says that the thinker that is going to think itself 'duplicates itself' (διχάσει γὰρ αὐτὸ ἑαυτὸ); In VI.7.39, 7–8 in thinking itself Intellect distinguishes 'itself from the intelligible by its relation of otherness to itself'. Plotinus is presumably making the same point also in V.1.7, 10–11.

seen Plotinus insisting on? In the former passage just quoted, he claims that 'number and many other things' are present in virtue of this duality, and in the latter that 'the same and the other, quality and the rest' are. He doesn't tell us how. Let us grant, however, that these things are present if the subject/object distinction is present.

Identity and difference, which are mentioned in the quote from V.3.15 above, are among the five 'greatest kinds' (*megista genê*)[34] from Plato's *Sophist*—and other late dialogues. The others are being (*to on*), motion (*kinêsis*), and rest (*stasis*). On Plotinian premises it is plausible enough to suppose that such features as the five kinds enter the scene along with the thinker and thought. Plotinus turns these 'greatest kinds' into the five highest kinds or forms of the intelligible world. They are coextensive and each presupposes the others.[35] That the distinction between thinker and object of thought entails the distinction between these forms is in fact explicit in VI.2.7–9, the fullest account of the 'greatest kinds'.[36] It actually turns out that motion and being are just different designations for thinker in act and object of thought:[37] there is motion (*kinêsis*) of thought from thinker to being, the object of thought; this motion comes to a rest (*stasis*) at determinate objects (VI.2.8, 20–1). And, as we have seen, there is *difference* (otherness) between the subject and the object presupposed; they nevertheless make up the *same* thing (VI.2.8, 11–13).

Let us for the time being not worry about the details of this picture.[38] In so far as Plotinus says anything about how this variety arises from this pair

---

[34] When Plato uses the expression *megista ... tôn genôn* in *Soph.* 254d he need not mean that he regards these as *the* greatest or the most important kinds; more probably he only means to say that they are very great, leaving it open that there also may be others that also are very great.

[35] For an account of Plotinus' interpretation of the 'greatest kinds' see Charrue (1978: 206–23), Brisson (1991), and Santa Cruz (1997).

[36] The 'greatest kinds' or some subset thereof appear in several other passages, e.g. II.6.1, 1–3; III.7.3, 9–11; V.1.4, 34; VI.6.9, 3 ff.; VI.7.13, 4 ff.

[37] In VI.2.7, 18–19, cf. 35–6 Plotinus says that motion is the activity/actuality of being. The idea is that being first becomes actual being when it is thought (cf. VI.2.8).

[38] What may be disconcerting in Plotinus' use of the 'greatest kinds' is whether and, if so, how, he thinks the kind of variety constituted by them amounts to a variety within the *object* of thought. For aren't motion and rest, the same and the different, more naturally interpreted as aspects of the activity of thinking, parts of the mechanism of thought, some sort of meta-notions, than as substantial, primary objects of thought, cf. Atkinson (1983: 94–7)? Yet it is fairly clear from VI.2, which contains the most detailed account of the structure of the intelligible sphere, that Plotinus thinks of the kinds from Plato's *Sophist* as genuine genera or forms which the intellect thinks: the rest of the intelligible sphere is either divisions of them or aspects of them. I shall not pursue this particular question in detail. Let it suffice to note that the solution I propose to the problem of the two kinds of otherness seems to me to suggest an answer to it.

of thinker and thought, it is along the lines just sketched. Let us instead focus on the question of how he thinks that a plurality within the object can be given by just this pair.

In order to come to grips with this question, we must pay due note to the fact that the original thought that arises when the inchoate intellect becomes Intellect is self-thinking. Plotinus regularly insists that self-thinking is the primary sense of thinking and that intellect's thought is self-thought (II.9.1, 48–50; V.3.6, 2; V.3.10, 26; 13, 14; V.6.1, 11). I suppose that in claiming self-thinking as the primary kind of thinking he means this kind of thought that doesn't have to search outside itself for its object is more unitary and, hence, prior to the sort of thought that has to do that (cf. II.9.1, 48–50). So the internality of the objects of thought is surely an aspect of Plotinus' notion of self-thinking: it thinks itself because what it thinks of is internal to itself. This, however, need not be all there is to self-thinking. I shall argue here below for a certain understanding of self-thinking in Plotinus, which I indeed think is provably his and which will at least go some way towards solving the puzzle about the two kinds of otherness.

7. Self-Thinking and the First Person

Let us start the inquiry into self-thinking by considering a recondite but interesting remark about it: 'But the thinker must not itself remain simple either, especially in so far as it thinks itself: for it will duplicate itself, even if it gives an understanding which is silent' (V.3.10, 44–6). This sentence, which belongs to the quote from V.3.10 on p. 81 above (for the Greek, see note 11), occurs directly after the passage about the 'touch and kind of contact' that we considered above. In the context the sentence serves the purpose of affirming that not only is the object of thought multiple but also the subject which thinks itself. But why? And what is it about self-thinking that makes it especially necessary for the thinker of self to split itself up?

I take it that if the thinker has an object of thought different from itself, it wouldn't have to split itself up in order to think this object: there is already a relation of otherness between it and the object, and this is a prerequisite of thought. Something which is going to think itself but doesn't stand 'in a relation of otherness towards itself' (VI.7.39, 6–8), must establish such a relation. So the inchoate intellect has to split itself, distance itself from itself, if it is to think itself (cf. V.1.7, 10–11). In the sentence referred to Plotinus says that the thinker has to duplicate itself. This may be slightly misleading, because before the splitting, that entity was not a thinker except potentially: the entity before the split is the inchoate intellect.[39] The split is its step from being a merely potential thinker into being an actual one.

So we have the inchoate intellect with its image of and longing for the One but without a full-blown subject/object distinction. Parting from the image it has got, it seeks to get hold of the One by thinking it, by seeing it intellectually; but in order to see anything, it must split itself up into a subject and object. The result of this, however, is not that this subject grasps its other half *per se*, the one which it has just split from. On the contrary, it does grasp itself in its entirety, subject and object together. This is a hypothesis that I shall seek to explore and support in the following paragraphs.

In order to see how this comes about let us consider a passage from V.3.13, 16–21, where Plotinus first describes the intellect's need to be itself and then goes on to say what its being itself consists in. I first quote the first half of the passage:

But that which is altogether simple and self-sufficient needs nothing; but what is self-sufficient in the second degree, but needs itself, this is what needs itself to think itself; and that which is deficient in relation to itself achieves self-sufficiency by being a whole, with an adequacy deriving from all its parts, present to itself and inclining towards itself.[40] (V.3.13, 16–21)

This passage occurs in a context where the One is contrasted with Intellect. The former has no need of thought or of self-perception, whereas the intellect has such a need, because it needs itself. We have previously seen that the intellect needs the One (see p. 74 above). Now we read in a similar context that it needs itself. One naturally suspects that it is somehow

---

[39] There is another passage where Plotinus refers to such a split in that which is about to think itself. In V.1.7, 10–11 he says that Ὧν οὖν ἐστι δύναμις, ταῦτα ἀπὸ τῆς δυνάμεως οἷον σχιζομένη ἡ νόησις καθορᾷ· ἢ οὐκ ἂν ἦν νοῦς. 'The things, then, of which it [*dynamis pantôn*=the One] is the productive power are those which the intellect sees, in a way cutting itself off from the power. Otherwise it would not be Intellect.' If *schizomenê* is middle rather than passive, there presumably is a reference to the emergence of a subject/object separation here too. For a discussion of the construction of the sentence, see Bussanich (1988: 48–9) and Atkinson (1983: 165–7).

[40] V.3.13, 16–21: Τὸ δὲ πάντη ἁπλοῦν καὶ αὔταρκες ὄντως οὐδὲν δεῖται· τὸ δὲ δευτέρως αὔταρκες, δεόμενον δὲ ἑαυτοῦ, τοῦτο δεῖται τοῦ νοεῖν ἑαυτό· καὶ τὸ ἐνδεὲς πρὸς αὐτὸ ὂν τῷ ὅλῳ πεποίηκε τὸ αὔταρκες ἱκανὸν ἐξ ἁπάντων γενόμενον, συνὸν ἑαυτῷ, καὶ εἰς αὐτὸ νεῦον.

a question of the same need, that it needs the One because it hasn't fully achieved itself (cf. V.3.10, 8–12 discussed on pp. 80–4 above). Here is a proposal as to how it may be a question of the same need: what needs the One needs it because it isn't the One itself, because it is not fully sufficient to itself; its not being fully self-sufficient means that it hasn't got everything to be itself, for that it needs the One; but it cannot have the self-sufficiency that pertains to the One; what it can and does get is something that enables it to be one (itself) in a second degree, namely to be a whole made up of parts. The sense in which it is made up of parts, however, is not that of independently existing parts, but parts that mutually presuppose one another, as the five highest genera do.[41]

Thus, the last quote gives us the sense of what being oneself amounts to for Plotinus: it consists in being one, and failing to be one *simpliciter*, it is one in the sense of being a unified whole. The intellect would very much like to be the One but it cannot, such has its nature become as a result of having parted from the One. So it does the next best thing, namely to be a whole, i.e. it becomes a unit consisting of parts that mutually presuppose one another and give self-sufficiency after a kind. This 'whole' is thought or the activity of thinking. The self-sufficiency regained consists in the Intellect's possessing itself in thought, i.e. it is a whole that knows itself, knows what itself is. Thus, we might say that the inchoate intellect's need is two-sided: it is its need of the One for being itself.

In the light of the passages mentioned above about the split between subject and object, we should say that the split is the intellect's attempt to grasp the One ending up, however, thinking itself. That is to say, the intellect regains a certain self-sufficiency but at the cost of absolute unity. It is now a thinker who thinks something like: 'I am', the 'I' and the 'am' being two different aspects of it, at once distinct and brought together in its thought. In thinking this, it already thinks a composite thing: itself thinking that it itself is.[42]

That Intellect's self-thought is in the first person seems to me to be confirmed by several passages—one of them being the direct continuation

---

[41] The account given here of the secondary self-sufficiency of Intellect as a totality consisting of integrated parts is close to Ham (2000: 232–3), though he and I differ on the interpretation of the subsequent lines 21–7.

[42] This formula, 'I am', stated as the result of thinking oneself, is of course reminiscent of Descartes's famous 'cogito, sum'. This is not the occasion to embark on a comparison between Plotinus and Descartes as to whether the similarity is deep or merely superficial. For what it is worth, I shall just express my hunch that it is not merely superficial.

of the last passage quoted about Intellect gaining its unity by becoming a unified whole. We shall consider that passage shortly. First, however, let us address the question about self-thinking and the first person in more general terms.

It is well known that Plotinus' doctrine of Intellect owes much to Aristotle and his followers, in particular Alexander of Aphrodisias (cf. Armstrong 1960 and Szlezák 1979). Aristotle and Alexander too speak of God and the active intellect as thinking itself and insist on the identity of the divine mind with its objects of thought. Alexander in fact plausibly identified the active intellect of *De anima* III, 5 with the divine mind of *Metaphysics* XII (Alexander *De an.* 89, 7 ff.). The relevant passages in Aristotle (*De an.* III, 4−5 *Meta.* XII, 7, 9) are obscure and much disputed as one might expect. It seems to me that whatever may be the exact correct interpretation of them, however, there is no indication that Aristotle (or Alexander) had in mind any kind of self-reflexive act of thought when they described divine thinking as self-thinking, and still less indications that a first-person stance plays any role in their conception of self-thinking. As Sorabji (1983: 147) puts it, 'There need be nothing narcissistic in the claim that God thinks of himself, or regressive in the claim that he thinks of his own thinking.' Other leading experts seem to agree. Kosman (2000: 323), for instance, argues forcefully and explicitly that Aristotle's notion of God's self-thinking and the description of his thinking as the thinking of thinking in *Metaphysics* XII, 9 'is not the description of an act of reflexive self-awareness' (see also Norman 1969). In Alexander this is even more obviously true. For the Peripatetics then the intellect is identical with its object of thought because the act of thinking is numerically identical with the object of thought, and the intellect acting is identical with its acts. The divine intellect is essentially an act of thinking and the object of its thought exists in this act. Since Intellect and its objects are identical, it follows trivially that the intellect thinks itself when it thinks its object. Plotinus too argues in a similar way for the identity of the intelligibles with Intellect, in V.3.5. This passage will be examined in Section 5 of the next chapter.

Plotinus' understanding of self-thinking, however, contains elements that go beyond anything reasonably attributable to Aristotle. His conception of self-thinking turns out to be reflexive—narcissistic if you wish—in a way Aristotle's is not.

As one would expect, Plotinus usually talks about Intellect in the third person, saying about it things such as: 'Intellect is second, after the One', or 'Intellect thinks itself', or 'Intellect is identical with its objects of thought'. On a few occasions, however, he imagines Intellect thinking. Interestingly, on those occasions Intellect thinks in the first person. That is to say, when Plotinus imagines such thinking, Intellect does not think thoughts in the third person like 'Being is Motion' or 'Justice is Beauty', as we might expect, but rather thoughts like 'I am'. It strikes me that in choosing such first-person expressions Plotinus is not employing a rhetorical or merely expressive device. The first person—or so I shall argue—is crucial for his conception of Intellect's self-thought or, which for him amounts to the same thing, its self-knowledge.

Evidence for this has already been presented in connection with the passage about the partless trying to "speak itself" in V.3.10, 31 ff. (quoted on p. 86 above). Let us resume the structure of Plotinus' argument here. He is arguing that the object of thought must contain variety and does so by showing the impossibility of thinking a partless object. In the course of this he claims that if this partless object were to think itself, thinking e.g. 'I am this', it would, in so far as it succeeded in thinking something about itself, be many, because the 'I' that thinks and what it thinks must be different. But if there were just these two different things, the 'I' and the 'this', 'number is already there and many other things' (lines 37–8).

There are two facts connected with Plotinus' reasoning here I wish to draw our attention to. First, that as a matter of course he renders thoughts expressing self-thinking by first-person statements that say what the subject of the thought is. This does not positively prove that self-thought is necessarily always of this form but it is an indication. Secondly, it is noteworthy that the duality of the subject and the object of the thought, the 'I' and the 'this' counts as evidence of the plurality of the object: that which thinks 'I am this' is thinking at least two things, in fact more, since two imply more.

Before attempting to explain the relevance of this, let us consider two more such first-person passages, starting with the lines from V.3.13 that continue the passage quoted above in connection with the inchoate intellect's need and its satisfaction.

For consciousness (*synaisthêsis*) of anything is a perception (*aisthêsis*) of something multiple, as the term itself bears witness to. And the thought which is prior turns inward to it [the intellect] which is obviously multiple.[43] For even if it only says just this, 'I am being' (*on eimi*), it says it as a discovery and plausibly, for being is multiple: since if it had an immediate grasp (*epibalêi*)[44] as if of something simple and said 'I am being', it would attain neither itself nor being.[45] (V.3.13, 21–7)

From the preceding lines it is clear that the word *synaisthêsis* ('consciousness') here replaces 'thinking oneself'. It is as if Intellect's turning to itself in order to discover itself leads to the thought 'I am being'. Thus, Intellect's self-thought is represented as a first-person statement about what the subject or thinker of Intellect's thought is. The passage aims at establishing the plurality of self-thought in order to show that self-thought does not pertain to the One. A question that arises is exactly how this is established. Here is a proposal: the thought 'I am' (or 'I am being') is complex, because it involves both an 'I', a subject, and its being. In the passage discussed above (V.3.10, 31 ff.) about the partless of the same treatise, the mere duality of 'I' and 'this' suffices to render the object of what 'speaks itself' multiple. We may take Plotinus to be making the same point here: Intellect thinks 'I am', and in so thinking it shows itself to be complex, consisting in a subject that thinks and an object that is being thought by this subject. This shows being itself to be multiple. For if the subject had 'had an immediate grasp' of an undifferentiated something, it would not have managed to think a thought and surely not discovered itself. In order to discover itself and being, it must think the complex thought of 'I am being'.

The remark in the present passage that if Intellect only says 'I am being', 'it says it as a discovery and plausibly, for being is multiple' is somewhat surprising, not to say disconcerting. Plotinus normally stresses that Intellect doesn't have to search for and discover its knowledge. So the word 'discover' is not a part of the regular vocabulary for Intellect. That sort of vocabulary belongs to discursive reason, whereas Intellect is non-discursive and possesses all its content all along. Likewise, the word 'plausibly' (*eikotôs*) is not one of Intellect's regular epithets, for its thought is better than merely 'plausible'. However, when the issue is the contrast between the One and

---

[43] I understand *ton noun* ('the intellect') as implied after *hauton* ('itself'). See H-S²'s note *ad loc.*

[44] On *epiballein* and *epibolê* see this chapter, n. 25.

[45] V.3.13, 21–7: Ἐπεὶ καὶ ἡ συναίσθησις πολλοῦ τινος αἴσθησίς ἐστι· καὶ μαρτυρεῖ καὶ τοὔνομα. Καὶ ἡ νόησις προτέρα οὖσα εἴσω εἰς αὐτὸν ἐπιστρέφει δηλονότι πολὺν ὄντα· καὶ γὰρ ἐὰν αὐτὸ τοῦτο μόνον εἴπῃ "ὄν εἰμι", ὡς ἐξευρὼν λέγει καὶ εἰκότως λέγει, τὸ γὰρ ὄν πολύ ἐστιν· ἐπεί, ὅταν ὡς εἰς ἁπλοῦν ἐπιβάλῃ καὶ εἴπῃ "ὄν εἰμι", οὐκ ἔτυχεν οὔτε αὐτοῦ οὔτε τοῦ ὄντος.

Intellect, as it in fact is in the present passage, Plotinus may use of Intellect the kind of language that suggests imperfection. When the contrast is not between non-discursive and discursive thought, but rather between non-discursive thought and the complete self-sufficiency of the Good, he is liable to use the language of search to characterize Intellect.[46] And, as he puts it in the lines just before our passage: 'What is self-sufficient in the second degree [i.e. Intellect], but needs itself, this is what needs to think itself' (V.3.13, 17–19). Intellect has to think itself in order to become itself. If we relate the 'discovery' to this aspect of Plotinus' thought here, we can see it as referring to this gaining of self, which Intellect (or rather Intellect's precursor, the inchoate intellect) had not achieved. But nobody gains what he already has or discovers what he already knows. Hence, 'discovery' indicates that there are genuinely two different notions, 'I' and 'being', that are discovered to be the same, to make up a whole. So understood the remark may give further support to my interpretation of the passage as a whole suggested in the preceding paragraph and to be further supported here below that being's multiplicity is ultimately derived from the complexity of the thought 'I am being'.

Plotinus continues the argument by noting that by saying 'being' one is implying many things. For being comprises many beings. This might arouse the suspicion that the plurality involved in the thought 'I am being' is derived from the innate and implicit plurality of being rather than from the plurality of subject and object in the thought. Now, evidently Plotinus thinks that being is in itself multiple in this way. However, in the quote above he says in explanation of why being must be multiple that even on the supposition that Intellect merely thought 'I am being', 'if it [Intellect] had an immediate grasp as if of something simple and said "I am being", it would attain neither itself nor being'. In this remark there is a contrast between 'itself' and 'being'; 'itself' and 'being' must be seen as at once the same (since the self *is* being) and different (since it is a question of finding each of them). So I take it that if Intellect found being to be multiple solely by finding a plethora of beings that didn't include 'itself', it would not have found itself in the sense of this sentence. The sentence is best understood in such a way that Intellect finds being to be multiple in virtue of the plurality of the very thought 'I am being'. If it gazed at variegated being

---

[46] In V.3.10, 49–50 Plotinus says, rather strikingly, that 'knowledge (*gnôsis*) is a kind of longing (*pothos*), and like a discovery made by a seeker (*zêtêsantos heuresis*)'. It is clear from the context that he is thinking of Intellect's knowledge, not of discursive reason.

that did not include the 'I', the subject, it evidently would not find itself either. In other words, I take this passage to contain the same idea about how plurality comes about as we saw in the previous passage in V.3.10.

In addition to the first-person passages in V.3.10 and 13 we have considered, there is yet another such passage in VI.7.38. which in some ways may be the most telling of them all. Since it is of such a great importance for the conception of self-thinking I am after, I shall investigate it in some detail. Plotinus is here considering an objection to his conception of the Good (the One): some people may think that the Good cannot be worth very much, if it doesn't have self-perception or self-awareness.[47] He lets such an objector pose the first question, which he then responds to:

But who is going to accept a nature that is not in a state of perception or awareness of itself?—What then will it [the Good] be aware of? Of 'I am'? But it *is* not.—Why then will it not say 'I am the good'? [48]—Again, it will be predicating the 'is' of itself. But it will say 'good' only with some addition.[49] For one could indeed think 'good' without 'is', if one did not predicate it of something else. But he who thinks that he is good will at any rate think 'I am the Good'. If not, he does indeed think 'good', but the thought that he himself is this will not be present to him. So the thought must be 'I am Good'.[50] And if the thought itself is the

[47] 'Perception of oneself' (*aisthêsis heautou*) and 'awareness of oneself' (*gnôsis heautou*) are here and in other similar contexts equivalent to 'thinking (of) oneself' (*noêsis heautou*), cf. the shift to *noein* and *noêsis* in the passage quoted.

[48] Or possibly: 'I am Good'. The sentence reads: Διὰ τί οὖν οὐκ ἐρεῖ τὸ ἀγαθόν εἰμι. The question is whether to read the definite article *to* as a kind of quotation mark or not. Elsewhere in this passage the definite article often clearly functions as a kind of quotation mark prefixed to sentences or words that the Good is imagined to think. If this is the case here, the thought quoted is only 'I am Good', not 'I am the Good'.

[49] The apparently contrastive 'but' (*alla*) may seem to come out rather awkwardly on my reading, which takes this sentence to follow a remark where Plotinus is speaking for himself. The following paraphrase, however, may help explain the meaning: But [given the opponent's premiss that the good has self-awareness], it will say 'good' only with some addition, i.e. unless something is added, the thought 'good' wouldn't constitute its self-awareness. It is as if Plotinus is imagining, without making this explicit, that the adversary, retreating a bit after being shown that 'I am the good' involves the use of 'is', proposes that if the Good only thought 'good' without any addition, it would have self-awareness. Plotinus then objects to this suggestion, insisting that if it is a question of self-awareness, the thought must be more complicated than that. This would explain both the talk of 'addition' and the 'but'.

[50] As opposed to Hadot (1987: 182, 357), who also divides the text of his translation into the objector's statements and Plotinus' responses, I take what starts with 'Again, ...' to the end of the passage to belong to Plotinus' response. Hadot takes the whole of 'But he who thinks... must be "I am the Good"' to belong to the objector's reply. But it must be Plotinus himself who insists that if there is thought, there is being, and that the Good can have no part in this. It is he too who insists that if the thought is merely of 'Good' in isolation, it fails to be self-thought, and that if the Good has self-thought at all, its thought would involve being. The point about being in relation to the Good is already

Good, it will not be a thought of himself but of Good, and he himself will not be the Good, but the thought will. But if the thought of the Good is different from the Good, the Good is there already before the thought of it.[51] (VI.7.38, 10–22)

Plotinus is here carrying out an imaginary discussion with someone who insists that the Good must have self-knowledge. It is already established in the preceding lines of the chapter that being, an 'is', cannot pertain to the Good. Now he argues that the Good does not have self-knowledge. The main steps of the argument as I read it run as follows: If the Good has self-knowledge (self-thought, self-awareness), this self-knowledge involves being, involves an 'is'. It may be granted (at least for the sake of argument) that it is possible to think 'Good' in isolation, not predicating it of anything. But if this is what the Good's alleged self-knowledge consists in, it will fail to know that it itself is this Good that it thinks. Hence, it would fail to have self-knowledge. So if it has self-knowledge, this must consist in the thought 'I am (the) Good'. But this cannot be the Good's self-thought, since this thought involves an 'is'. As we shall see shortly, this last observation is of crucial importance. The last part of the argument, however, is clearly quite interesting for our purposes too. Moreover, it is somewhat bewildering. So let us consider it as well.

Plotinus claims here that even if the Good itself should consist in 'the thought itself', the thought 'will not be a thought of himself but of Good, and he himself will not be the Good, but the thought will' (18–20). On the other hand, if the Good and the thought of it are different, the Good will be itself quite independently of the thought of it (20–2).

Two questions immediately spring out at the reader: who is this 'he' who is introduced here? And what does Plotinus have in mind by 'the

settled: being cannot pertain to the Good. If the opponent is still insisting, as Hadot's translation and commentary suggest, that not only does the Good have self-awareness but this self-awareness involves being, the opponent is question-begging (because the question about being in relation to the One is already settled) and, moreover, Plotinus doesn't respond to this longish objection. The opponent's point is that the Good has self-thought, not that its thought involves being.

[51] VI.7.38, 10–22: Ἀλλὰ τίς παραδέξεται φύσιν οὐκ οὖσαν <ἐν> αἰσθήσει καὶ γνώσει αὐτῆς; Τί οὖν γνώσεται; "ἐγώ εἰμι"; Ἀλλ' οὐκ ἔστι. Διὰ τί οὖν οὐκ ἐρεῖ τὸ "ἀγαθόν εἰμι"; Ἢ πάλιν τὸ "ἔστι" κατηγορήσει αὐτοῦ. Ἀλλὰ τὸ "ἀγαθὸν" μόνον ἐρεῖ τι προσθείς· "ἀγαθὸν" μὲν γὰρ νοήσειεν ἄν τις ἄνευ τοῦ "ἔστιν", εἰ μὴ κατ' ἄλλου κατηγοροῖ· ὁ δὲ αὐτὸ νοῶν ὅτι ἀγαθὸν πάντως νοήσει τὸ "ἐγώ εἰμι τὸ ἀγαθόν"· εἰ δὲ μή, ἀγαθὸν μὲν νοήσει, οὐ παρέσται δὲ αὐτῷ τὸ ὅτι αὐτός ἐστι τοῦτο νοεῖν. Δεῖ οὖν τὴν νόησιν εἶναι, ὅτι "ἀγαθόν εἰμι". καὶ εἰ μὲν νόησις αὐτὴ τὸ ἀγαθόν, οὐκ αὐτοῦ ἔσται νόησις, ἀλλ' ἀγαθοῦ, αὐτός τε οὐκ ἔσται τὸ ἀγαθόν, ἀλλ' ἡ νόησις. Εἰ δὲ ἑτέρα τοῦ ἀγαθοῦ ἡ νόησις τοῦ ἀγαθοῦ, ἔστιν ἤδη τὸ ἀγαθὸν πρὸ τῆς νοήσεως αὐτοῦ.

thought itself'? The reference of 'he' and 'himself' here must be to the subject of the supposedly self-directed thought, its thinker as distinct from the thought itself. As to the second question, Plotinus has just said that if the Good had self-knowledge, its thought would have to be 'I am the Good'. (Since such a thought involves plurality, the Good can of course not have such a thought.) It is tempting to identify 'the thought itself' with this very thought that 'I am the Good'.[52] This, however, leads to some strange results. The 'am' in 'I am the Good' is the 'am' of identity: if this thought as a whole is identical with the Good and the thought is of the Good (as admitted), it is also a thought of the 'I' who thinks the thought. Moreover, according to its content this very thought is a thought the subject utters in the first person about itself. It is hard to see how it could fail to be of the 'I', the thinker. So, if this is what Plotinus intends, his claim that the thought would not be a thought of him, the subject, seems to be quite unwarranted.

In fact, I shall propose a different interpretation of what Plotinus means by 'the thought itself' here. I suspect this is elliptical for 'the thought of the Good itself', cf. line 21, where 'the thought of the Good' seems to be a paraphrase of 'the thought itself' in line 19. Thus, Plotinus is considering the proposal that the thought itself of the Good is the Good, perhaps as a part of the thought 'I am the Good'. In the latter case, there would be a thinker who thinks 'I am the Good', and the Good itself is identified with the 'the Good' part of the thought. Plotinus' claim about it is that it would fail to be the thinker's self-thought, since the thinker would be no part of the thought of the Good. So the point would be similar to what we saw in the preceding lines about the thinker's failing to know its identity with what it thinks, and, hence, its failure to know itself.

The whole passage we have been considering is of course explicitly about the One, something which does not think itself according to Plotinus. It is, however, revealing for our purposes on account of what it says about what the One would say if it had perception of itself, knowledge of itself, or thought of itself, i.e. if the One had that crucial feature the Intellect has and the objector misses in the One. So we can use the passage to become clearer about Plotinus' conception of self-knowledge or self-thinking of Intellect. So, to put it succinctly, the self-knowledge here denied of

---

[52] Hadot (1968: 182, 357) adopts this interpretation. I do not understand his explanation in the commentary (357) of how one who thinks 'I am the Good' fails to think the 'I'. It strikes me as a non sequitur.

the One is without doubt just the kind of self-knowledge insisted on for Intellect.

Plotinus' demand that 'the thought that it itself is the Good' must be present to the Good if it were to have self-knowledge is quite telling. It shows that he conceives of the self-thinking of Intellect as including the awareness that the subject of the thought is something or other. So according to this passage nothing could 'think itself' in the relevant sense without it being the case that the subject of the thought conceives of itself as the object of the thought; which in itself suffices to make its thought complex.

Thus, this passage confirms what V.3.10 and 13 strongly suggest, namely that if we were to render discursively the self-thinking of Intellect, it would be appropriate to do so by statements in the first person which say what the Intellect is: 'I am F' would be the characteristic form (allowing that 'F' may hide further complexities). Here in VI.7.38, since it is a question of the Good's self-awareness, the matter is naturally presented in terms of the Good's awareness of being good or being the Good (which awareness, as we have seen, Plotinus rejects). In Intellect's case, however, the first thought naturally is of being. In order to keep open the possibility that Intellect also thinks of other things, things that would in fact be comprised by being without being being itself, I shall in what follows usually present its thought simply as 'I am F'. For the present, what exactly Intellect thinks of itself is not my main concern.

I insert the qualification, 'if we were to render discursively the so-called self-thinking of Intellect', because, as we shall see in Chapter IV, it is not so clear that Intellect's non-discursive thought is by means of statements. Let us, however, ignore that issue for the time being, and proceed as if it was quite unproblematic to report on Intellect's thought by ordinary statements. After all, Plotinus often does this himself. In any case, I take it that the foregoing shows that we have fairly clear evidence for the claim that Plotinus actually thought of first-person statements which say what the subject is as appropriate to report Intellect's thought, however inadequate any sort of propositional account of its thought may be.

Let me try to make clearer what the point of Plotinus' use of the first person is. First of all, statements of the form 'I am F' serve to indicate that Intellect is talking about itself. In fact it strikes me that in Plotinus' case these statements are self-identifying statements by means of which the subject asserts its identity or essential character. Moreover, as Anscombe

(1975) has noted, by using the first person a speaker implies that he takes himself to be talking about himself, the latter occurrence of 'himself' being understood in a special way that is tied to the first person. By contrast, a speaker who refers to himself in the third person does not imply this. If such an implication is to be understood in the latter case, the additional premiss that the speaker knows that he is the one referred to in the third person is required. This, however, need not always hold. Odysseus, for instance, may know (e.g. by reading, in a later incarnation, the Myth of Er at the end of Plato's *Republic*) that Odysseus chose wisely from among the life-sketches available to him on the plain yonder, even if, after having drunk from Lethe, the river of forgetfulness, he may not know that he is Odysseus. On the other hand, if he afterwards noted 'I chose wisely', he would thereby imply that he, the speaker, knew that he himself was that person who made the wise choice. We need not, in fact, resort to such fanciful examples: John Smith learns from reading a newspaper from his hospital bed that a man of 33, John Smith, was seriously wounded in a terrorist attack; he tells his wife about this. He is in fact referring to himself but he doesn't realize that he is this John Smith spoken of in the paper.

The fact that Plotinus consistently uses the first person when imagining Intellect thinking, together with the understanding of self-thinking as involving knowing oneself to be that which one thinks, which emerged from VI.7.38, shows that the self-thinking Plotinus is after is reflexive in a way Aristotelian self-thinking is not. In fact, Intellect's self-thinking is at once reflexive in the sense that Intellect is self-conscious of its thoughts, and self-directed in the sense that the thoughts are directly and straightforwardly thoughts about Intellect's identity.

The pattern suggested by these first-person passages that we have seen also indicates that Plotinus' concern about self-thinking is not merely to note that in thinking Intellect is aware of its thoughts, knows that and what it is thinking.[53] By his first-person mood Plotinus is not making the

---

[53] In a very interesting article Gerson (1997) deals with some of the same issues as I address in this section. I think that in important respects he and I are on the same track. The idea that Plotinus' self-thinking is somehow essentially reflexive is common. There are very significant differences in how Gerson and I conceive of this, however. Gerson's central point is that self-thinking in Plotinus consists in reflexivity, which he understands as infallible knowledge of one's occurrent epistemic states (pp. 160–3). Thus, he connects self-thinking to Plotinus' claim that in thinking the Intellect thinks that it thinks (cf. II.9.1). As I see the matter, knowing that one knows or thinking that one thinks is not

Kantian point that any apprehension is reflexive, that whatever we think we are, or may become, aware of ourselves thinking the thought.[54] On this supposition, any thought seems trivially to become a self-thought, which is a view Plotinus evidently does not hold (cf. V.3.3–4). As already emphasized, Plotinus indeed believes that in Intellect's self-thought the thinker is aware of itself thinking what it is: for it itself is one element in the content of the thought, an element which together with what it thinks it is, being, makes the thought complex. This does, however, not rely on a tacit appeal to the reflexivity of all thought. Intellect's thoughts are specifically its thoughts about what it itself is, not its thoughts about whatever (which it apparently doesn't have either, it is rather egocentric in its thoughts). As was argued above, the reflexivity of Intellect's thought follows from the very conception Plotinus has of self-thinking, not the other way around.

Plotinus evidently conceives of the subject of thought and the object as inseparably connected. As we have seen, of undifferentiated entities there can be no thought. So there is no such thing as an 'I' in isolation or being that is not being being thought. In fact the subject and what it thinks are constituted in its act of thinking. Before it thinks there is no separation between it and what it thinks nor is anything conceived of as distinct from anything else. The subject and what it thinks itself to be come together as inseparable moments in an act of thought. I shall resume this issue of the intimate connection between thought and object in the next chapter.

So there is reason to believe that Intellect's thoughts, discursively rendered, are thoughts of the form 'I am F' by which Intellect identifies itself, says what it is. If such are its thoughts, it will think of itself as subject in every one of its thoughts. If, as suggested above, the subject and what it thinks it is are constituted in the thought, Intellect is the thoughts it has about what itself is.

With the preceding in mind let us consider yet another passage, this time from II.9—the treatise Porphyry gave the title 'Against the

sufficient for the kind of self-thinking Plotinus is after. I may think that '5 + 7 = 12' and I may, *ipso facto* think that I think this thought. So there is, or may be, some sort of reflexive knowledge involved in having this very thought. But even if thinking this thought should thus carry with it awareness of the thought, it doesn't follow that the subject thinks that it itself is the truth that 5 + 7 = 12. The kind of self-knowledge Plotinus envisages for Intellect, on the other hand, is such that it is an integral aspect of its thought that it is about itself.

[54] Cf. Kant's famous remark: 'Das: "Ich denke" muss alle meinen Vorstellungen begleiten können' (*Kritik der reinen Vernunft* B 51).

Gnostics'.[55] Gerson (1997) rightly sees the first chapter of this treatise as an important source on Plotinus' views on self-reflexivity. Here Plotinus considers and rejects views on the intellect, held by some unnamed thinkers, according to which there is a marked distinction between a thought and the thought that one thinks the first thought. Apparently, some of the philosophers he is taking issue with would take this distinction to the extreme of positing two intellects, one that thinks, and another one that thinks that the first intellect thinks (33–4).[56] Plotinus refutes this strong doctrine and then considers a weaker one along the same lines, which holds that thinking and thinking that one thinks differ notionally, differ *epinoiai* (dative) (41). That is to say, assuming that Plotinus' rendering of this position is correct, 'thinking' and 'the thought that one thinks' differ notionally in such a way that the notion of thinking as such does not include the consciousness that one thinks (*mê parakolouthounta hoti noei* (43–4)). He then proceeds to refute this too. The first consideration he advances against this view is that it doesn't even hold for us in our everyday lives, 'who always watch over our impulses and discursive thoughts' (44–5). The implication seems to be that these mundane states normally include a consciousness of one being in these states. He then proceeds to the case of Intellect, saying:

But certainly when the true Intellect thinks itself in its thoughts and its object of thought does not come from the outside, but it is itself also its object of thought, it necessarily in its thinking possesses itself and sees itself: it sees itself not as without intelligence but sees itself as thinking. So that in its primary thinking it would have also the thinking that it thinks as one being;[57] and it isn't double, even notionally, there in the intelligible world.[58] (II.9.1, 46–52)

---

[55] This treatise forms a part of a whole consisting of III.8, V.8, V.5, and II.9, which apparently were originally written as a single treatise. Their division and titles are the work of Plotinus' student and editor, Porphyry.

[56] See Armstrong's note *ad loc.* Dodds (1963: 168) speculates that Numenius (cf. Fr. 22 Desplaces = Proclus, *In Tim.* III, p. 103, 28–31 Diehl) is the source of the idea of two intellects one of which thinks and the other one thinks that the former thinks. I agree with Armstrong that the Numenian fragment is too obscure to make anything out of it in this direction.

[57] The sentence, 'So that in its primary thinking it would have also the thinking that it thinks as one being' is not altogether transparent, but I think there is no doubt that Plotinus means to say that thinking and thinking that one thinks make up a single entity.

[58] II.9.1, 46–52: "Ὅταν δὲ δὴ ὁ νοῦς ὁ ἀληθινὸς ἐν ταῖς νοήσεσιν αὑτὸν νοῇ καὶ μὴ ἔξωθεν ᾖ τὸ νοητὸν αὐτοῦ, ἀλλ' αὐτὸς ᾖ καὶ τὸ νοητόν, ἐξ ἀνάγκης ἐν τῷ νοεῖν ἔχει ἑαυτὸν καὶ ὁρᾷ ἑαυτόν· ὁρῶν δ' ἑαυτὸν οὐκ ἀνοηταίνοντα, ἀλλὰ νοοῦντα ὁρᾷ. "Ὥστε ἐν τῷ πρώτως νοεῖν ἔχοι ἂν καὶ τὸ νοεῖν ὅτι νοεῖ ὡς ἕν ὄν· καὶ οὐδὲ τῇ ἐπινοίᾳ ἐκεῖ διπλοῦν.

I find these lines extremely interesting. Let us start by noting that the thought in question here is evidently the kind of thought Plotinus often refers to as self-thinking (cf. 'is itself also its object of thought'). First, he postulates that in Intellect's thought the object does not come from outside and that in thinking Intellect 'sees itself'. In other words, what it sees is something internal to itself, not an external object. So far this may suggest only an 'Aristotelian' kind of reasoning that bases self-thinking merely on the identity of the thinker and the object. The way he proceeds to account for how the object appears to the subject, however, indicates that he has something more in mind: the object, which already is said to be Intellect itself, is seen not as something void of thought but 'it sees it as thinking'. In other words, it is the object of thought that is seen as thinking here. On an 'Aristotelian interpretation' this would render Plotinus' thought rather mystical: if Intellect thinks itself not *per se* but merely in virtue of the object of thought being identical with the subject, why should this object be seen as thinking? If Intellect thinks e.g. Beauty itself or a mathematical truth, these objects are readily seen to be thoughts on the 'Aristotelian' model. But that they should be seen as thinking something, doesn't make much sense.

Let us test the hypothesis proposed above that Intellect's self-thinking, discursively rendered, has the form 'I am F' and see how it would match the present passage. Well, one whose thought is 'I am F', may readily be said to see himself thinking. For the object of the thought is 'I am F' or 'I being F'; but this object is the very thought 'I am F'; so, in having this thought the thinker will be aware of himself thinking F of himself. So he will be aware of himself being (thinking that he is) F. That this is so follows from the the first-person, self-directed character of the thought in question. Consider, by contrast, the supposition that Intellect thought something like 'Justice is beautiful'. Plotinus indeed thinks, and plausibly so, that anyone who has a thought of this sort will be aware of having it or at least can attend to it. That this should be so does not, however, follow from the very content of the thought as the I's being aware of having the thought 'I am F' follows from the the very content of that thought.

I am in other words suggesting that expressions of the sort 'sees itself thinking' as we have here in II.9.1, are intended to capture both what I have called the first-person character of Intellect's thought and its self-directed character. Plotinus is naturally understood as presuming that the self-thought in question is of that character, a first-person, self-identification of the thinker. Of course the thinker is aware of having that self-identifying thought. Not only that, it is the kind of thought one couldn't have without *eo ipso* being conscious of having it. Thus, I tend to agree with Plotinus that in the case of the kind of thought in question, there is no room for even a notional distinction between thinking and being aware of what one thinks, thinking that one thinks.

Let us now, once again, resume the issue of the two kinds of otherness. Let us suppose with Plotinus that self-thinking is the primary kind of thought. It being primary means, I take it, that it comes first among thoughts in the process from the One downwards. Given Plotinus' usual way of looking at things, this also means that it is the most complete and unitary kind of thought. Now, the proposal was that 'self-thought' is to be interpreted as thinking 'I am F'. Moreover, it is thinking that one is F in such a way that one's being F is constituted by this thought. In this thought, 'I am F', one can see the 'I' performing a double role. Because for Plotinus 'I am F' is equivalent with 'I think I am F' or 'I think myself as F', we might say that the 'I' in 'I am F' hides an 'I think', an 'I' as a subject of thought. But this subject is also a part of the object, along with 'being F', for 'I am F' is what is being thought, *to nooumenon*. This means that 'I' is both subject and object of the thought. The otherness between the 'I' and the 'F' is what makes the object plural. This otherness is in a way the same otherness as the one that differentiates the subject and the object. For even if the object is the whole of 'I am F' and the subject is 'I', the subject and object differ only in virtue of 'F'. So the otherness between the 'F' and the 'I' accounts for both the subject object distinction—without the F, the subject wouldn't manage to think about itself at all, couldn't take itself as an object (cf. V.3.10, 31 ff. and p. 86ff. above).

So self-thinking, the primary kind of thought, as interpreted here above necessarily involves both kinds of otherness. We may even go further than that and say that they coincide: it is the difference between the F and the 'I' which underlies both the subject/object distinction and the original objective plurality. This is good news. For if the two kinds of otherness not only are present in, but even coincide in the primary kind of thought, lesser thoughts will possess them both as well. Indeed, according to Plotinus, they do possess them. They, however, do so in a less unified way than Intellect's self-thought does in that when thought no longer is self-thought, the subject of the thought is something different from the object, an object which, however, is bound to be complex in its own right. I won't pursue the issue here but Plotinus would no doubt hold that a thought of the form 'A thinks BC' is more complex than a thought of the form 'A thinks AB'.

It may be objected against the admittedly complicated account given of self-thinking and the two kinds of otherness in the preceding paragraphs that Plotinus himself nowhere presents such an account. So it may seem far-fetched to attribute something like this to him. To this I would respond that given the first-person nature of Intellect's thought, the interpretation is, despite the appearances, not really far-fetched. And there is solid textual support for the claim that Intellect's self-thought is essentially in the first person. Admittedly, there are not many instances showing this, but I consider those that are to provide strong evidence for this view. Once we adopt the view that Intellect's self-thought is to be represented by 'I am F' type of statements, however, we readily and intuitively see that the two kinds of otherness coincide in this case. Plotinus may well have taken the obviousness of this for granted. What turns out to be somewhat complicated is to work this out in detail.

The present hypothesis has the obvious merit of making some sense of some features of Plotinus' accounts of the genesis of Intellect that otherwise may remain puzzling: (1) The hypothesis enables us to see how Plotinus may have considered himself as introducing only one otherness at the stage of Intellect's self-thought. That otherness, the difference between the 'I' and the 'F', indeed functions in two ways, but it is the same difference in each case. (2) The hypothesis also straightforwardly makes sense of Plotinus' insistence that the first thought is self-thought: its thought is the thought of what it itself is. (3) We saw above that the inchoate intellect is in need of the One and in need of itself, and that this need is satisfied, to the extent it can be satisfied, by its thinking itself. These claims do perhaps not necessitate the understanding of self-thinking advocated for here, but the hypothesis makes good sense in their light. For 'I am being' is seen to be a discovery and constitution of self in thought in as straightforward a way as one could possibly have. It seems to me that alternative interpretations would have to tell a more complicated story to do justice to the claim that something in need of itself finds itself.

3

Intellect and Being

In this chapter I shall address some philosophical issues that have to do with the relationship between cognition and its objects. This involves inquiring into the connection between Plotinus' epistemology and his psychology, on the one hand, and his ontology, on the other. Interesting questions arise with respect to his views both as regards the relation between sense-perception and the sensible object and that of thinking and the intelligible object. One set of questions concerns realism versus idealism and subjectivism: is there in general an essential connection between cognition and object in Plotinus such that the mode of cognition in some sense determines the object? This would imply idealism of some sort. One may also ask whether the immediate object of cognition is always something belonging to the subject of cognition as opposed to something extra-mental. Such a subjectivist position would place the extra-mental beyond the direct reach of cognition and might involve a radical scepticism about it. Or is Plotinus neither an idealist nor a subjectivist and objects appear to be such and such because they are such as they appear independently of the mode of apprehension? Different stories may of course have to be told about intelligibles and sensibles with respect to these questions. So I shall in fact argue. Still it is interesting to inquire whether there are any common principles underlying Plotinus' views on both sensibles and intelligibles in this regard. This too I shall take up here below.

1. Cognition, Images, and the Real

Before we jump into particular issues, let me sketch the form these questions assume in Plotinus. For him the Intellect is at once the locus of the real or real being, and the locus of perfect knowledge and understanding. Its knowledge, being the highest possible kind of knowledge, is naturally of the real. Everything else is an image, an external act of the real (or an image of an image). It follows that any cognition of things of the latter sort is not knowledge of the truly real but is cognition of images. Hence, for instance sense-perception, which has sensibles as its object, and discursive reason, which belongs to the order of soul and does not grasp the primary intelligibles—more on this in Chapter 4—have something less than the fully real as their object. This is in itself unproblematic, provided we are clear about what counts as fully real for Plotinus.

There is a second consideration, however, which purports to show that only Intellect *can* know the real things themselves. Plotinus suggests that cognitive powers that are not identical with their object are for that very reason bound to apprehend at most an image of whatever they set out to grasp. The reasoning behind this, which is evident e.g. in the first chapter of V.5 and in chapter 5 of V.3, seems to be that powers that do not possess their object, must be acted on by the object; since they are acted on by the object they receive only an image of it. Since Intellect is the only cognitive power which primarily possesses its object, it alone can know its object itself.

The two preceding considerations, both of which result in the view that only Intellect knows the real things, may appear to be independent of one another. The first one proceeds on the assumption that some things are the real things, others are images of them. Knowledge of the former is knowledge of the real things, because this is what these things are, and cognition of the latter is a cognition of images because images is what they are quite independently of how they are apprehended. Considerations of the nature of cognition or cognitive powers do not enter into this at all. The second consideration, on the other hand, relates the question of cognition of images vs. cognition of the real things to the question of whether the objects are internal to the cognizing faculty or not. Since the real things on this view turn out to be necessarily internal to a cognitive faculty, some kind of idealism seems to follow: what is internal to a cognitive faculty must be a mental item of some sort.

If the preceding two kinds of considerations are independent of one another in this way, it seems that something may be real according to the one but not according to the other. Consider a hypothetical case according to which the ontologically primary things happen to be external to a given faculty, of which it then, by the second consideration, can at most cognize an image. Suppose also that this same faculty possesses innately some objects that by the first consideration are ontologically secondary and, hence, images. If this is a possible case, it seems that this faculty in one sense knows images, in another sense the real things. This is because the expression 'the real things', as I have been using it, is ambiguous. In the former instance, it refers to what comes first in the order of things ontologically speaking, in the latter it refers to the real thing in the sense of the thing itself which is to be apprehended as opposed to an image of it belonging to the cognizing subject. Plotinus, however, does not explicitly distinguish between these considerations. There is reason to believe he actually thought that what is real in the first sense must coincide with what is real in the second sense. It will be one of our main tasks in this chapter to explore how this is so. Let me, however, give some indications about how the story is going to unwind.

There is actually a further distinction to be made within what I have referred to as 'the ontologically primary'. Given that one goes in for a scheme of ontological orders of firsts, seconds, thirds, and even more, as Plotinus and all other Platonists do, the first are bound to be ontologically primary for the trivial reason that they are first: there is nothing prior of which they could be an image. Ontologically primary things in this sense are, however, not trivially primary in the sense of satisfying all the criteria of what fully is. The Greek philosophers from Parmenides through to Plato, Aristotle, and the Stoics developed some ideas about what really is must be like. There is no single list, agreed upon by all parties, but the features of independence or self-sufficiency (*autarkeia*), stability, unity, and even life could, I think, be accepted by all in the mainstream of Greek philosophical thought to which Plotinus belongs. For the Platonists and Aristotelians in particular that which is real being in the sense of possessing all or most of these features is also ontologically primary in the sense that there is no being prior to it. This is of course no coincidence, since one of the criteria of real being is independence. That which is ontologically secondary or tertiary depends on what is prior. That is why it is secondary or tertiary.

In Plotinus' view Intellect is both ontologically primary and satisfies the other traditional demands on real being. Moreover, it both is 'the real thing' and knows the real thing in the sense of the second set of considerations above: for it knows itself. In fact, I take it that Plotinus holds that only something like Intellect, a knower who innately possesses its object, has a chance of satisfying the criteria of real being and of being ontologically primary. This is due to the conditions of unity and life that what truly is must satisfy. This is the story in the broadest and most abstract outline. It remains to see the details.

2. The Nature of Sense-Perception

Plotinus normally speaks as a non-representational realist about the objects of sense-perception: what we perceive is qualities of external objects, qualities that exist out there independently of us. He even makes a point of insisting that what we see is an external object out there, rejecting certain theories about the transmission between object and perceiver in vision on the ground that the theories would entail that we do not see the objects themselves (IV.5.3, 21–2). He writes, against a view that holds that we see by receiving physical impressions of the objects we see, that 'if we received impressions (*typos*) of what we see, there will be no possibility of looking at the actual things we see, but we shall look at images and shadows of the objects of sight, so that the objects themselves will be different from the things we see' (IV.6.1, 29–32). And there are several other remarks that clearly point to direct realism.

Nevertheless, there are also some indications to the contrary. First, certain features of Plotinus' theory of sense-perception may be difficult to reconcile with direct realism. Second, there are some passages that at first glance at least speak against perceptual realism. Third, there are considerations speaking for the view that Plotinus holds that what is out there, if anything at all, is quite different from what appears to our senses. I shall now take up these issues in turn.

Before proceeding, however, let us have an outline of Plotinus' views on sense-perception, which are presented in a fairly systematic way in IV.4.23 (see also III.6.1). The elements involved in sense-perception are the following: an external qualified object (or the quality of such an object) is what is perceived; the subject of sense-perception is the individual soul and its role is described either as judging (*krisis*) or the reception of the form (*eidos*) of the object. I have argued (Emilsson (1988: 137–40) that these are different descriptions of the same phenomenon. For perception to occur the soul must come into contact with the external object. The soul by itself, being an intelligible thing, cannot do this: alone, it only grasps intelligibles and in any case it cannot be affected by sensibles (IV.4.23, 4–33). But to perceive through the senses is to apprehend sensibles, extended spatial phenomena, and the soul must somehow come into contact with these. This it does by means of ensouled sense-organs: these are affected by the object of perception. This sensory affection, which Plotinus also describes as 'assimilation', is transmitted to the soul. By the stage at which it reaches the soul, it is no longer an affection (*pathos*) but a form or judgement.

Plotinus' usual story about sense-perception is along these lines. One question that obviously arises is how he reconciles the realism which he insists on with the role he assigns to sensory affections. It is for instance hard to see how he could be a realist if he also holds that what we immediately perceive is the sensory affections and that the sensory affections are different from the external objects of sense-perception. In my book, *Plotinus on Sense-Perception* (Emilsson 1988), I discuss the inner workings of Plotinus' account of sense-perception and argue for an overall interpretation which seeks to do justice to his realistic intuitions.

Now I shall not repeat the details of my previous account here, only summarize the points that are of direct concern to us now. (1) The affection (or assimilation) in sense-perception is a sensation, a non-conceptual, phenomenal presence of the external quality to the senses. (2) This phenomenal quality is in a way identical to, in a way different from, the quality as it exists in the external corporeal object. It is the same quality without the matter or bulk, and hence it is not the quality in its normal corporeal mode. The phenomenal quality is not a purely intelligible item, however, since it retains the spatial features of the corporeal—we do perceive things extended in space. We can perhaps describe this by saying that the quality the sense-organ takes on is the quality of the object but in a hybrid mode of being in between the corporeal and the intelligible, having some features in common with each. In Emilsson (1988: 133 ff.) I present some evidence that Plotinus actually held such a view, even if he does not express it explicitly in terms of different modes of being. (3) The judgement attributed to the soul is a judgement about the external object, not about the affection. So the idea is that Plotinus can with some plausibility retain his realism: even if the soul is immediately aware of the affection, the judgement (the perception itself) is about what is external, and the affection, the quality the organ takes on, is in the way indicated above identical with the external quality.

I still think that an interpretation along these lines is the best available one. Certain difficulties however deserve a fuller treatment than I gave in my previous account and it should be admitted that Plotinus' is a vulnerable sort of realism: a sceptic would jump with a wedge in hand at the distinction between the affection and the external corporeal quality. In the next section we shall inquire whether Plotinus himself gets into such a sceptical mood in the first chapter of the celebrated treatise 'That the intelligibles are not outside Intellect and on the Good' (V.5. (32)).

3. Evidence for Subjectivism or Idealism

I mentioned above that there are some Plotinian passages that may seem to state or imply antirealism about sense-perception. For instance Plotinus writes in one place: 'And soul's power of perception (*aisthêsis*) need not be of sensibles, but rather it must be receptive of the impressions produced by sense-perception on the living being; these are already intelligible entities' (I.1.7, 9–12). Obviously, there are two kinds of perception at stake in this passage: the soul's perception and that of the living being. Blumenthal (1971: 71–2) has suggested that the *aisthêsis* attributed to the organism is a mere sensation and that of the soul fully-fledged sense-perception. In that case, the passage would affirm antirealism or at least a denial of direct realism. It is also possible, however, to take the *aisthesis* attributed to the living being to be simply sense-perception (including, but being more than, sensation), and that of the soul to be a non-sensory apprehension of mental representations, the kind involved in memory and in discursive thinking, the highest stage of the human soul. There are ample instances in Plotinus of *aisthêsis* being used to refer to non-sensory apprehension (VI.7.5, 18–20; VI.7.35, 38; VI.7.38, 10). In my view, the latter interpretation gives a better sense to the passage in its context and has the advantage of acquitting Plotinus of the charge of holding that sense-perception is an apprehension of intelligible things, which is both counter-intuitive and contrary to his normal teaching. For even if in Plotinus' view sense-perception, *qua* judgement and form in the soul, involves intelligible forms or impressions, it need not thereby be necessary to ascribe to him the claim that sense-perception is *of* something intelligible. Moreover, this latter interpretation is easily harmonized with other significant passages about sense-perception: he elsewhere clearly attributes sense-perception as a whole, the sensory affection and the judgement or reception of intelligible form in the soul, to the organism or compound of soul and body.

The passage which is by far the most worrisome for a realist interpretation is V.5.1—the treatise Porphyry entitled 'That the intelligibles are not outside Intellect, and on the Good'.[1] I shall now consider it at some length. As will become clear, its examination will lead us beyond the theory of sense-perception to the theory of Intellect and questions of metaphysics.

Plotinus first raises the question of the conditions for ascribing perfect infallible knowledge of what is real to Intellect. He will argue that only if the object of Intellect's thought—the Ideas, what is ontologically primary—is internal to Intellect itself, will it have such knowledge of them. We shall come to this doctrine in its own right in due course. But in the first chapter he remarks that Intellect's knowledge cannot be founded on demonstration.[2] For even supposing that some of Intellect's knowledge is founded on demonstration, not all of it can be so founded. Some at least must be immediately evident. This is of course just a statement of the familiar point emphasized by Aristotle (see *An. post.* II, 19) that not everything can be demonstrated, something must be given without demonstration; and if the demonstration is supposed to yield knowledge, what is given without demonstration must be known to be true without any further proof. Then Plotinus goes on to ask from where 'they' (these are some unnamed philosophers) suppose Intellect comes to have the self-evidence (*to enarges*) about that which they admit to be immediately known. He then continues with the passage containing the crucial remark for our concerns:

But anyhow, what they admit to be immediate, whence do they say its self-evidence comes to it? From where will it get the confidence that things are so?

---

[1] This treatise is along with III.8 (30), V.8 (31), and II.9 (33) a part of a whole that Porphyry split into four treatises placing them in different slots of the *Enneads*. In Chapter 2 we had occasion to consider aspects of II.9 and in the next chapter aspects of V.8 will be in focus.

[2] The reference to knowledge based on demonstration (*apodeiksis*) here indicates that it is Peripatetics or Platonists under Peripatetic influence that are Plotinus' target here rather than e.g. the Epicureans, whom Bréhier (1931: 119) in his 'Notice' on V.5 and others suggest. See Emilsson (1988: 118–19).

For it may even be doubted about that which seems clearest in sense-perception, whether it has its apparent existence not in the substrates but in the affections, and intellect and reason are needed as judges. For also if it is admitted that what sense-perception is to grasp is in sensible substrates, what is known through sense-perception is an image (*eidôlon*) of the thing, and sense-perception does not grasp the thing itself: for that remains outside.[3] (V.5.1, 9–19)

What does Plotinus mean by the claim that the senses know only an image of the object?[4] And what does he mean by 'the thing itself' which he says remains external? At first sight the point of Plotinus' remark may seem to be that in sense-perception we grasp only a *subjective* representation, something that pertains to us as perceivers, and that this is contrasted with the object as it exists externally, independently of us. What we are directly aware of in sense-perception would then be an image or representation, existing in our sense-organs, of the external object. Furthermore, it seems to speak for such an antirealist interpretation of our passage that in this same chapter, V.5.1, Plotinus argues along the following lines: if the intelligibles are external to Intellect, Intellect must receive an impression of them if it is to know them at all; it would in that case be just like sense-perception; what Intellect would then know is a mere impression (or representation) and not the intelligibles themselves; but Intellect does know the intelligibles themselves, which, therefore, must be internal to Intellect. The implication seems to be that a power of cognition that does not primarily contain the objects it knows, must somehow acquire them. But it cannot acquire these objects themselves, and must therefore make do with representations that pertain to it, the power of cognition. Given that this is the line of argument

---

[3] V.5.1, 9–19: Ἀλλ' οὖν, ἃ συγχωροῦσιν αὐτόθεν, πόθεν φήσουσι τούτων τὸ ἐναργὲς αὐτῷ παρεῖναι; Πόθεν δὲ αὐτῷ πίστιν, ὅτι οὕτως ἔχει, παρέξεται; Ἐπεὶ καὶ τὰ ἐπὶ τῆς αἰσθήσεως, ἃ δὴ δοκεῖ πίστιν ἔχειν ἐναργεστάτην, ἀπιστεῖται, μή ποτε οὐκ ἐν τοῖς ὑποκειμένοις, ἀλλ' ἐν τοῖς πάθεσιν ἔχει τὴν δοκοῦσαν ὑπόστασιν καὶ νοῦ δεῖ ἢ διανοίας τῶν κρινούντων· ἐπεὶ καὶ συγκεχωρημένου ἐν τοῖς ὑποκειμένοις εἶναι αἰσθητοῖς, ὧν ἀντίληψιν ἡ αἴσθησις ποιήσεται, τό τε γινωσκόμενον δι' αἰσθήσεως τοῦ πράγματος εἴδωλόν ἐστι καὶ οὐκ αὐτὸ τὸ πρᾶγμα ἡ αἴσθησις λαμβάνει· μένει γὰρ ἐκεῖνο ἔξω.

[4] O'Meara (2000: 244–5) argues, partly criticizing my previously published views on this passage (Emilsson 1988: 118–21; 1996: 220–3), that these lines from V.5.1 constitute a sceptically inspired rejection of 'sensualist and externalist theories (whose proponents are referred to indifferently as "they")' and thus clear the ground, by elimination, for Plotinus' non-sensualist conception of knowledge characteristic of transcendent Intellect'. I am in principle not unsympathetic to such a reading. I, however, stick to my previous view which takes the 'sceptical' remarks about sense-perception here to express Plotinus' own views. My main reason for holding on to this view is the beginning of chapter 2 of V.5, which seems to me difficult to make sense of unless we take Plotinus to be reporting his own views here in chapter 1.

for the internality of the intelligibles, one naturally takes the 'image' in the passage quoted above to be an image pertaining to the faculty of sense.

However, not everything is as it seems here. Such antirealist reading of the passage quoted above also runs into difficulties on examination: Plotinus seems in fact to be making two points in denial of the supposition that Intellect gets its self-evident premises from sense-perception: first, considering sense-perception alone, it may be doubted whether what is perceived is external or just in the affections; reason and intellect are needed as judges; secondly, granting that what it apprehends is external, it is nevertheless an image. So one would suppose that the image mentioned here is in fact something external. But what would then be the 'thing itself' which remains external? A natural answer not involving antirealism is provided by the first lines of chapter 2 of the same treatise. Here Plotinus summarizes the main points established in chapter 1 and it becomes clear that by the 'image' (eidolon) that sense-perception grasps he means the qualitative features of each thing as opposed to the essence or quiddity of which these are an expression. So one would expect that 'the thing itself' in our original passage from chapter 1 is the imperceptible and separate essence of the thing, as opposed to the qualified matter which constitutes the sensible object. Such a view, according to which the perceptible qualities of an object are representations or images of an intelligible Being, which is the real thing, is a standard Plotinian view as is the claim that sense-perception fails to grasp essences. The following passage shows this particularly well:

So called [sensible] Being is not an essence (ti) but a quale; and the formative principle (logos), of fire, for instance, indicates rather the essence, but the shape it produces is rather a quale. And the formative principle of man is the essence, but its product in the nature of body, being an image (eidôlon) of the principle, is rather a quale. It is as if, the visible Socrates being a man, his painted picture, being colours and painter's stuff, was called Socrates. In the same way, therefore, since there is a rational principle according to which Socrates is, the perceptible Socrates should not rightly be said to be Socrates, but colours and shapes which are representations of those in the principle.[5] (VI.3.15, 26–37)

[5] VI.3.15, 26–37: κινδυνεύει ἡ λεγομένη αὕτη οὐσία εἶναι τοῦτο τὸ ἐκ πολλῶν, οὐ τὶ ἀλλὰ ποιὸν μᾶλλον· καὶ ὁ μὲν λόγος εἶναι οἷον πυρὸς τὸ τὶ σημαίνων μᾶλλον, ἣν δὲ μορφὴν ἐργάζεται, ποιὸν μᾶλλον· καὶ ὁ λόγος ὁ τοῦ ἀνθρώπου τὸ τὶ εἶναι, τὸ δ' ἀποτελεσθὲν ἐν σώματος φύσει εἴδωλον ὂν τοῦ λόγου ποιόν τι μᾶλλον εἶναι. Οἷον εἰ

Sensible qualities are just this: they are expressions in matter of the activity of an imperceptible and separate inner nature or essence (*logos, to ti*). Another passage from the early treatise V.9. (5), where Plotinus deals with the internality of the intelligibles to Intellect as in V.5, supports this understanding of 'image'. He has affirmed that Intellect thinks the real beings and raises the question whether it thinks them 'somewhere else'. In response to this he says:

[It will] surely not [think them] in sensible objects, as they suppose. For the primary object of each kind is not the sensible object: for the form on matter in the things of sense is an image (*eidôlon*) of the real form, and every form which is in something else comes to it from something else and is a likeness (*eikôn*) of that from which it comes.[6] (V.9.5, 16–19)

The early treatise V.9. (5) is less sophisticated than V.5, but it presents the same general doctrine about the internality of the intelligibles to Intellect. Here the sensible object is rejected as the ontologically primary object and Plotinus explains its image character in terms of its being 'in something else', i.e. in some matter which takes on the form, and 'from something else', i.e. the intelligible cause, without a word about the nature of sense-perception or antirealism about the cognition of external objects. Thus, the word 'image' here has clearly the meaning I have suggested for V.5.1.

So there are difficulties on internal grounds for an antirealist reading of our passage: such a reading squares badly with Plotinus' regular position, and another interpretation naturally suggests itself. Nevertheless, there remains the difficulty of the contrast between intellection and sense-perception in Plotinus' argument for the internality of the objects of intellection: this may still count in favour of an antirealist reading. So let us ask: is there a way of interpreting Plotinus' contrast between intellection and sense-perception in V.5.1 without attributing to him an antirealist view on the latter? It should give us grounds for pause before attributing such a position to him on this

---

ἀνθρώπου ὄντος τοῦ Σωκράτους τοῦ ὁρωμένου ἡ εἰκὼν αὐτοῦ ἡ ἐν γραφῇ χρώματα καὶ φάρμακα ὄντα Σωκράτης λέγοιτο· οὕτως οὖν καὶ λόγου ὄντος, καθ' ὃν Σωκράτης, τὸν αἰσθητὸν Σωκράτη <ὀρθῶς λεκτέον οὐ Σωκράτη> ἀλλὰ χρώματα καὶ σχήματα ἐκείνων τῶν ἐν τῷ λόγῳ μιμήματα εἶναι. This is the text of H-S² which involves an emendation suggested by Igal in line 35.

[6] V.9.5, 16–19: Οὐ γὰρ δὴ ἐν τοῖς αἰσθητοῖς, ὥσπερ οἴονται. Τὸ γὰρ πρῶτον ἕκαστον οὐ τὸ αἰσθητόν· τὸ γὰρ ἐν αὐτοῖς εἶδος ἐπὶ ὕλῃ εἴδωλον ὄντος, πᾶν τε εἶδος ἐν ἄλλῳ παρ' ἄλλου εἰς ἐκεῖνο ἔρχεται καί ἐστιν εἰκὼν ἐκείνου.

account that in V.3, where he also argues for the internality of the objects of thought to Intellect and contrasts intellection with sense-perception, there is no suggestion of this sort of subjectivism. In fact the sense of 'internal' Plotinus seems to be after here for the objects of Intellect is a stronger sense than the one in which sensory images can be said to be internal to the faculty that apprehends them. For the apprehension of such images counts for him as cognition of something external too (V.3.1–3).

In fact I believe there is a plausible interpretation that avoids subjectivism while doing justice to the contrast Plotinus wishes to draw between thinking at the level of Intellect and sense-perception. This is basically an expansion of the interpretation cursorily stated above which identifies the contrast between the representation and the thing itself in our passage with the contrast between sensible qualities and the nature or essence of the thing, the immediate intelligible cause of sensible qualities. As a preliminary to the full statement of this interpretation, we must recall certain aspects of Plotinus' metaphysics. In Chapter 1 we had an account of Plotinus' distinction between internal and external activity and sketched how these two kinds of act pervade the stages of the Plotinian world: the One has a totally self-contained internal activity and an inchoate Intellect has an external act, which is an image of the One itself; this inchoate Intellect converts to its source, whereby it becomes informed; this is Intellect's inner activity, identical with Intellect's Being. This internal activity in turn has Soul as an external act. Plotinus describes the inner act as the real thing itself, and the outer act as its image or representation. This kind of process continues at soul-levels below the hypostasis Soul till we reach immanent sensible forms and matter which have no external activity and progression comes to an end. So, not only is the relationship between sensible qualities and the underlying nature or *logos* that produces them that of image and original, the image/original relation here is a part of the double activity schema. This is quite clear for instance from chapters 1–7 of III.8. Formative principles produce sensible qualities and shapes (outer activity) as a result of reverting to and contemplating their immediate cause (inner activity).

Let us now consider what we have just ascertained together with one tenet of Plotinus' realism: (1) The internal activity of the formative principle is the cause of sensible qualities; the qualities are external acts and, thereby, images of formative principles. (2) In sense-perception the quality taken on by the sense-organ is the same quality as the one that exists externally (though in a different mode of being cf. p. 128 above). It follows from these two premises that in sense-perception there is no further activity from the object side in addition to the activity of the formative principle: it is not as if the formative principle first causes the external quality which then in turn acts separately on the senses; rather, there is just one activity: the internal act of the formative principle with a sensible quality as a concomitant by-product. So, metaphysically speaking, the quality the sense-organs take on is still the external act of the object's formative principle.

In Chapter 2, in connection with a discussion of why knowledge of the One is impossible (cf. pp. 77–8 above), I appealed to the principle that a power of cognition that does not by itself possess the internal activity of its objects can at most apprehend these objects through their external activity, i.e. their images. It is time to appeal to this principle again and give it some support as a Plotinian doctrine. In Plotinus' view, a power which does not innately possess the internal activity of its object must be affected by the object; to affect is to have an effect in something else, which by definition is the work of an external, as opposed to an internal, activity. Plotinus does not explicitly state such a principle. It seems plausible to suppose, however, that a principle along these lines is what underlies Plotinus' arguments for the internality of the intelligibles to Intellect in V.5.1 and in V.3.5. I shall come back to that issue later on in this chapter. But in any case, if Plotinus adheres to such a principle, he has good reasons for contrasting sense-perception and intellection in the way he does in V.5.1: the faculty of sense does not possess the intelligible causes of sensible objects, i.e. it does not possess the internal activity that constitutes the intelligible essence of these objects. What these objects are in themselves is external to the faculty of sense. This faculty can, however, be acted on by these objects in such a way as to come to share in their external activity. Or to resort to more Plotinian language, the objects themselves, i.e. the imperceptible *logoi*, may act externally in the sense-organ of a sentient being. To hold this is not to deny that the same external act may exist as an objective quality or quantity of a body.

Objections: I have maintained that, through sensing, the faculty of sense comes to apprehend the external qualities themselves, whereas it cannot apprehend the internal nature of the sense object. Isn't this a violation of the principle just stated that a cognitive power can at most apprehend images of what is external to it, for indeed we have said that the senses apprehend the external qualities themselves? For doesn't this principle dictate that we know images of the qualities? And secondly, if the senses can know something external to themselves by taking on or sharing in that very thing itself, why shouldn't Intellect be able to know the intelligibles themselves in an analogous manner, even if they are originally external to it?

These questions would, I think, be based on a misunderstanding. Responding to them may however clarify the position I am urging. The first question presupposes that qualities in their turn have a sort of inner and outer activity, and that, by the above-mentioned principle, their inner activity is beyond our reach; what we grasp through sense-perception, then, is the outer activity of the qualities, not the outer activity of the object's formative principle. I see no reason for supposing this to be Plotinus' view. To my knowledge, Plotinus nowhere explicitly discusses what is the real agent in sense-perception, whether it is the quality itself or the underlying formative principle. He does say, however, that the perceptible manifestations of (the last) formative principles are dead, by which he means that the cycle of inner and outer activity has come to an end: 'This forming principle, then, which operates in the visible shape, is the last, and is dead and no longer able to make another' (III.8.2, 30–2). Qualities, I should think, are not active in their own right according to Plotinus. It is true that he does say that opposite qualities in matter affect one another (III.6.9, 25–6). This is, however, compatible with holding that the real agent in such cases is a formative principle, a view he also expresses in the same treatise (III.6.17, 21–3).

This is also what is suggested by the mirror analogy he invokes and makes much use of in III.6.7 in order to explain the relations between matter, sensible corporeal forms, and their intelligible causes: these relations are to be seen by analogy with a mirror, the image that appears in it and the real object reflected in the mirror (III.6.7, 40–3). Furthermore, Plotinus has a peculiar theory about the transmission from object to percipient in sight and hearing, a theory which holds that such transmission takes place through *sympatheia*.[7] Many details of this theory are obscure, but it is clear that *sympatheia* is a process involving psychic agency. It is not a matter of visible or audible quality doing something entirely on its own. So, even if

---

[7] See IV.5.5; cf. Emilsson (1988: ch. 3) and Gurtler (1988: ch. 3).

the evidence is meagre, what there is suggests that qualities are not active in their own right in sense-perception (cf. II.4.9, 6–12).

Now, to the second question: why shouldn't Intellect be able to know the intelligibles themselves, even if they were external to it, if the senses can know something external to themselves by taking on that very thing itself? Let us suppose for the sake of argument that Intellect were in a similar situation to that of the faculty of sense. It might in that case know the intelligibles by participating directly in their external activity. Intellect would then know this external activity itself as opposed to an image of it (just like sight knows the objective colour itself rather than an image of it). Presumably the cognition the soul has of Intellect is of this sort: it knows the primary intelligibles at the level of Intellect by sharing in (in fact by being) the external activity of the primary intelligibles (cf. V.1.3; V.3.4). But on the present hypothesis, in another sense Intellect would not know the intelligibles themselves at all, since it would fail to know them through their internal activity. Given an account along the lines suggested here above of how in a sense we perceive an external item itself and how in another sense that external item is not 'the thing itself', Plotinus has indeed a reason to contrast sense-perception and intellection: sense-perception turns out to be of what is external to it, and we have explained how the object of sense-perception is bound to be of an image, because it is of what is external. If this account holds, Plotinus' celebrated doctrine that the intelligibles are internal to Intellect should be interpreted as the claim that Intellect's primary activity and that of the intelligibles is one and the same activity. In other words, Intellect knows the intelligibles by their internal activity, and this could not be the case unless Intellect and this activity were identical.

It is tempting to elaborate on this. The claim that a given form of cognition is of an object internal to the cognizing subject means that the object's inner activity and that of the subject are the same. Likewise, the claim that a form of cognition is of something external means that the activity which is the object is not identical with the activity of the cognizing power in question. So, this latter type of cognition is bound to be of the external act of the object, and hence of an image of it. Since subject and object coincide only in Intellect's cognition of the intelligibles, every other form of cognition is of images.

We have arrived at this position through fairly abstract reasoning that has taken place well above the texts. But in fact Plotinus says as explicitly as one might hope for that the activity of the intelligibles and that of Intellect are the same: 'But being is activity: so both [being and Intellect] have one activity, or rather both are one thing' (V.9.8, 15–16). In the same vein he claims in V.3.5 that the intelligible is a kind of activity and that life and thinking are not imposed upon it from the outside. And he continues: 'If then it is activity, and the first activity and fairest, it is the first intellection and substantial intellection: for it is the truest; but an intellection of this kind which is primary and primarily intellection will be the first Intellect' (V.3.5, 36–9). He is claiming here that the intelligibles are essentially active, that their activity is intellection and that this intellection is the universal Intellect. In other words the activity of the intelligibles and that of the Intellect are identical. The same doctrine underlies the striking analogy of sight seeing itself and light mingling with light that he uses to illustrate Intellect's thinking in V.3.8.

What about the second aspect of the claim above, that cognition of what is external is cognition of the external activity of the object? Can we see evidence for such a view elsewhere in Plotinus' thought?

Plotinus' primary use of the double activity model is to account for the generation of the hypostases and his accounts of this are the obvious place to look. In this context our question becomes the question of whether e.g. Intellect, by 'looking' towards its source, apprehends the One through the latter's external activity. And a parallel question may be raised about the generation of Soul from Intellect. But we have already answered this question: Intellect indeed knows the One through the latter's external act (see pp. 75–7 above). And the same seems to be asserted of the soul's cognition of Intellect (V.3.4). However, since the external act of the higher hypostasis also constitutes the lower hypostasis, the cognition of this external act is at the same time cognition of the lower hypostasis itself. The relevance of this for our present concerns is that an apprehension of a higher hypostasis may well be an objective apprehension of its external activity and at the same time of something pertaining to the lower hypostasis itself.

So far I have argued that Plotinus is not a subjectivist in the sense that what we apprehend in sense-perception are subjective images of the external world. Subjectivism should, however, be kept distinct from subjective idealism. A subjective idealist, as I am interpreting the term, maintains that there is no external world independent of us, and it questions the meaningfulness of such a notion. A subjectivist holds that what we perceive are images that pertain to us, and he is liable to say that the external world as it is in itself is unknowable. So the subjectivist is likely to be a sceptic about the nature of external objects as they are independently of being perceived; he may even doubt the existence of the external world; but as I use the term 'subjectivist' he is not one who denies the meaningfulness of the notion of an independently existing external world.

If my contentions about V.5.1 above are correct, Plotinus never sustains doubt about the general adequacy of sense-perception as a mode of cognition of external qualities or objects. He does not sceptically contrast what is given in sense-perception with physical objects as they are independently of being perceived. He does hold, nevertheless, that sensibles (physical objects) are not the sorts of things one can have knowledge about (V.9.7, 5–6; 13, 10). But the reasons for this have more to do with the nature of sensibles as such than with the faculty of sense-perception. The sensible object is a conglomerate of qualities in matter (cf. VI.3.15, p. 132 above). This conglomerate is indeed an image of an intelligible archetype. However, the archetype is not given in the conglomerate as such. As Gerson (1994: 105) notes, the archetype and the image are only homonymous: they have only the name in common in the same way as a house and a picture of that house can both be called 'houses'. A picture of a house is hardly intelligible as a picture of a house without prior knowledge of real houses. Similarly the intelligible Socrates, Socrates' soul, is not given in Socrates' perceptible image.[8] To this we may add that Plotinus frequently contrasts the togetherness of everything in the intelligible realm—often quoting Anaxagoras' (fr. B 1) phrase, *homou panta*, 'everything together'—with the dispersion in the sensible realm (I.1.8, 8; III.2.2, 18–23). Such remarks indicate the spatiality of sensibles and contrast it with the non-spatiality of intelligibles, but they also have a bearing on epistemology. The togetherness in Intellect turns up in accounts of how Intellect can grasp the intelligibles and their connections all at once (V.8.6). The dispersion characteristic of sensibles also means that there can be no understanding of the connections between sensibles and sensible features. There are only separate particular facts (VI.4.1, 17–29) and the sensible object as such does not contain any explanation of the relations between these particulars (II.6.1, 6–12; III.2.2, 18–23). One must

---

[8] For discussions of the sensible object in Plotinus, see Strange (1992), Gerson (1994: 85–95), and Wagner (1996).

inquire into their intelligible causes for an explanation to the extent it is to be had. All this disqualifies the sensible object as an object of understanding.

If the preceding account holds, Plotinus is not an idealist about the sensible world either: if sense-perception reveals to us objective features of the sensible world, there is an objective sensible world and the world we sense is not a creation of our senses. Unless, of course, Plotinus is a subtle idealist of the Kantian type who redefines the notions of objectivity and externality in some such a way that the sensible world is somehow constituted by, or defined in terms of, our cognitive faculties, perception or thought or both, but is still external and objective. I can see no hints of such a line of thought in Plotinus, however.

Nevertheless, it must be admitted that Plotinus himself often uses the kind of language germane to idealism about the sensible realm. So let us consider the matter further. Plotinus holds, and in fact emphasizes, that the qualities and quantities in matter, i.e. the directly perceptible features of things, are in some sense unreal. He for instance writes: '[Sensible Being] is a shadow, and upon what is itself a shadow, a picture and a seeming' (VI.3.8, 36–7). The 'shadow' on which sensible Being rests is matter. Such language may suggest idealism in the sense that trees and houses only appear to be out there but really they are not there at all. Our previous remarks about Plotinus' notion of an image (see p. 132 above) should however keep us from hastily jumping to such a conclusion. At least a part of the explanation of the language suggesting non-reality is that in such passages the sensible is contrasted with the intelligible. The latter is what is real and original, and the sensible, being a mere dependent image of the intelligible, is a shadow and an appearance of it. The passages that suggest the non-reality of the sensible are usually also associated with a certain view of the relationship between matter and sensible features: the features that appear in matter are not genuine properties of it for matter has no proper form of its own. Indeed Plotinus goes as far as inviting us to see the relationship between the intelligible archetypes, their sensible images and matter on analogy with an ordinary physical object, a mirror image of that object and the mirror. As already noted, the features that appear in matter fail to belong to matter similarly to the way colours appearing in a mirror fail to be genuine properties of the mirror (cf. III.6.7, 40–3).

However we are to understand Plotinus' views here in detail, two facts seem evident: first that by itself the mirror analogy does not suggest that the features which appear in matter are unreal in the sense of being somehow the products of *our* senses and, second, that the analysis of what is involved in the use of the mirror image explains the language of shadows and unreality without necessitating idealism. So it seems that we can make sense of his claim that the external sensible world is unreal without attributing to him any sort of idealism about the sensible world.

So we have come to the conclusion that sensible features are objective in the sense of being there independently of us as perceivers, even if they are somehow unreal, mere appearances of reality. It would be desirable to be able to give an account of their lack of reality that goes beyond Plotinus' mirror analogy. This is not the occasion to penetrate into this question, and I shall only give the gist of the answer that seems most promising: on scrutiny the sensible object breaks down, fails to be a genuine object at all. There is just matter, which turns out to be nothing positive at all, and features in it which cannot be *its* features, since matter is no determinate object, and hence, trivially, there is no object there to have the features. Nevertheless, it may seem to us that there is a real object out there with the features that appear to us. But this would be a mistake similar to mistaking a mirror image for a real object.

4. The Identity of Subject and Object in Intellect

We have already mentioned Plotinus' famous thesis that the intelligibles are internal to Intellect—the Internality Thesis, as I shall hereafter call it. We have also seen, especially in connection with V.5.1, that this claim about the intelligibles is contrasted with the externality of the objects of sense-perception. The Internality Thesis in V.5 is connected with the view that Intellect knows the things themselves as opposed to images of these things (cf. V.3.5; V.8.4–5). According to the line of interpretation suggested above, knowing 'the things themselves' implies that the activity constituting the object of Intellect's cognition and the activity constituting the subject are identical. We have also seen that this is indeed Plotinus' view.

In this and the subsequent sections of this chapter we shall consider in greater detail Plotinus' notion of knowledge of the things themselves in relation to other claims it typically appears together with. Knowing the things themselves is described by Plotinus as Intellect's self-knowledge and as its self-thinking (V.3.5, 45–6; V.9.5, 14–16); at the same time Intellect's knowledge is the knowledge of what is ontologically primary. In fact the universal Intellect is the only stage in the Plotinian hierarchy where identity of subject and object of cognition, complete knowledge of the ontologically primary things themselves, and self-knowledge obtain. Before us, then, lies the difficult task of getting clearer about how these claims fit together. This will involve us in a rather detailed study of some very difficult but still rewarding passages from V.3, especially chapter 5. Before I proceed to consider these, I shall dispose of some preliminary difficulties that Plotinus' position may seem to invoke.

One may ask why Intellect's knowledge isn't knowledge of images since Intellect knows the One's external activity and the One's external activity is an image of the One itself. The answer is that with respect to the One, Intellect's knowledge is indeed knowledge of an image, as Plotinus himself in fact clearly asserts (e.g. at V.6.5, 12–16; V.3.11, 8). This does not prevent this cognition from being knowledge of the things themselves, because the things Plotinus calls real or ontologically primary beings (*ta onta*)—the paradigms of all other existences—first come about at the stage of Intellect. So, to put it succinctly, Intellect's knowledge of the image of the One is the cognition of what is ontologically primary: the image of the One is the first and primary being.

Secondly, given my account of apprehension of images and of the things themselves in terms of apprehension of external and internal activity, one may wonder why cognition at the level of soul does not qualify as apprehension of the things themselves. It was asserted that if a cognitive power does not possess the internal activity of its objects, it can at most apprehend images of these objects expressed through their external act (see p. 137 above). Soul has an internal act of its own, an act which comes about when it turns towards intellect. The objects of its cognition in this internal act are somehow what constitutes Soul. Does Soul know these objects themselves or mere images of them? Surely the constitution of Soul is described in cognitive terms very much like the generation of Intellect from the One: an external act of intellect seeks to grasp its source, intellect itself, and fails to do so (V.1.4–5).[9] Or rather, it fails to apprehend

---

[9] See V.1.4–5. The relationship between Soul and Intellect may be more complex (or less consistent) than the account given here suggests. This account, however, has solid textual support. But

Intellect as the latter is in itself while succeeding in grasping an image of it, its external manifestation. So far, so good: this is just a repetition of the account of the relation between Intellect and the One, and we readily see that Soul will have to settle for a cognition of a mere image of Intellect, as Plotinus indeed maintains (cf. V.3.3–4). Yet the question remains, given my account here above, whether the soul's cognition of an image of intellect doesn't constitute the soul's self-knowledge and knowledge of objects pertaining to the psychic realm *themselves* (as opposed to of images of these psychic objects). This must surely be the soul's internal act and one might for that reason expect identity of subject and object. So why doesn't Soul grasp *psychic* objects themselves?

Let the following admittedly simplified answer to this question suffice at this stage. It is a given of Plotinus' ontology that the truly real objects are the intelligible objects at the level of Intellect. The soul does not grasp *these* objects themselves, but only images of them. Hence, the soul does not grasp the real objects themselves. Furthermore, there is not full identity of subject and object when the soul apprehends what it gets from intellect, because the agent on the object side is intellect, and this agent, abiding in its own internal act, is beyond the soul's reach. One might say, similarly, that that there is not full identity between subject and object in the relation between the One and Intellect, because Intellect fails to grasp the One as it is in itself. Yet, in this case, Intellect cannot be blamed for not grasping the things themselves or what is most real, because in the case of the One as it is in itself there are no beings to grasp: the One is according to Plotinus beyond being. So the relations between the One and Intellect and between Intellect and Soul are not analogous on all scores. Plotinus however nowhere denies that what the soul grasps in its internal act are the images it gets of Intellect themselves (as opposed to images of these images). Actually, according to the logic of V.3.5 that I shall turn to more closely shortly, if he were to deny this, it looks as if he would be involved in a vicious regress: in order to apprehend anything the soul would have to apprehend an image of an image of an image *ad infinitum*.

So according to Plotinus there exists a type of cognition that is identical with its object or, in other words, cognition in which the activity constituting

---

as Blumenthal (1974) has shown, the difference between the unembodied hypostasis Soul and Intellect is by no means clear.

the object of cognition and the one constituting the subject are one and the same. Moreover, the objects known in this cognition are what Plotinus considers the real beings. Thus, in this doctrine of Plotinian metaphysics, psychology and epistemology come together, actually merge. I shall now address this fusion. One may approach this subject via several routes. I shall proceed by first considering some central passages from V.3 and V.5 where the fusion appears. Then I shall address the issue more generally, considering among other things certain problems that seem to emerge for Plotinus.

5. The Puzzles of *Ennead* V.3.5: Self-Thinking Revisited

In chapter 5 of V.3 Plotinus seeks to combine three central ideas in his account of Intellect: that of Intellect's self-knowledge; the notion of the intelligibles as the ontologically primary beings as opposed to mere images or representations; and the unity of subject and object in intellection. We shall have V.3.5 as a central Plotinian source for most of what remains of this chapter. I shall start with presenting and expounding the bulk of it. In the subsequent sections we shall try to see how he seeks to accomplish the amalgamation of these key notions.

In V.3.5 Plotinus begins by addressing questions relating to self-knowledge. If Intellect is to have genuine self-knowledge, it cannot be the case that it knows itself in the sense that one part, the subject side, just knows the other, the object side of thought. In that case Intellect as a whole would not know itself completely, for the subject-side would not know itself at all (1–16). This observation, which seems to show awareness of a sceptical argument preserved in Sextus Empiricus (see p. 170 below), combines nicely with the account of self-knowledge given in the previous chapter: according to the latter account, self-knowledge is a subject's knowledge of what itself is, expressed by statements of the form 'I am F'. That the subject itself is included in the object of the thought is quite crucial on this account. We see Plotinus insisting on this very point here. In the subsequent lines (16–22), which are the most obscure part of the text, Plotinus considers the hypothesis that Intellect, being divided into a subject- and an object-side, is able to include the subject side of itself by an addition from itself. Presumably, he has in mind something like the following: suppose Intellect were divided into a subject-side which knows the intelligibles and an object-side which constitutes what is known; suppose also that in addition to this knowing, the intellect, 'by some sort of addition from itself' (*prosthêsei par' hautou*), apprehends itself as a thinking subject. If so, Plotinus continues,

it at the same time adds what it sees. If then the things contemplated are in the contemplation, if what are in it are impressions of them, then it does not have them themselves; but if it has them themselves, it does not see them as a result of dividing itself, but it was contemplator and possessor before it divided itself.[10] (V.3.5, 17–21)

This is of course fairly obscure, so that any interpretation is likely to be less than certain. What is clear, though, is that Plotinus is attempting a *reductio* of the idea that Intellect is divided into a subject-side and an object-side such that the subject as such is not included in the object of the thought but only known by some kind of 'addition' directed at itself. He wishes to reject the hypothesis he has stated, that the intellect originally comes divided into a subject void of objects and objects void of thought, even if Intellect's apprehension of itself as a thinker is provided for by the assumption of an addition from the thinker whereby it apprehends itself.

I take it that Plotinus' conception of the division between the subject and object on the hypothesis he is arguing against is such that the subject and the object are quite apart, the subject not containing the object at all and the object as such void of thought. It would be quite unexpected and contrary to his usual practice if he meant to reject any distinction between subject and object.[11] We shall later in this chapter consider how subject and object, albeit distinct, nevertheless are always entwined.

---

[10] V.3.5, 17–21: 'Αλλ' εἰ καὶ τὸν τεθεωρηκότα, ὁμοῦ καὶ τὰ ἑωραμένα. Εἰ οὖν ἐν τῇ θεωρίᾳ ὑπάρχει τὰ τεθεωρημένα, εἰ μὲν τύποι αὐτῶν, οὐκ αὐτὰ ἔχει· εἰ δ' αὐτὰ ἔχει, οὐκ ἰδὼν αὐτὰ ἐκ τοῦ μερίσαι αὐτὸν ἔχει, ἀλλ' ἦν πρὶν μερίσαι ἑαυτὸν καὶ θεωρῶν καὶ ἔχων.

[11] Crystal (2002) devotes the last chapter of his book to refuting my alleged view that self-thinking in Plotinus is incompatible with a distinction between subject and object (see also Crystal (1998)). He (2002: 180) quotes a sentence from Emilsson (1995: 32) saying with respect to the present passage (V.3.5): 'Thus we have a claim to the effect that a subject object distinction in the intellect is incompatible with its self-knowledge.' I admit that I expressed myself somewhat carelessly here. Such a sentence is indeed no longer in Emilsson (1996), which also presents my views on the same topic. However, as indeed should be clear from e.g. another passage from Emilsson (1995) also quoted by Crystal, this time approvingly (p. 191 n. 53), it was never my intention to suggest that Plotinus ever supposed that there is absolutely no distinction to be made between thinker and object of thought. Rather, my position was, and is, that the subject and object are not to be conceived of as independently existing parts of Intellect.

What is the point of the first hypothetical sentence 'If then the things contemplated are in the contemplation'? It is, I presume, that if the addition to the subject that is to apprehend the subject itself does not include the original object but a mere 'impression' of it, the subject's supposed original apprehension of its object too would have been of a mere impression. This is so because the addition's apprehension of the subject is of the subject along with everything that pertains to it, including its object; this apprehension, being an internal apprehension of a subject of itself, must be non-representational and truthful. Hence, what is thus apprehended in it must be equally real or 'ontologically primary' as what the subject grasped in its original grasp of its object. On the other hand, if the supposed addition, in apprehending the subject, apprehends the object itself as opposed to an impression of it, then the original apprehension the subject had of its object was of the object itself, the ontologically original item. So if the addition apprehends mere images, Intellect's apprehension of its objects was not knowledge of primary beings in the first place. But Intellect, it is assumed, does have knowledge of the intelligibles and the intelligibles are the primary beings.

The mode of thought of this passage seems to square nicely with our first-person account of self-thinking in the previous chapter. For if the thought in question is something like 'I am being', we can readily see how this kind of thought would escape the problems involved in the hypothesis Plotinus rejects: there would not be any need for an addition to the subject in charge of apprehending the thinker, because an apprehension of the thinker would already be included in the original apprehension of the object, which is me being being. I am not adducing this difficult passage as evidence for the first-person interpretation of self-thought, but on the best interpretation

In the previous works I was not concerned with the question what the difference between subject and object might be; the focus was on their unity. I always assumed, however, that some distinction is to be made. In the present work, however, I do address this question and I am now willing to speak of them as 'aspects' or 'parts mutually presupposing each other' of Intellect (see pp. 159 below). Crystal (2002: 189–92) seems indeed to agree. So I don't think Crystal and I have a real quarrel, at least not on this score. I am very much in agreement with what he says about the role of the *megista genē* (2002: 194–6) in differentiating Intellect (cf. p. 106 above). I also think he rejects Gerson's view on self-thinking for the right reasons. As to Crystal's own solution of the dilemma about self-thinking in V.3.5 ('Sextus's dilemma' as he calls it), however, I am somewhat at a loss to understand what he means, in particular how subject, object, and activity of thought are supposed to be wholes that do not differ 'at the level of substance' but are nevertheless different 'active states or dispositions (*energeiai*)'. See Crystal (2002: 198–9), cf. Crystal (1998: 279–283).

of the passage I can come up with it seems to fit fairly well. Moreover, Plotinus' initial concern here in V.3.5, how to include the thinking subject in Intellect's thought, surely speaks in favour of an interpretation of self-thought according to which the thinking subject indeed is included.

However, in the remainder of chapter 5 of V.3 Plotinus gives an account of self-thinking which does not ostensibly depend on self-thinking being a first-person self-identification. Let us see the rest of chapter in full (with the exception of lines 21–8 which we shall deal with in Section 9 below):

But if the act of thought and the intelligible are one, how because of this will that which thinks think itself? For the act of thought will in a way encompass the intelligible, or be the intelligible, and Intellect will not yet be clearly thinking itself. But if Intellect [in the sense of act of thought] and the intelligible are the same—for the intelligible is some kind of activity: for it [the intelligible, the object] is certainly not a potentiality and not unintellectual either,[12] nor is it without life, nor again are life and thought brought in from outside to something else, as if to a stone or something lifeless—then the intelligible is the primary Being. If then it is activity, and the first activity and the fairest, it is the first act of thought and substantial act of thought: for it is the truest; but an act of thought of this kind which is primary and primarily intellective will be the first intellect; for this intellect [subject][13] is not potential, nor is it one thing and its act of thought another: in this way again its substantiality would be potential. If then it is activity and its Being is activity, it is one and the same with its activity; but being and the intelligible are also one with the activity. All together are one, Intellect, act of thought, the intelligible. If therefore its [Intellect's] thought is the intelligible object, and the intelligible object is itself [i.e. Intellect, subject], it will itself think itself. For it will think with the thought which it is itself and it will think the intelligible object, which is itself. In both ways, then, will it think itself, in that the thought is itself and in that the intelligible object, which it thinks in the thought which is itself, is itself.[14] (V.3.5, 28–48)

[12] There is a textual problem here. I accept an emendation, suggested by Theiler and followed by H-S², of γε νοητόν to γ' ἀνόητον.

[13] The word 'Intellect' (nous) is at least doubly ambiguous in Plotinus. The official doctrine is that nous embraces that which thinks (to nooun), the act of thought (hê noêsis), and the object of thought (to noêton). Intellect is the totality of these. He, however, often contrasts 'Intellect' with the object of thought. This admittedly often occurs in contexts where he is arguing that they are in fact identical; nevertheless, the fact that this needs to be argued for shows that he is presuming at least a notional difference. When there is such contrast, 'Intellect' may refer to the act of thought or it may be the subject of the thought, as for instance it clearly is in line 43 of V.3.5, where nous, noêsis, to noêton are all said to be one. Here nous clearly picks up to nooun of line 29, 'that which thinks'.

[14] V.3.5, 28–48: Ἀλλ' εἰ ἡ νόησις καὶ τὸ νοητὸν ἕν, πῶς διὰ τοῦτο τὸ νοοῦν νοήσει ἑαυτό; Ἡ μὲν γὰρ νόησις οἷον περιέξει τὸ νοητόν, ἢ ταὐτὸν τῷ νοητῷ ἔσται, οὔπω δὲ

The crucial aspect of this account is the abolition of the notions of mind and objects of thought as something existing prior to and independently of thought, in favour of an account that takes thinking activity as the basic notion: intellect is the activity of thought, and the intelligibles, as well as the thinker, exist as aspects of this thinking activity. Plotinus first argues for the identity of the activity of thinking with the object of thought and then for the identity of the activity and the thinker; the identity of the thinker and the object follows from this, as is explicitly stated in the last part of the quotation. That the object of thought is identical with the activity of thinking has already been established in the previous lines of V.3.5. The point is, however, repeated: because the object of thought is not potential, and life and thought are integral to it, it is the same as the act of thought (33–4). This object, being the same as the act of thought, is a substantial act, i.e. the act constitutes a self-contained primary being. The Intellect as thinker too is identical with this activity of thinking because this intellect is in no way potential, i.e. the thinker is what it is merely through its activity of thought (39–41). There is no remainder to the thinker that is not actual in the thought.

The account of self-thinking given here may seem to be essentially Aristotelian: as Szlezák (1979: 126–35) has carefully demonstrated, there are several resonances to *Metaphysics* XII, 7 and 9, the main passages on divine thinking.[15] In the Aristotelian version of the argument the conclusion

ὁ νοῦς δῆλος ἑαυτὸν νοῶν. Ἀλλ' εἰ ἡ νόησις καὶ τὸ νοητὸν ταὐτόν—ἐνέργεια γάρ τις τὸ νοητόν· οὐ γὰρ δὴ δύναμις οὐδέ γ' ἀνόητον οὐδὲ ζωῆς χωρὶς οὐδ' αὖ ἐπακτὸν τὸ ζῆν οὐδὲ τὸ νοεῖν ἄλλῳ ὄντι, οἷον λίθῳ ἢ ἀψύχῳ τινί—καὶ οὐσία ἡ πρώτη τὸ νοητόν· εἰ οὖν ἐνέργεια καὶ ἡ πρώτη ἐνέργεια καὶ καλλίστη δή, νόησις ἂν εἴη καὶ οὐσιώδης νόησις· καὶ γὰρ ἀληθεστάτη· νόησις δὴ τοιαύτη καὶ πρώτη οὖσα καὶ πρώτως νοῦς ἂν εἴη ὁ πρῶτος· οὐδὲ γὰρ ὁ νοῦς οὗτος δυνάμει οὐδ' ἕτερος μὲν αὐτός, ἡ δὲ νόησις ἄλλο· οὕτω γὰρ ἂν πάλιν τὸ οὐσιῶδες αὐτοῦ δυνάμει. Εἰ οὖν ἐνέργεια καὶ ἡ οὐσία αὐτοῦ ἐνέργεια, ἓν καὶ ταὐτὸν τῇ ἐνεργείᾳ ἂν εἴη· ἓν δὲ τῇ ἐνεργείᾳ τὸ ὂν καὶ τὸ νοητόν· ἓν ἅμα πάντα ἔσται, νοῦς, νόησις, τὸ νοητόν. Εἰ οὖν ἡ νόησις αὐτοῦ τὸ νοητόν, τὸ δὲ νοητὸν αὐτός, αὐτὸς ἄρα ἑαυτὸν νοήσει· νοήσει γὰρ τῇ νοήσει, ὅπερ ἦν αὐτός, καὶ νοήσει τὸ νοητόν, ὅπερ ἦν αὐτός. Καθ' ἑκάτερον ἄρα ἑαυτὸν νοήσει, καθότι καὶ ἡ νόησις αὐτὸς ἦν, καὶ καθότι τὸ νοητὸν αὐτός, ὅπερ ἐνόει τῇ νοήσει, ὃ ἦν αὐτός.

[15] Szlezák (1979: 128–9) also notes that Plotinus does not slavishly follow Aristotle in V.3.5. He detects a 'tiefgreifende Kritik an der in dem zitierten Satz des Aristoteles durchscheinenden Priorität des Objekts vor dem Subjekt. ... Ein wirkliches Sich-selbst Denken ist nur möglich, wenn der Nus nicht nur durch Hinwendung zum Denkobjekt selbst νοτός wird ... sondern wenn zudem das Denkobjekt seinerseits geisthaft und energetisch ist.' I agree with this assessment. I, however, have some doubt that Plotinus' insistence on the spiritual and energetic nature of the object of thought will sufficiently counterbalance the feeling that the object holds priority of place—unless we understand this spiritual and energetic nature of the object along the lines of the 'first-person interpretation' of Chapter 2.

is presented in such a way that the identity of thinker and object comes as a conclusion of theoretical considerations. Aristotle says that 'it must be of itself that divine thinking thinks' (*Meta.* XII, 9, 1074b 33). The way he phrases this, as well as the foregoing argumentation, suggests that Aristotle does not conceive of the identity of the divine intellect and the object of its thought as an identity expressed by a first self-reflexive thought: as we noted in the previous chapter, there is nothing in Aristotle's considerations that suggests that the divine mind must think that it as the subject of the thought is identical with its object. For all Aristotle says or suggests, the divine mind is indeed identical with its objects of thought but it may know nothing about this identity. This is not to say, of course, that the Aristotelian divine mind doesn't know what it is thinking or that it is thinking. There is nothing against presuming that it knows that and what it thinks, whatever that may be. But there is a crucial step from this to the claim that it knows that it is thinking *of* itself in the sense characteristic of self-thoughts in the first person.

The only aspect of the passage just quoted that might point to the first-person account in the previous chapter is the claim that life and thought are integral to the *object* of thought. It is not altogether easy to see how this claim can be made plausible on the Aristotelian account.[16] If it were to be made plausible, this would have to be along the following lines: since that which thinks obviously is alive and thinking, and since that which it thinks is internal to the thought, that which it thinks, the object, shares in the thinker's life. This is not totally implausible but nevertheless a questionable argument. The reason is that the object and the subject are still different aspects of Intellect; life pertains to the subject as such; it seems to pertain to the object only parasitically. I shall, however, not pursue this further.

If, on the other hand, we presuppose the kind of account of self-thinking given in the previous chapter, the intelligent nature of the object is obvious

[16] Plotinus' view that Intellect's object of thought is alive is undoubtedly rooted in Plato's *Sophist* 248e–249a, where it is claimed that being must have life and intelligence. The relevance of the *Sophist* to Plotinus here is emphasized and elaborated by Hadot (1999) and Szlezák (1979: *passim* but especially 122–5), though their interpretations differ in some ways, see Szlezák (1979: 129, n. 405). In *Metaphysics* XII, 7, 1072b 26–7 Aristotle also asserts that 'life also belongs to God; for the actuality/activity (*energeia*) of thought is life, and God is that actuality/activity'. Aristotle, however, doesn't say specifically that the *object* of thought is alive (though this seems to follow, if the activity is identical with the object and the activity is a kind of life). On Plotinus' interpretation of this passage of the *Sophist*, on the other hand, being is the object of thought, and being is in the *Sophist* 249a said to have life.

and unproblematic: on that account, the subject itself is an aspect of the object of thought: it is the 'I' in 'I being'. Since this aspect of the object is straightforwardly the same as the subject, it is something not without life and thought (cf. V.3.13, 23–36). It is possible, although I shall not insist on the point, that this indicates that Plotinus has his first-person account in mind throughout this passage without making this explicit.

Are we faced with two accounts of self-thinking in Plotinus? According to the one, self-thinking would essentially be thinking in the first person saying what the subject thinks itself to be. According to the other, the self-thinking of Intellect follows from the identity of thinker and object (where the object need not specifically contain the subject), each of which turns out to be an aspect of the same activity of thought. This latter account does not in itself presuppose that Intellect thinks in the first person. The identity of thinker and object seems to be guaranteed for any thoughts Intellect may have, not just its thoughts specifically about itself from a first-person view. This account does not even presuppose that Intellect (as subject) is aware of the fact that it itself is identical with its object.

Can Plotinus have it both ways? Yes, he can. He could certainly believe in the Aristotelian considerations that establish the identity of the thought and the object of thought on independent grounds and superimpose that doctrine with what I have labelled the 'first-person account'. There is no incompatibility in the two accounts, except in so far as they differ in their understanding of what self-thinking amounts to. The superimposed account entails that Intellect's thoughts are self-thoughts in a stronger sense than the other account requires: the subject cannot fail to know that it is thinking of itself.

Plotinus may also have thought that what we have labelled the 'Aristotelian' account follows from the 'first-person account' or he may have seen the 'Aristotelian' account in light of his own first-person account. In particular, he may have thought that the identity of activity in subject and object, which is the crucial aspect of the 'Aristotelian' account, is an integral part of the 'first-person account'. He may or may not be presuming this in the passage above. Even if there is little that positively points to the latter account in this passage, there isn't anything that counts directly against it either. And surely the whole passage can be read from the point of view of the 'first-person' account. This holds in particular for the crucial lines of the passage that argue for the identity of the thinker with the act of thought in terms of the actual as opposed to the potential nature of the thinker. We shall see here below how this may be so.

In order to see this, let us recall an important point from the previous chapter: the two kinds of otherness coincided because the thinker had as its object itself thinking what it is: in thinking itself it saw itself as that which it thought itself to be, i.e. being. Let us recall also the warnings in the previous chapter that even if Intellect's thought may be rendered as being paradigmatically of the form 'I am being', the 'I' and the 'being' always come as a pair: there is no such thing as the subject or the object of thought in isolation. So the thinker thinks 'I am being', capturing in this thought itself being being, thus capturing itself in this thought. This is the primary activity of thinking. Each side, the thinker and what the subject thinks itself to be, is a necessary part of this activity. At the same time, each of them may be said to be established in the activity: the thinker, because in its activity of thinking it becomes a determinate being, gets an identity; the object because it is constituted and subsists in the activity. The last part of this claim will be further supported and elaborated below in Section 6.

It pertains to the 'Aristotelian' account that the identity of subject and object holds because of the identity of activities constituting the subject and the object, respectively. As to the identity of the act of thought with the object, there is no discrepancy between the two accounts. The object subsists in the act on both accounts and for the same reasons: there is no external object (except for the One which is not an 'object'); hence the object must be native to the thought. The identity of the thinker with the thought, on the other hand, makes even better sense on the 'first-person' account of the previous chapter than on the 'purely Aristotelian account': 'I am being' holds because of the identity of the activity of thinking which constitutes the 'I' and the one constituting 'being'. This is what really makes the thinker *be* being.

This calls for some elaboration. What could it mean to say that the activity of thinking constituting the 'I' is identical with the activity constituting being? In the first place, what is the activity of thinking constituting the 'I'? Well, the thinker, the 'I', is something only when and in so far as it thinks what it is. So it is constituted as a determinate being in the act of thought that says what it is, that it is being, for example. This is a restatement of what was asserted in the previous chapter that there is no such being as a pure subject (see p. 109). I am in other words interpreting the ground given for the identity of thinker and object in V.3, 'for this intellect [subject] is not potential, nor is it one thing and its act of thought another' (V.3.5, 39–40) as an expression of the view that the subject is actualized in its self-identifying thought. So there is a thinking activity in which the subject is actualized. (The same, as already noted, holds for the object: it too is actualized in a thinking activity, i.e. the thought that thinks what the subject *is*.) The act of thinking 'I am being' thus at once establishes the subject and the object, which is 'me being', and it is the same activity in both instances.

6. Being and Thought

In the previous chapter as well as in this one, I have insisted that for Plotinus subject and object, thinking and being, are really equals. That is to say, neither thinking nor being 'comes first' logically or temporally, they enter the scene 'at the same time'. Since this view is not universally shared and has been challenged in the scholarly literature, let us consider, and hopefully bury, the view that being is prior to thought.

Plotinus often states in clear terms that thinking and being are coextensive. In V.1.4, for instance, he writes:

For [Intellect and being] are simultaneous and exist together and the one does not abandon the other, but this one is two things, Intellect and being together, the thinker and what is thought, intellect as thinking, being as that which is thought. For there could not be thinking without otherness, and also sameness.[17] (V.1.4, 30–5)

He, however, is also liable to assert that thought establishes being.[18] He even does so in the very same context as he asserts their equality, e.g. just three lines above the passage just cited. In the same context it is made clear that the thinking and the being have the same cause, i.e. the One. So whatever he precisely means by saying that the intellect in its thought

---

[17] V.1.4, 30–5: "Ἅμα μὲν γὰρ ἐκεῖνα καὶ συνυπάρχει καὶ οὐκ ἀπολείπει ἄλληλα, ἀλλὰ δύο ὄντα τοῦτο τὸ ἓν ὁμοῦ νοῦς καὶ ὂν καὶ νοοῦν καὶ νοούμενον, ὁ μὲν νοῦς κατὰ τὸ νοεῖν, τὸ δὲ ὂν κατὰ τὸ νοούμενον. Οὐ γὰρ ἂν γένοιτο τὸ νοεῖν ἑτερότητος μὴ οὔσης καὶ ταὐτότητος δέ.

[18] Cf. V.1.4, 28: ὁ μὲν νοῦς κατὰ τὸ νοεῖν ὑφιστὰς τὸ ὄν ('Intellect establishing being in thinking it'). See also VI.7.40, 10–12; VI.7.41, 18–19; V.9.5, 13.

'establishes being', he cannot mean to suggest that the intellect is first established and in turn causes being: what is responsible for both at once is the One (cf. V.1.4, 28). Presumably, the point of saying that the Intellect establishes being is just the already familiar one that being and beings come about in the act of thought. This, however, does not make the thinker prior, because there is no intellect prior to the act of thought either: the intellect is in its very nature an active, thinking intellect and this already presupposes being as that which it thinks.

It might be retorted concerning this last point that though the inchoate intellect does not actually think, it nevertheless is an intellect; since being comes to be when the inchoate intellect turns into an actually thinking intellect, i.e. Intellect, the inchoate intellect may be said to be prior to being.

Several remarks in response to this are in order. First, let us note with Lloyd (1987: 182) that the inchoate intellect is no more a potential thinker than it is a potential being. As noted earlier (Chapter 2: pp. 73–4), the inchoate intellect does not involve a full-blown subject/object distinction. Hence, thinking and being do not arise from an empty thinker that has to be acted on by something external in order to be actualized. They arise together with the subject/object split (cf. p. 108 above). The present objection assumes that being in Intellect is a descendant of the inchoate intellect and tries to thereby make being look posterior to something mental or intellectual. But, as we noted, the inchoate intellect isn't really any more a potential intellect than it is a potential being. Hence, it might with equal plausibility be said that potential being turns into an actual being when the inchoate intellect becomes actual. In short, the objection fails to show that something specifically of the nature of a mind or intellect (as opposed to being) is prior to being.

This, I think, takes care of the present objection about the priority of the inchoate intellect to being. There is, however, another objection lurking in the background here. We noted above (p. 148) in connection with V.3.5 that Plotinus insists on the actuality of Intellect. It supposedly involves no potentiality. This is tantamount to saying, on the one hand, that Intellect is not acted on by its object as if from the outside, on the other that as subject Intellect always thinks, that there is no move from potentiality to actuality. But how are we to square this with the notion of the inchoate intellect? For what else is the inchoate intellect, it might be asked, than a potential thinker and potential being? And if it is, Intellect indeed seems to arise from a potential intellect. Contrary to what the passages stressing the actuality and self-sufficiency of Intellect may make one believe, Intellect has humble origins in something that is indeed incomplete and needy. So our question becomes: how can Plotinus claim both that Intellect involves no potentiality and is sufficient to itself and at the same time maintain that it originates in the inchoate intellect which is anything but actual and self-sufficient?

Let us consider self-sufficiency and actuality separately. As we saw in Chapter 2, Section 3, Intellect is self-sufficient only in a relative way: it needs the One, and its so-called self-sufficiency amounts to the fact that the intelligible beings do not depend on any prior beings. That is to say, the intelligible Horse, say, is self-sufficient as a horse in the sense that there is no horse prior to it. It does not take another horse as its model. To put it generally, there are no beings prior to the beings in Intellect; so far as being is concerned Intellect is self-sufficient. This is not to say that it is absolutely self-sufficient, that it depends on nothing.

Let us then turn to actuality. The native actuality of Intellect may seem to be threatened by the inchoate intellect's state of potentiality; Plotinus cannot both hold, it might be said, that Intellect is essentially active and actual and also originally potential and in need of the One. The answer to this is basically the same as the answer to the concerns about self-sufficiency: when he insists that Intellect is essentially actual, involving no potentiality, he means that all the intelligibles are fully whatever they are; so far as their character is concerned there is nothing prior to them which gives them the form which they are. So the intelligible Horse is not at some stage only potentially a horse and then made into an actual one by some prior horse. The Aristotelian Principle of Prior Actuality does not apply. But again, none of this is to deny that Intellect is actualized by the One. That is, however, not an actualization by means of a prior actuality. The same point is convincingly argued, though in somewhat different terms, by D'Ancona Costa (1996).

Let us now turn to some passages where Plotinus may seem to assert, and indeed has been taken to assert, that being is prior to thought.[19] In V.9.8, for instance, there is an interesting passage that superficially read may

---

[19] Cf. Oosthout (1991: 63–5). Atkinson (1983: 93–4) thinks Plotinus is inconsistent about the priority relations in thinking and being. He seems to mean that while passages speaking of intellect establishing being assert the priority of thought, other passages, e.g. V.9.8, 8–11 and VI.6.8, 17 ff. assert the opposite. What Plotinus ought to say, according to Atkinson, is what he also often says, namely

suggest that being is prior to thought. Plotinus is discussing the question whether Intellect is prior to being or vice versa. He writes:

If then Intellect was thought of as preceding being, we should have to say that Intellect by becoming actual and by thinking perfected and produced the beings; but since it is necessary to think of being as before Intellect, we must assume that the beings have their place in the thinking subject, but that the activity of thinking is in the beings, as the activity of fire is in fire already existing, so that they may have Intellect in a unity in themselves as their activity.[20] (V.9.8, 8–15)

He seems here to affirm that being must be conceived of as preceding Intellect. That this primacy of being should lead to the conclusion that 'beings must have their place in the thinking subject', however, is baffling: why should the placement of beings in the thinking subject follow from the primacy of being over Intellect? Such an arrangement would rather suggest the dependence of being on Intellect than the converse. However this is to be resolved, what Plotinus continues to argue here is his normal doctrine about the equality of thought and being. In the end, he puts the blame for making either Intellect or being primary at the cost of the other on us, on our dividing thought:

And being is activity: so both [being and Intellect] have one activity, or rather both are one thing. Being and Intellect are therefore one nature; so therefore the beings and the activity of being and Intellect are of this kind; and the thoughts of this kind are the form and shape of being and its active actuality. But they are thought of by us as one before the other because they are divided by our thinking. For the dividing intellect[21] is a different one, the undivided and non-dividing Intellect is being and all things.[22] (V.9.8, 15–22)

that there are 'no distinctions at all between Intellect and Being'. There is a fine discussion of the issue in Lloyd (1986: 180 ff.).

[20] V.9.8, 8–15: Εἰ μὲν οὖν προεπενοεῖτο ὁ νοῦς πρότερος τοῦ ὄντος, ἔδει τὸν νοῦν λέγειν ἐνεργήσαντα καὶ νοήσαντα ἀποτελέσαι καὶ γεννῆσαι τὰ ὄντα· ἐπεὶ δὲ τὸ ὂν τοῦ νοῦ προεπινοεῖν ἀνάγκη, ἐγκεῖσθαι δεῖ τίθεσθαι ἐν τῷ νοοῦντι τὰ ὄντα, τὴν δὲ ἐνέργειαν καὶ τὴν νόησιν ἐπὶ τοῖς οὖσιν, οἷον ἐπὶ πῦρ ἤδη τὴν τοῦ πυρὸς ἐνέργειαν, ἵν' ἐν ὄντα τὸν νοῦν ἐφ' ἑαυτοῖς ἔχῃ ἐνέργειαν αὐτῶν.

[21] 'The dividing intellect' must be discursive reason, what is referred to in the previous line as 'our thinking'.

[22] V.9.8, 15–22: Ἔστι δὲ καὶ τὸ ὂν ἐνέργεια· μία οὖν ἀμφοῖν ἐνέργεια, μᾶλλον δὲ τὰ ἄμφω ἕν. Μία μὲν οὖν φύσις τό τε ὂν ὅ τε νοῦς· διὸ καὶ τὰ ὄντα καὶ ἡ τοῦ ὄντος ἐνέργεια καὶ ὁ νοῦς ὁ τοιοῦτος· καὶ αἱ οὕτω νοήσεις τὸ εἶδος καὶ ἡ μορφὴ τοῦ ὄντος καὶ ἡ ἐνέργεια. Ἐπινοεῖταί γε μὴν μεριζομένων ὑφ' ἡμῶν θάτερα πρὸ τῶν ἑτέρων. Ἕτερος γὰρ ὁ μερίζων νοῦς, ὁ δὲ ἀμέριστος καὶ μὴ μερίζων τὸ ὂν καὶ τὰ πάντα.

The point here is that we, presumably by virtue of the limitations of our lower intellect, i.e. our discursive reason, have a difficulty with thinking of Intellect and being as a union of equals and tend to take either one, or actually rather to take being, as the primary concept.[23]

Another passage that seems to affirm the primacy of being in relation to Intellect is VI.6.8, 17–20. Here Plotinus says:

If then one should take being first, since it is first, then intellect, then the living being—for this seems already to encompass all things—but intellect comes second, for it is the activity of Being (*ousia*).[24]

This passage seems to assert, even if only in an innocent looking, brief insertion, 'since it is first', that isn't elaborated, that being comes before Intellect. Here there is nothing in the context as there was in the previous such passage we considered that warrants us to explain the remark away, incidental as it may seem to be. What occurs to me is that this is a case of non-standard terminology by which Plotinus uses the terms being (*on*) and Being (*ousia*) to refer to the undifferentiated content of the inchoate intellect rather than to the totality of Intellect's content. Other possible instances of such a use are to be found in V.2.1, 11[25] and VI.2.8, 14. In the latter passage Plotinus speaks of being as 'that towards which and that from which' there is an intellectual gaze (*blepsis*). In so far as being is that *from which* (*aph'hou*) the gaze takes place, it may seem that 'being' here is the

---

[23] In the chapter before this one, V.9.7, Plotinus says: 'It is, then, incorrect to say that the Ideas are thoughts, if what is meant by this is that when Intellect thought, this particular Idea came into being or is this particular Idea; for what is thought (*to nooumenon*) must be prior to this particular thought [of this particular Idea]. Otherwise, how would it come to thinking it? Certainly not by chance nor did it happen on it casually' (V.9.7, 14–18). This passage too might be taken to indicate the priority of being to thinking or at least that the Ideas are not thoughts. Plotinus' point here, however, is not to deny that Ideas are thoughts *simpliciter* (such a view in fact is implicit in the context (cf. lines 8–11)) but to deny a particular version of such a view. Precisely what that version amounts to is unfortunately somewhat unclear. It seems to me that the following is presumably what he has in mind: it is not the case that we have Intellect in place and it, as it were subsequently, comes to think of the particular Ideas which first then and thereby come into existence. The Ideas are internal to it, as it were from the very beginning. Seen in this way, Plotinus is here affirming the mutual dependence of thought and object on which we have insisted.

[24] VI.6.8, 17–20: Εἰ δὴ τὸ ὂν πρῶτον δεῖ λαβεῖν πρῶτον ὄν, εἶτα νοῦν, εἶτα τὸ ζῷον—τοῦτο γὰρ ἤδη πάντα δοκεῖ περιέχειν—ὁ δὲ νοῦς δεύτερον—ἐνέργεια γὰρ τῆς οὐσίας.

[25] This is the passage that was used as a launching point for the themes of this book. It is quoted at the beginning of Chapter 1. Plotinus says there with respect to the One's emanation that 'its halt and turning towards the One constitutes Being, its gaze upon the One, Intellect'. On the face of it, at least, Intellect and Being are here presented as distinct phases of the process from the One, cf. Atkinson (1983: 93).

first offspring of the One before any split into subject and object, before thinking in fact. If so, such a use is quite exceptional, for being in Plotinus is as a rule a manifold bound up with the activity of thought.

Despite this last passage we brought up, it seems to me that the texts overwhelmingly favour a view according to which being and thinking are coextensive and on an equal footing and that the reasons for maintaining this given by Plotinus are in general the same. So I do not agree with Bussanich's (1988: 231) verdict on this issue that Plotinus 'has not worked out crucially important issues in his theory of ontological derivation'. There may be unclear or unresolved aspects of the theory and an occasional anomaly but Plotinus is fairly consistent about the matter.

7. The Difference and Identity between Subject and Object

We may recall from Chapter 2 that Plotinus insists that the duality of Intellect in contradistinction to the absolute unity of the One consists precisely in the presence of a subject/object distinction in Intellect (see p. 84 above). How are we to reconcile this with the claim we have been considering in V.3.5, a claim which is to be found all over the *Enneads* where Intellect is at all discussed, that the thinker and the object of thought are really identical? So far we have been focusing on how they can be said to be the same; less has been said about how they differ, although some relevant remarks have been made both in this chapter and in the previous one. It is time to address this question directly. Let us start with disposing of one untenable view about the relationship.

One might think that the distinction between subject and object in Intellect is something that *we*, being confined to a lower, discursive mode of thinking, are bound to impose upon Intellect in our thought about it, even if there really is no such distinction in Intellect itself: the fact that we feel forced to employ it shows something about *our* discursive concepts but does not adequately reflect the state of affairs in Intellect itself.[26] We saw in the discussion of V.9.8 above about the respective primacy of being

---

[26] Atkinson (1983: 93) seems to understand Plotinus' remarks about our dividing way of thinking in V.9.8, 19–22 (quoted p. 155 above) in such a way that there is really no distinction at all between

and thinking that Plotinus himself suggests that it is due to our limitations that we feel forced to place the one or the other first. So he is liable to make moves of this sort. The point here about the limitations of human discursive thought, however, has to do with the need for giving priority to the one or the other rather than seeing thinking and being as a unified pair of equals. There is no implication that the distinction between subject and object is as such due to our discursive thinking. But might it be the case that the very distinction between subject and object is something that we, because of our shortcomings, must impose upon the matter in our attempts to come to some conception of it, whereas in the nature of things there isn't one?

I do not think so. Consider again a passage from V.1.4 cited on p. 152 above:

> but this one is two things, Intellect and being together, the thinker and what is thought, the one is intellect as thinking, the other being as thought. For there could not be thinking without otherness, and also sameness. (31−5)

Plotinus asserts here, as indeed is clear from numerous other passages (see e.g. V.3.10, 45−6, V.6.1, 4−13, VI.7.39, 4−5) that though one, thought and being are nevertheless two. In such passages about the genesis of Intellect, where it is asserted that there must be a thinker and also an object of thought, there is no hint that the distinction between the two is illusionary or somehow due to us or our discursive limitations. It lies in the nature of Intellect that without distinctions it would collapse into the One. So the distinction between subject and object in Intellect as such is not due to our discursive mode of thinking. It is a quite different matter whether discursive sentences such as 'I am being' adequately render the thoughts in Intellect. As we shall see in the next chapter, they presumably do not.

Nevertheless, even if what has just been said may be quite true, the distinction between subject and object may well be one that it is appropriate to call a notional or conceptual distinction as opposed to a real one. More must be said, however: merely to note that there is a conceptual but not real distinction is in itself not particularly helpful. There are indeed various ways in which there may be a conceptual but not a real distinction between

Intellect and being, subject and object, and that the apparent distinctions are due to our discursive mode of thought.

subject and object, only some of which would be of use to elucidate Plotinus' text.

As a first approach to this let us recall that Plotinus clearly believed in both of the two following claims: that thinker and thought are identical and that they differ. Taken at face value, this seems to be a contradictory claim. For nothing can differ from itself—or can it? Well, as anyone at all familiar with Frege's distinction between 'sense' and 'reference' knows, true identity statements may assert the identity of 'different' things, i.e. the identity of a reference conceived under two different senses. Is that how subject and object differ for Plotinus? Yes and no. It is true that he is naturally interpreted as meaning that the subject and the object have the same reference: the act of thought. And they clearly have a different sense, differ in *epinoia* (cf. Heiser 1991: 40–1). Yet, there is more to say about how they differ than just that.

As we have seen, Plotinus conceives of Intellect as a whole consisting in an activity in which subject and object are primary parts or aspects. My conjecture is that subject and object differ in being different aspects of this whole and that they are identical by making up this same whole. The relationship is, however, even closer than this indicates. For, as several times noted already, these parts mutually presuppose each other. Neither one can exist and be what it is separately. So, as Crystal (1998 and 2002: 190 ff.) also notes, even if subject and object are distinct moments of Intellect, they are complementary and do not make sense in isolation; together they make up a unity but each taken in itself is something incomplete, a non-entity, without the other.

Thus, the relation between subject and object in Intellect might be thought to be analogous to that between such pairs of notions as 'top and bottom', 'verbal phrase and nominal phrase' as interdependent components of a sentence, or, perhaps more fittingly, triples like 'a producer, an act of production, and a product': just as there is no product without a producer engaged in an act of producing and no producer engaged in the act of producing without something being produced, so there is no object of thought without a thinker engaged in the act of thinking and no act of thinking without there being an object thought of.

It might be objected that in general the existence of an object that can be thought does not depend on its being thought of, nor does the existence of a thinker depend on his actually being engaged in thinking. As we have already seen, however, Plotinus has reasonably clear and, given the set-up of Intellect, convincing answers to such objections. Against the former, he argues that antecedent being would render Intellect's thought a thought of images, an unacceptable conclusion for Intellect. Against the latter he would say, appealing to the Aristotelian principle that actuality is prior to potentiality, that the thinker must be understood in terms of its acts and moreover that the thinker in question here, the divine Intellect, is not an intermittent thinker, but one who is always engaged in thinking (cf. p. 154 above). If he pressed the first-person account on this point, he would say that the thinker first becomes an identifiable thinker through its thoughts of itself that define what it is. Thus, even if Plotinus might agree that in some cases thinker and object of thought may exist independently of each other, given the special constraints on the primary case of the thinker and thought at the level of Intellect, this is not so.

8. Subordinate Intelligibles and Subordinate Intellects

We noted above that Plotinus holds that the intelligible object is alive and intelligent (see p.147 ff. above). Sometimes, he even goes as far as saying that each intelligible, each Idea is an intellect: 'And Intellect as a whole is all the Ideas, and each individual Idea is an individual intellect'[27] (V.9.8, 3–4), and in VI.7.17 we find him saying:

What is this 'one defined'? Intellect. For defined life is Intellect. But what is this 'many'? Many intellects. For all [the many] are intellects, taken as a whole they are Intellect, taken individually they are intellects.[28] (VI.7.17, 25–7)

I take it that the claim that the intelligible object is alive and intelligent is intricately tied up with the doctrine of its being an intellect. Let us now directly face the question in what sense each of the intelligibles can be said to be an intellect. How is for instance the intelligible Horse an intellect? In connection with the claim that the intelligibles are alive and active we saw (p. 151 above) that this does not mean that an intelligible is to be conceived

---

[27] V.9.8, 3–4: Καὶ ὅλος μὲν ὁ νοῦς τὰ πάντα εἴδη, ἕκαστον δὲ εἶδος νοῦς ἕκαστος.

[28] VI.7.17, 25–7: Τί οὖν τὸ "ἓν ὡρίσθη"; Νοῦς· ὁρισθεῖσα γὰρ ζωὴ νοῦς. Τί δὲ τὸ "πολλά"; νόες πολλοί. Πάντα οὖν νόες, καὶ ὁ μὲν πᾶς νοῦς, οἱ δὲ ἕκαστοι νοῖ. For the idea that Intellect contains individual intellects, see also VI.2.22, 27; VI.4.4, 19; VI.6.15, 14.

of as an intellect in its own right independently of the subject that thinks it: it is not the case that we have an intelligible object, which is already an intellect in its own right, and in addition a subject of thought and an act of thought of which our intelligible object is an aspect. Such a view would indeed lead to an infinite regress: if the intelligible object is an intellect in its own right, independently of any subject that thinks it, by the force of Plotinus' own logic about thinking and objects of thought, the question arises with respect to that intelligible itself, whether it, being an intellect, would not consist of a subject and an object; the answer must be that it does; this object would in turn presumably also be an intellect, and so on *ad infinitum*.

So the claim that each intelligible is an intellect must be made sense of in some other way. Let us try to pursue this curious doctrine more fully. In order to do so, we should first provide a sketch of the basic structure of Intellect. Thereafter, we must address the question how a subordinate intelligible such as the intelligible Horse fits into this structure as an intellect in its own right.

On the top there are, as previously noted (see Chapter 2, Section 2), the highest kinds from Plato's *Sophist*: being, identity, difference, motion, and rest. These are intermingled, each presupposing all the others, yet each a distinct thing. This totality is further divided up into kinds of natural objects, such as the Heavens, the Earth, natural substances, plants, and animals. Beauty and, it seems, such Aristotelian kinds as Quality, Quantity, and Relation also have their place in the intelligible structure (cf. VI.2.18–19). Together the five highest genera and the subordinate species and aspects of them such as Beauty, Quality, and Quantity comprise the Intellect or the Living Being which is the totality of all there is and in fact, in Plotinus' view, the totality of all there must be and can be (VI.7.12–14; VI.2.19–22).

The details of the picture of exactly how the subordinate genera are derived from the first five are by no means perspicuous. Certain recurring points may, however, be granted. (1) The relationship between the five highest genera and subordinate ones is to be seen as analogous to the relationship between a science and particular theorems of the science, or particular sciences and universal science (VI.2.20, 16 ff.; cf. V.9.8, 5–8). Plotinus evidently believed that a theorem of a science somehow contains the science as a whole, i.e. that somebody who really understands a given theorem has potentially the whole science available to him—otherwise the case would be 'like a child talking' (cf. IV.9.5, 20–1). Conversely, the science as a whole contains the particular theorem. So in Intellect the subordinate part contains the whole and the whole contains the part. I shall return to this analogy in Chapter 4, Section 3. (2) The subordinate kinds are conceived of as differentiations within the overarching ones. Given that one starts with the five highest intermingled genera, and given that the division is primarily a division of kinds of being, and given in addition the Aristotelian principle that differences within a genus must come from outside the genus (cf. Aristotle, *Cat.* 5, 2b 20)—otherwise we would end up saying e.g. that a species of animal is differentiated from other animals by a feature which itself is a kind of animal—given all this, it follows that the differentiations of being for Plotinus ultimately come from the other highest genera (cf. VI.2.19, 4–5). In practice this must mean that they come from 'motion' and 'otherness', since these are the kinds that provide some contrast to being. (3) Sometimes this idea of differentiation is expressed by means of a metaphor of 'unfolding' or 'eliciting' (*exelittein*), suggesting the idea of something seemingly uniform which nevertheless implicitly contains internal differences that may be brought to light (III.8.8, 34–8; V.3.10, 52). This is also described in terms of an increasingly narrowing focus: the general is likened to the broad outlines, the more particular to the details that appear within when the focus is narrowed (VI.7.14). (4) Plotinus also uses the terms 'movement' (*kinēsis*), 'process' (*proodos*), or 'activity' (*energeia*) to describe the unfolding of the contents of Intellect (cf. VI.7.13). These appear to be near synonyms in such contexts. It is as if the overarching entity must act out all the powers it contains—in terms of (1), as if the science works out all its theorems. In any case, the overarching entities contain powers (*dynameis*) that are not actualized or unfolded (cf. (2)) at the higher level. The clearest statement of this is probably VI.2.20 (cf. VI.2.5, 12–14). (4) As we saw in (1), the more general (higher) is contained in the more particular but not absorbed by it or reduced to it. This is what in Chapter I (p.28 ff.) was described in terms of the 'remaining' of the internal act (cf. Lloyd 1990: 81–2). Thus, the overarching genus is not parcelled out in the subordinate one; it remains as something in itself. This is of course a version of the Platonic doctrine of the separation of the Ideas, which Plotinus also asserts as holding within the intelligible sphere.

(5) A subordinate kind, for example the Horse, is a mind that thinks the Horse, thinks itself.[29]

With this in place, let us now embark on a speculative excursion exploring what (1)–(5) may lead to with respect to the claim that each Idea is an intellect. Take any intelligible that comes into being, let us say the Horse. The Horse is a species of Animal or of the Living Being. For the Horse to come about, the Animal has to proceed (or something has to proceed from the Animal). Its proceeding involves first a movement constituting otherness between the Animal and a subject of thought, a thinker that distances itself from it—this is an application of what I take to be said in general terms in VI.7.13, especially lines 10–31. This otherness constitutes the Animal as an object of thought for this subject. By the conditions of intellectual vision stated in the previous chapter, that any object of thought must appear as varied, the Animal will appear as varied. So differences will be perceived within the Animal, constituting the kinds of Animal there are. This movement and alienation from the Animal together with the appearance of the species is what Plotinus calls activity (actualization) (cf. VI.7.13, 11–12), in this case, activity of the Animal. This is an example of working out all the powers (cf. (2) above).

Let us allow ourselves to be a bit speculative about what being the intelligible Horse consists in. Please imagine that you are the intelligible Horse; you are conscious of actually being the Horse; this consciousness is a matter of your having left a higher genus, that of Animal, and now being in a position of seeing the Animal, as among other things, the Horse. You expound just that alternative. Your being conscious of being the Horse will involve having the thought that constitutes the Animal with the specific difference of the Horse: 'I am the equine sort of animal,' you, being the sort of intellect you are, will say to yourself. My hunch is that in Plotinus' view, a subject's leaving the Animal and proceeding to the animal species of Horse is a matter of establishing the same sort of otherness as is involved in the differentiation of the Horse within the Animal genus: for the differentiation of a subject which thinks the equine sort of Animal is the very same thing as the equine sort of animal. Thus, I am suggesting

---

[29] Cf. VI.7.9, 22–5: 'In the intelligible world even what is called non-rational is rational, and the unthinking is intellect, since the thinker of horse is an intellect, and the thought of horse is an intellect.' Ἐκεῖ δὲ καὶ τὸ ἄλογον λεγόμενον λόγος ἦν, καὶ τὸ ἄνουν νοῦς ἦν, ἐπεὶ καὶ ὁ νοῶν ἵππον νοῦς ἐστι, καὶ ἡ νόησις ἵππου νοῦς ἦν.

that talk of leaving the Animal, or proceeding from it, already involves a determinate attitude towards it: acting out one specific possibility that the Animal contains. Thus, differentiation or movement of the genus Animal means thinking differences within that genus—otherwise nothing can be said to have moved from Animal at all (cf. VI.7.13, 10–12). But the fact that such differences within Animal have been thought also shows the presence of a new subject, i.e. a subject whose thought is characterized by exactly the differentiations of Animal that have appeared. In other words, there being a partial mind which is the Horse means that there is the thought, and hence the thinker, who says something like 'I am the Horse!' or perhaps better 'I am the Animal with the equine sort of differentiation!'

Such an account is never given in this systematic way by Plotinus himself but something along these lines is what I think he may be having in mind in e.g. VI.7.13. At any rate, in one of his most detailed accounts of the generation of the intelligibles after the primary intelligible genera in VI.7.13–14, the systematic distinction between the 'outward' and the 'inward' (or 'epistrophic') movements seems to be abandoned: both are subsumed under the notion of activity in such a way that it is clear that activity involves both a separation from, and an engagement with, what precedes it.

If this is at all on the right track, the intelligible Horse is indeed a mind that thinks itself (and so is and does each of the other subordinate intelligibles). We can by now begin to make sense of the apparently bizarre statements to the effect that each intelligible, each Idea, is an intellect. If, say, the intelligible Horse is the act of thinking equine thoughts, i.e. the thoughts that define equinity, the Horse is intellectual (*noeros*) in the sense that it is a thought of a certain sort. Plotinus, however, goes further than this and asserts that each intelligible is an intellect. The reason why he occasionally calls a partial intelligible an intellect is presumably the fact that the partial intelligible is a thought, and any thought is somebody's thought and involves a subject component, a thinker or 'seer', who thinks the thought. If the hypothesis of the previous chapter about the basic first-person form of Intellect's thought is correct, the thinker of any partial intelligible will think something of the kind of 'I am that partial thing'.

It is clear from numerous passages that though distinct, the intelligibles are interlocked into one another so that there is no question of any one of them being a separate, totally independent intellect. This means that the thought which is the Horse will e.g. include the thought of Animal, but with a differentiation. Ultimately, the self-thought of the Horse involves everything else. Thus, the intelligibles constitute a kind of holistic system. The nature of this system will be the theme of Section 4 of the next chapter.

9. Truth in Intellect

Intellect makes no mistakes. Its getting things right is a function of two features: (a) there being no external object against which Intellect's thought would have to be matched and with reference to which it might possibly be corrected; (b) knower and known are in such an intimate union that no wedge can be inserted between them. Such ideas are developed in V.3.5, a chapter we already have had several occasions to visit. Here Plotinus insists that truth in Intellect 'must not be of something else'. He says:

For, if [Intellect and the intelligible] are not the same, there will be no truth; for the one who is trying to possess what *is* (*ta onta*) will possess an impression that is different from what is, and this is not truth. For truth ought not to be truth of something else, but to be what it says.[30] (V.3.5, 23–6)

The claim that truth ought to be what it says is particularly noteworthy (cf. also V.3.6, 23–36). This is of course metaphorical talk, for literally speaking truth in Intellect *says* nothing at all.[31] But what is it that truth 'says' and why this choice of figurative expression? There is a similar but fuller statement of the same point in V.5.2, 13–24:

And then again, [Intellect] will need no demonstration and no confirmation that this [the intelligibles] is so, for itself is so and itself is manifest (*enargês*) to itself.... So that [in Intellect] there is also the real truth, which does not agree with something else, but with itself, and says nothing other than itself, but it is what it says and it says what it is. Who then could contradict it?... For the contradictory statement would lead to the preceding account, and even if one dressed it up as different, it is brought into conformity with and is one with the original statement: for you could not find anything truer than the truth.[32] (V.5.2, 13–24)

---

[30] V.3.5, 23–6: καὶ γάρ, εἰ μὴ ταὐτόν, οὐκ ἀλήθεια ἔσται· τύπον γὰρ ἕξει ὁ ἔχων τὰ ὄντα ἕτερον τῶν ὄντων, ὅπερ οὐκ ἔστιν ἀλήθεια. Τὴν ἄρα ἀλήθειαν οὐχ ἑτέρου εἶναι δεῖ, ἀλλ᾽ ὃ λέγει, τοῦτο καὶ εἶναι.

[31] For a different view of what saying in Intellect means, see Heiser (1991: chapter 6).

[32] V.5.2, 13–24: καὶ γὰρ αὖ οὕτως οὐδ᾽ ἀποδείξεως δεῖ οὐδὲ πίστεως, ὅτι οὕτως—αὐτὸς γὰρ οὕτως καὶ ἐναργὴς αὐτὸς αὑτῷ—καὶ εἴ τι πρὸ αὐτοῦ, ὅτι ἐξ αὐτοῦ, καὶ εἴ τι

Thus we have here that truth in Intellect 'says what it is' in addition to being what it says. The expression 'does not agree with something else' corresponds to the claim that 'truth ought not to be truth of something else' in the former passage. In both cases Plotinus is contrasting truth at the level of Intellect with another, more familiar kind of truth, which evidently does 'agree with something else' and is 'of something else'. But what sort of truth is it that agrees with itself? Now, the regular Greek word for truth, *alêtheia*, may also mean 'reality', 'what is real and genuine' as opposed to what is forged or derivative. One may wonder whether it isn't this sense of *alêtheia* that is involved here. Surely, 'the real thing' is not real in virtue of agreeing with something else and it would be quite proper for Plotinus to assert that Intellect contains 'the genuine article'. Indeed, I suppose the notion of *alêtheia* Plotinus wishes to attribute to Intellect here is in part that of 'the real thing': truth in this sense is not primarily supposed to say something, but *to be* something.

There is, however, more to Plotinus' view. To put it simply: truth in Intellect is not merely supposed to be but also to 'say'. This is the feature that truth in Intellect has in common with ordinary truth and suggests that *alêtheia* in Intellect belongs not merely to the order of reality or being but also and at the same time to the cognitive order. This should of course not come as a surprise, for as we have seen in previous sections being itself is according to Plotinus of the order of thought.

One might understand the claim that 'it says what it is and it is what it says' simply as an utterance of ordinary truthfulness: Intellect says something, and this is what it happens to be; Intellect is something and this is what it says it is. This is, however, not the point. Intellect, somehow, in saying what it is is what it says, and vice versa: in being what it is it says what it is. In other words, its thought coincides with its being. So, the notion Plotinus is after here is a notion of something in which reality and thought converge: the real is the content of the thoughts in Intellect, which, as the final lines

μετ' ἐκεῖνο, ὅτι αὐτός—καὶ οὐδεὶς πιστότερος αὐτῷ περὶ αὐτοῦ—καὶ ὅτι ἐκεῖ τοῦτο καὶ ὄντως. "Ὥστε καὶ ἡ ὄντως ἀλήθεια οὐ συμφωνοῦσα ἄλλῳ ἀλλ' ἑαυτῇ, καὶ οὐδὲν παρ' αὑτὴν ἄλλο λέγει, <ἀλλ' ὃ λέγει>, καὶ ἔστι, καὶ ὃ ἐστι, τοῦτο καὶ λέγει. Τίς ἂν οὖν ἐλέγξειε; Καὶ πόθεν οἴσει τὸν ἔλεγχον; Εἰς γὰρ ταὐτὸν ὁ φερόμενος ἔλεγχος τῷ προειπόντι, κἂν κομίσῃ ὡς ἄλλο, φέρεται εἰς τὸν ἐξαρχῆς εἰπόντα καὶ ἕν ἐστιν· οὐ γὰρ ἄλλο ἀληθέστερον ἂν εὕροις τοῦ ἀληθοῦς.—As usual, this is Armstrong's translation modified. The translation is based on a slight emendation proposed by Theiler and followed by H-S[2] and Armstrong.

of the quotation show, could not be corrected with reference to anything else. These thoughts are not thoughts of something else nor are they true because they agree with some other reality against which they may be tested. On the contrary, they constitute what is real. Hence, they are not true in the ordinary sense which takes truth to consist in a correspondence between a thought and reality. Nevertheless, these thoughts may also be said to be true in the sense that through them something is known to be such as it is, namely these thoughts themselves.

So if forced to explicate what these thoughts 'say' and 'to whom', the answer must be that they make their own content known to Intellect (subject). But Intellect, we have seen, is just these thought acts. In fact, according to the conclusions of Chapter 2, Intellect's thoughts are self-identifying thoughts that it cannot fail to be conscious of. So the conclusion is that thoughts in Intellect are self-conscious and self-evident without referring to anything external. Plotinus indicates this himself, for in the first part of the passage just quoted he says that Intellect is manifest to itself. This I take to be the point of the claim that truth in Intellect 'says what it is'.

Several further comments on this are in order. It is clear and well known that Plotinus' Internality Thesis owes much to Aristotle and his followers: basically, Plotinus follows Alexander of Aphrodisias in unifying the account of God as a pure thinker in *Metaphysics* XII and that of the active intellect in *De anima* III, 5.[33] The Platonic Ideas become for him acts of thought which constitute the universal divine Intellect.[34] This means that, say, the Platonic Idea of the Horse is for Plotinus a certain act of thought which has the characteristics we have been describing: it is the Horse and 'says so'. And this is the primary Horse both in the sense that it is the cause of horses on all lower stages in the Plotinian hierarchy and in the sense that it is the original horse: there is no prior Horse on which this thought depends; the Horse is, one might say, created in this act of thought (cf. V.9.5, 13–14).

Despite Plotinus' debt to Aristotle in this area, there is an epistemological strain in Plotinus' Internality Thesis which is absent or at least not prominent in Aristotle. As noted above, Plotinus' original concern in V.5, where he

---

[33] For Plotinus' debt to Alexander Aphrodisias here see Armstrong (1960), cf. Szlezák (1979: 135–43).

[34] On Middle Platonic precursors to Plotinus here see Jones (1926) and Rich (1954). It is important to note, however, that the identification of the realm of Ideas (being) with Intellect is not merely an Aristotelizing trait in Plotinus: he thought he had Platonic support for this in *Sophist* 248e 8–249a 9, where being is endowed with intelligence (*nous*) and life. See Hadot (1999) and Szlezák (1979: 122–5).

most explicitly argues for the Internality Thesis, is how to answer the question why Intellect will never 'be in error and believe what is untrue'. He also says that if the intelligibles are external and Intellect 'only receives in itself images of the truth, it will have falsities and nothing true' (V.5.1, 56–8). What is Plotinus' epistemological worry here? Is it just that anything less than direct knowledge of the ontologically primary is not good enough for Intellect, it being assumed to be an ideal knower, as anything less would violate the Platonic principle that knowledge is of the fully real? Or is there something about images in addition to failing to be primary that makes them epistemically suspect or inadequate?

In Plotinus' view there is. First, let us note that image-making in Plotinus' metaphysical sense of the term is not exact copying but always involves a loss. Images have their intelligible content, and hence their identity, entirely in virtue of their archetypes. On a purely ontological level this means 'remove the archetype and the image will perish' (III.6.13, 37–8; VI.4.9, 38–41). On an epistemological level, this means that for a mind without access to the archetype everything it encounters becomes something less than epistemically transparent and self-explanatory.

We can see the germs of such a view in Plotinus' first treatise 'On beauty'. Recognition of sensible forms depends on the prior possession of these forms in the soul of the person who judges. The architect pronounces the external house before him beautiful by using the form of beauty he has in his soul 'as we use a ruler for judging straightness' (I.6.3, 4–5). In V.5.1 the claim that knowledge of images depends on knowledge of the original is quite explicit and used as an argument for the Internality Thesis. Plotinus is in the following passage exposing the consequences of the view that the intelligibles are external and Intellect receives images of them:

But how, also, will it know that it really grasped them? And how will it know that this is good or beautiful or just? For each of these will be other than it, and the principles of judgement on which it will rely will not be in itself, but these too will be outside, and that is where truth will be.[35] (V.5.1, 28–32)

So, as all Platonists will agree, the Ideas are the principles of judgement, and if the divine Intellect does not already possess these principles, it would

---

[35] V.5.1, 28–32: Πῶς δὲ καὶ γνώσεται, ὅτι ἀντελάβετο ὄντως; Πῶς δέ, ὅτι ἀγαθὸν τοῦτο ἢ ὅτι καλὸν ἢ δίκαιον; Ἕκαστον γὰρ τούτων ἄλλο αὐτοῦ, καὶ οὐκ ἐν αὐτῷ αἱ τῆς κρίσεως ἀρχαί, αἷς πιστεύσει, ἀλλὰ καὶ αὗται ἔξω, καὶ ἡ ἀλήθεια ἐκεῖ.

not recognize images of these Ideas for what they are, i.e. images of just these Ideas. This argument evidently assumes that no image contains the principle for what it is, is self-evident, 'says what it is'. Presumably this is so because Plotinus holds that just as it is a defining characteristic of images that they depend on their causes for their being, recognition of their intelligible content refers to and presupposes knowledge of something else, namely the originals. Plotinus' view here may perhaps be summarized as follows: the full intelligibility of any image depends on the thinker's possession of—actually on its being—the primary intelligible which the image expresses. The image, because it is an image, necessarily expresses the primary intelligible 'in something else', i.e. in some matter or potentiality which expresses but is not identical with the intelligible content of the image. So in the case of images judgement would have to be that something ('the matter') is F—this matter being by definition different from the thinker and the intelligible content. Only in case of Intellect is there a coincidence of subject and content.[36]

This does not mean that we always ascend to Intellect in every mundane cognitive activity. We normally understand the world around us by means of concepts or images belonging to the order of soul.[37] But the question can be raised about the concepts belonging to the soul themselves, how a thinking subject recognizes the intelligible content of his concepts. It turns out that these concepts are themselves images that express through something else—words or mental pictures—some intelligible content (cf. previous note). They are not intelligible in virtue of themselves. This leads to the postulation of a level of intelligible content in itself, not expressed through anything else. This is a thought which constitutes the intelligible content there is. This is also 'the ontologically primary' as the last quotation clearly shows: there is nothing prior to it to which one could appeal to question it.

Plotinus' epistemological concerns we have been considering here are likely to be modified by the sceptical tradition. The dilemma he sets out to

---

[36] Plotinus' view that images are always 'in something else' (*en allôi*; *en heterôi*) seems to be based on Plato's *Timaeus* 52c, cf. V.3.8, 13–14.

[37] Plotinus does not have any one word he systematically uses to refer to such concepts or images in the soul, but chooses an expression according to the context. He often uses *logos*, cf. V.1.3, 7–8; I.2.3, 27, IV.3.30, 9, but also 'form (*eidos*) in the soul', cf. I.1.8, 19, 'impression' (*typos*), cf. I.1.7, 12 and p. 29 above, and 'representation' (*eidôlon, eikonisma*) of Intellect, cf. I.4.10.

solve in V.3.5 and we considered in Section 5 above about Intellect's self-knowledge, parallels a dilemma mentioned by Sextus Empiricus, where Sextus argues that Man's self-knowledge is impossible (*Adv. math.* VII, 284–6, cf. Wallis 1987: 917–25). The argument in V.5.1 we just considered and the notion of truth in Intellect which 'says what it is and is what it says' is probably also prompted by sceptical considerations: it may be an attempt to block the kind of sceptical move which consists in insisting on a criterion for the validity of any proposed criterion (cf. Sextus Empiricus, *PH* 1, 166). Plotinus' theory of divine thoughts is clearly meant to make such thoughts self-validating. In general it seems to be instructive to see Plotinus' epistemological concerns—his contrast between cognition of images or impressions and knowledge of the things themselves as well as his insistence that genuine knowledge is identical with its object and true just in virtue of itself—in the light of sceptical considerations. His theory is so construed that it is supposedly impossible to put any wedge between Intellect and the object of its cognition.

10. The Notion of the Given

It is enlightening to compare Plotinus' account of Intellect's perfect knowledge with some later ideas in the history of philosophy. Wilfrid Sellars (1963: 69–70; 129–34; 156–61) launched an attack on what he called 'The Myth of the Given'. In particular he has traced in the tradition of empiricism a notion, mostly implicit rather than explicit, of items which are at once supposed to be items of a certain kind and instances of knowledge of that kind. That is to say, in the empiricist tradition a given sensation (sense datum, impression, sensum, phenomenal quality, or whatever it is called) is supposed to be at once, say, something green and an awareness of or knowledge of something green. Such items may seem to provide a solid foundation of meaning and knowledge, for they seem to bridge the gap between what is and what is within the reach of our minds: the very same thing is an F and our direct awareness of F. Plotinus' notion of the intelligible as something which 'says what it is and is what it says' shares the formal features of Sellars's notion of the given: the Plotinian intelligible *is* at the same time something (e.g. Beauty) and the thought of (awareness of) what it is. It must be said in Plotinus' praise that he shows a keen understanding of what it takes for there to be a given and, as opposed to the empiricist's view, his account of it cannot be rejected on the ground that the proposed givens (the intelligibles) fail to be so. Sensual images or impressions of qualities must have a conceptual or 'intelligible' content in order to function as givens in an epistemologically relevant sense. As Sellars has shown, it is, however, most unlikely that any such conceptual content is given in virtue of a mere sense impression. Plotinus, on the contrary, designs his account of Intellect's thoughts in such a way that this kind of attack would not succeed. As we have seen, the epistemic principle or criterion of, say once more, beauty must at once be that very thing of which it is the principle, namely beauty, and in being beauty it must somehow 'say' that that is what it is. Plotinus sees to it that it is not possible to separate the intelligible content from the thing which has the intelligible content in question or from the 'mind' which grasps it. One might say that his programme is precisely to reduce both the thing and the mind to the content as thought.

Plotinus' doctrine of the givenness of the contents of Intellect and the problems he hopes to solve by it have a parallel in another modern philosophical issue (which ultimately is closely related to the question of the given): recent discussions of scepticism about meaning and self-knowledge prompted primarily by Saul Kripke's *Wittgenstein on Rules and Private Language* (1982: 41–53).[38] The main contention of this scepticism is that there do not seem to be any facts about us thinking subjects that determine the meaning of the expressions we use, whether in mental or in spoken language. In surveying candidates for determinants of meaning, Kripke briefly mentions Platonism in connection with Frege's views. Frege's Platonism is a non-Neoplatonic kind of Platonism, according to which mathematical objects exist as Platonic 'Ideas' independent of any mind. Expressions have a certain 'sense' associated with them that is likewise an objective non-mental thing. This sense determines the reference of a sign, which in the case of mathematics is a 'Platonic' objective mathematical entity, e.g. the plus function. But for people to grasp the sense associated with a sign, they must have appropriate ideas in their minds associated

---

[38] The givens of the empiricist tradition are, according to Kripke, one main set of candidates Wittgenstein considers and rejects as items to which we can refer in order to determine meaning. According to Kripke, this is what Wittgenstein's famous private language argument is meant to show, cf. Kripke (1982: 41–53).

with the sign. According to Kripke it is in relation to the alleged function of these mental ideas that Wittgenstein's sceptical problem about meaning sneaks in for a Platonist of the Fregean sort:

[The sceptical problem] arises precisely in the question how the existence in my mind of any mental entity or idea can constitute 'grasping' any particular sense rather than another.... For Wittgenstein, Platonism is largely an unhelpful evasion of the problem of how our finite minds can give rules that are supposed to apply to an infinity of cases. Platonic objects may be self-interpreting, or rather, they may need no interpretation; but ultimately there must be some mental entity involved that raises the skeptical problem. (Kripke 1982: 54)

Suppose one is willing to go along with Platonism in holding that Platonic objects are in themselves self-explanatory (or need no interpretation), while insisting that what anybody, including God, can have access to is at best certain representations of them. Suppose in addition that one believes that no representation (image, impression) is self-authenticating. This is very much the position Plotinus finds himself in with respect to scepticism about Intellect's knowledge. Given the availability of the Aristotelian doctrine of divine thought, the natural move would be to maintain that the Ideas, the ontologically primary beings, are in fact internal to Intellect, are its thoughts which it immediately knows.

In saying this I am not suggesting that Plotinus saw right through the sceptical problem about meaning that preoccupied Kripke's Wittgenstein and other contemporary philosophers, and proposed a solution to it. However, there are interesting common features. First of all, Kripke's point against Fregean Platonism is analogous to one objection Plotinus raises against classical 'objective' Platonism, according to which the Ideas are extra-mental. Plotinus seems to have held that no representation (image) of F, whether a mental representation or expression of it or a material embodiment of it in nature, can show the general nature it represents in such a way that one could read off what is represented from the representation alone. This is evident for instance from his remarks in V.5.1, 28–33 considered above that if Intellect had mere representations of the intelligibles, it would not be able to recognize the Just for the Just or the Beautiful for the Beautiful (cf. also lines 49–50 and p. 168 above). Intellect would have no way of knowing what the representation it received represented unless it had independent access to what it represents as a self-authenticating criterion. In Plotinian language this is so because no representation 'is what it says and says what it is'. The self-authenticating aspect of Intellect's thought functions in Plotinus to preclude any kind of scepticism and indeterminacy as to what is what in Intellect. Nothing less is required if Intellect is to be able to have knowledge of the real and, which is the same, of the content of its own thought. To what extent this might provide solid grounds for the thought of lesser, human minds is a different issue that I shall leave untouched here.

11. Plotinus' Idealism

Where do the conclusions of the preceding sections leave us with respect to the fusion of the topics of self-knowledge, the internality of the intelligibles, and knowledge of what is real?

The Internality Thesis amounts to the claim that the object of Intellect's thought doesn't act on it from the outside. The claim that Intellect has self-knowledge means, at the very least, that what it knows when it knows its object is itself. In this way the Internality Thesis and Intellect's self-knowledge are really different labels for the same idea. If we bring to this the first-person considerations from the previous chapter about the nature of Intellect's self-knowledge, we will have to add that not only is the object of Intellect's knowledge internal to it and identical with it, Intellect is aware of this identity. Not only that, actually, Intellect's constituting thought will be an 'assertion' about its identity. That thought will include its subject as a part of its object. For this reason the object is *eo ipso* partly internal to the thinker. In so far as it isn't, in so far as there is being or some 'F' that the thinker thinks itself to be, that aspect of the object will be shown to be internal too, for very much the same reasons as on the simpler 'Aristotelian' account.

But as we saw in Section 5, Plotinus also insists that Intellect's self-knowledge (the notion he starts from) and the claim that Intellect's knowledge is of ontologically primary beings are intimately connected. How?

Let us first notice that the primary reason Plotinus gives for why discursive thought fails to provide genuine self-knowledge is that even when it grasps something it receives from Intellect, this is still a grasp of an image, not the genuine article so to speak *in propria persona* (cf. V.3.3–4). Underlying his way of reasoning about this matter there is an assumption well known in Plotinus' Platonic-Aristotelian tradition: to know something is to know its principles and causes. So, if discursive reason itself and all its contents are ontologically derivative, however much discursive reason may be aware of itself, in the absence of an understanding of its principles and causes, its cognition will fail to be full self-knowledge (cf. V.3.4, 25 ff.). The content of the cognition will be an image of the thing and not the thing itself.

Furthermore, genuine self-knowledge and knowledge of the ontologically primary must satisfy the same conditions: in both cases the subject of the cognition must be identical with its object. In the former case this is because otherwise we have knowledge of part by part and the thinker would fail to know itself as a thinker. In the latter case, this is because if the object was external, the thinker would only know an image of it, and the genuine article would remain outside.

So while the sensible object is in no way defined in terms of sense-perception, the faculty by which we apprehend such objects, the intelligible object is defined in terms of thinking. Since the intelligible object is also the ontologically primary object, Plotinus becomes a kind of idealist after all.[39] As we have seen, there are epistemological reasons for this: Plotinus believes that Intellect's knowledge is infallible and self-authenticating and

---

[39] Burnyeat (1982: 16–18) attempts to cast doubt on the view that Plotinus was an idealist in 'any interesting sense'. He gives two grounds for this doubt: (1) matter for Plotinus is independent of form, like pre-existing darkness which is illuminated. (2) With respect to Plotinus' notion of the One's self-knowledge (if he had such a notion; Burnyeat leaves the question open), Burnyeat claims that 'it would be misleading and partial to describe the ultimate monism as a monism of mind'. I disagree on both points. As to (1) see O'Brien (1991), who very convincingly shows that matter is indeed caused by the One. As to (2), even if it may be conceded that it would be misleading to call Plotinus' view 'a monism of mind', since the Plotinian One isn't a 'mind', it would hardly be misleading to call it a 'monism of the spiritual'. For the One, as noted in Chapter 2, pp. 70–1, is a mental or spiritual entity of sorts. Even more importantly, however, in his inquiry into the presence of idealism in antiquity Burnyeat does not consider Plotinus' identification of primary being with acts of thought—what should count as idealism if not that doctrine? Interestingly, he also passes over, as a possible germ of idealism, the Aristotelian view of God as at once an intellect and a being in the most primary sense. This does not give us idealism in the sense that everything that in some way exists is mental nor even the weaker thesis that absolutely everything has a mental cause. However, Aristotle's views here connect the notions of being or substance and that of thought in a remarkable way and were, as we have seen, developed by Plotinus and other Platonists in an idealistic direction: for Plotinus absolutely everything that is has a mental cause (assuming that the One is in a sense mental) and everything that deserves to be called fully real is thought of some sort, cf. III.8. This whole Platonic-Aristotelian idealistic tradition in turn greatly inspired the main philosophical movement that goes under the name of idealism in modern times, i.e. German idealism, cf. Beierwaltes (1972 and 2002) and Vieillard-Baron (1979).

he thinks that this requires the identity of the objects of this kind of knowledge with the acts of thinking these objects. So far this sounds as if the Internality Thesis results merely from the request for secure knowledge on behalf of the divine mind. This is however only one half of the story. Plotinus is of course not only concerned with showing that there can be something given in an epistemic sense; he is also and no less concerned about showing that there can be real things, substances or essences, i.e. things that satisfy traditional Greek criteria of ontological primacy. The most important of these is self-sufficiency: that which stands in need of nothing for being what it is, is ontologically primary. From the account above we can see that in Plotinus' view thoughts at the level of Intellect satisfy the conditions: each of them is fully actual, fully is what it is, and in general they satisfy all the important conditions of Platonic Ideas. They are self-sufficient and essentially active things. So Intellect's thoughts have both the required epistemological properties and satisfy the conditions of being. Is this sheer metaphysical luck?

One way to put our question is to ask: given Plotinus' general outlook, might there be something which satisfied the conditions of the ontologically primary without being epistemically primary? Does Plotinus give us any arguments for the view that the ontologically primary must be a mind of the sort of his Intellect? We can indeed extract the following kind of argument: the intelligible, i.e. the ontologically primary, must be identical with some inner activity which constitutes it; that activity must not involve any potentiality for otherwise this would not be the ontologically primary activity, and the only activity which does not is a thinking activity of the kind we have described. An argument along these lines seems to lie behind for instance V.3.5, 33–48. One premiss here is of course that the only conceivable pure activity is thinking, and for this we do not get much explicit argument.

I suspect that behind Plotinus' view here there lies an intuition which connects the notions being, meaning or intelligibility, and mind: what a thing is, is what is intelligible about it and the source of intelligibility must be a thought. The primacy of thinking for Plotinus lies already in the quasi-intellectual attributes of the One and in the fact that the external activity of the One is an inchoate intellect.

4

Discursive and Non-discursive Thought

In the two previous chapters we have considered the genesis of Intellect and to some extent its internal structure, with the relationship between thinker and thought especially in view. In this chapter I wish to focus more on the kind of unity characteristic of the intelligible world in contrast to the degree of unity of the embodied soul and the sensible world. I shall approach this topic by attempting to clarify Plotinus' distinction between ordinary inferential or discursive thought, which he normally refers to as *dianoia* or *logismos*, and the kind of thought characteristic of Intellect that is non-discursive or, as it is sometimes called, intuitive. His most usual terms for the latter are *noêsis* ('intellection') and *theoria* ('contemplation'). Among its characteristics are veracity, certainty, and immediacy. I shall spell out these and other traits of it in some detail below.

Plotinus is not the first Greek philosopher to distinguish between higher forms of thinking and less perfect forms: in *Republic* VI, 509 d–511 d Plato famously distinguishes between the kinds of thought involved at the two upper levels of the Divided Line: the lower of the two, characteristic of the mathematical disciplines, he calls discursive thought or *dianoia*, while the higher one, which is associated with dialectic, is called *noêsis*. Aristotle too makes some such distinction between higher and lower thinking. Though the terminology is not fixed, *nous* and its cognates are used of the higher kind of thought, though they may also be used in a wider sense that covers reasoning and inferences (see Kal 1988: 9). Thus, it is *noûs* or *noêsis* that are involved in the non-inferential grasp of first principles in *Posterior analytics* II, 19, in divine thinking in *Metaphysics* XII, and in the passages about the intellect in *De anima* III, 4–6.

While Plotinus certainly draws on sources such as those just mentioned, it is equally clear that he develops and modifies the Platonic and Aristotelian material to suit his own purposes. Plotinus turned the notion of non-discursive thought into an extremely rich and many-faceted concept and, as is clear from the two previous chapters, it plays a fundamental role in his philosophy.

The idea that there are different modes of thought, the highest one of which is non-inferential, veridical, and vision-like, haunts both medieval and early modern philosophy, clear examples being intuition in Descartes and Spinoza, and Kant's notion of *intelligibile Anschauung* (which he rejects, for us humans). In our times, this notion is to a large extent lost at least in professional, systematic philosophy. Some bits and pieces of the ancient notion, however, survive or have been reinvented here and there, e.g. in notions such as 'tacit knowledge' or that of 'intuition' as in 'our moral intuitions' or 'our pre-philosophical intuitions'. There is, however, nothing in current philosophical thought that comes close to satisfying all the conditions of Plotinus' notion of non-discursive thought.

1. Non-discursive vs. Discursive Thought: the Main Contrasts

I shall now proceed by comparing and contrasting discursive and non-discursive thought with the aim of making a list of their contrastive characteristics. Thus, the focus here will be on the differences between the two. I shall not attempt anything like an exhaustive account of each. In previous chapters, however, most of the important features of non-discursive thought have been presented. We just haven't yet sought to bring them together.

Many of the contrasting features emerge in the following striking but difficult passage in V.8.6, 'On the Intelligible Beauty':

The wise men of Egypt, I think, also understood this, either by scientific or innate knowledge, and when they wished to signify something wisely, they did not make use of the impressions of letters that pass through the order of words [*logoi*] and statements [*protaseis*] or those that imitate the sounds and enunciations of propositions [*axiômata*], but by drawing likenesses [*agalmata*] and inscribing in their temples one particular likeness of one particular thing, they manifested the non-discursiveness of the object, since each likeness would then be a kind of knowledge and wisdom, an underlying subject which comes all at once [*athroon*], and not a discourse [*dianoêsis*] or deliberation [*bouleusis*]. But afterwards, [others], starting from it [the wisdom] in its all-at-once state, discovered an image [*eidôlon*] of it in something else, already unfolded and speaking it discursively and giving the reasons [*aitiai*] why things are such as they are, so that, because what has come into being is so beautifully disposed, anyone who knows how to admire it expresses his admiration for this wisdom, how it, without possessing the reasons why Being is such as it is, gives them to that which is made according to it.[1] (V.8.6, 1–15)

First, a few remarks about my understanding of this passage in general. Though neither *noêsis* nor *theoria* occur here, the context leaves little doubt that the kind of thought that the wisdom and knowledge inherent in the Egyptian likenesses is likened to is *noêsis*, Intellect's kind of thought. As indeed the passage makes clear, in giving Egyptian likenesses on temple walls as a paradigm of knowledge and wisdom, Plotinus is of course not implying that true knowledge or wisdom are likenesses of any sort. Rather the point is that in comparison with phonetic or other more discursive forms of representation, the Egyptian likenesses resemble the intelligible object itself. So I take it that Plotinus is saying that the wisdom of the Egyptian priests was non-discursive and they thought it more appropriate to express this wisdom by likenesses that contain the elements of the wisdom all at once and all together than in writing, which separates these elements and expresses them by mere images that fail to show the true features of the thing.

The latter half of the passage (after 'afterwards') is not altogether lucid. Though there is no formal grammatical sign of a change of subject between the first and the second half, the required sense doesn't permit that the same Egyptian priests who made the likeness later discovered its wisdom in a discursive form. Those who discovered this must be some other people, as Armstrong indicates in his translation. But what exactly did these other people discover? It is said that they started from the wisdom in its 'all-at-once' state but 'discovered an image of it in something else.' This image must

---

[1] V.8.6, 1–15: Δοκοῦσι δέ μοι καὶ οἱ Αἰγυπτίων σοφοί, εἴτε ἀκριβεῖ ἐπιστήμῃ λαβόντες εἴτε καὶ συμφύτῳ, περὶ ὧν ἐβούλοντο διὰ σοφίας δεικνύναι, μὴ τύποις γραμμάτων διεξοδεύουσι λόγους καὶ προτάσεις μηδὲ μιμουμένοις φωνὰς καὶ προφορὰς ἀξιωμάτων κεχρῆσθαι, ἀγάλματα δὲ γράψαντες καὶ ἓν ἕκαστον ἑκάστου πράγματος ἄγαλμα ἐντυπώσαντες ἐν τοῖς ἱεροῖς τὴν ἐκείνου <οὐ> διέξοδον ἐμφῆναι, ὡς ἄρα τις καὶ ἐπιστήμη καὶ σοφία ἕκαστόν ἐστιν ἄγαλμα καὶ ὑποκείμενον καὶ ἀθρόον καὶ οὐ διανόησις οὐδὲ βούλευσις. Ὕστερον δὲ ἀπ᾽ αὐτῆς ἀθρόας οὔσης εἴδωλον ἐν ἄλλῳ ἐξειλιγμένον ἤδη καὶ λέγον αὐτὸ ἐν διεξόδῳ καὶ τὰς αἰτίας, δι᾽ ἃς οὕτω, ἐξευρίσκον, ὥστε καλῶς οὕτως ἔχοντος τοῦ γεγενημένου θαυμάσαι εἴ τις οἶδε, θαυμάσαι ἔφη τὴν σοφίαν, πῶς αὐτὴ αἰτίας οὐκ ἔχουσα τῆς οὐσίας, δι᾽ ἃς οὕτω, παρέχει τοῖς ποιουμένοις κατ᾽ αὐτήν. I follow Igal in emending the text in line 7 to *ekeinou ou* instead of the manuscripts' *ekeinou*. And against H-S² and Armstrong I read *auto* rather than *hauto* in line 11.

be a discursive representation of the wisdom, and it is suggested that this image gives the reasons why things are such as they are. The original priests, on the other hand, did not possess the reasons in a discursive way. Nevertheless, they managed to make such a beautiful and well-ordered likeness that anyone who understands it must admire the priests' non-discursive wisdom.

This is a paraphrase that shows how I read the passage. I am not overly confident about all of it, but I don't think that plausible alternative interpretations will seriously affect the points to be made here below.

We see here that non-discursive knowledge does not involve inferences (cf. VI.2.21, 32–9; VI.7.1–2). It does not contain the reasons why Being is such as it is. In a different text Plotinus says that in Intellect the reason for a thing's being such and such is a part of the being of each thing, that the fact and the reason why coincide (VI.7.2, 8–12). This may seem to contradict the present statement, but it really doesn't. In substance Plotinus is making very much the same point in VI.7.2 as here in V.8.6: in the former passage he is saying that Intellect does not possess the reason why in a distinct form separated from that which it is a reason for; the reasons that are discovered 'afterwards' in V.8.6 are such separated reasons. I shall return to this point below. In any case, we may affirm that:

(1) Non-discursive thought is not inferential.

We see in our passage that non-discursive thought is 'all at once' or 'collectively' (*athroon*). Borrowing Anaxagoras' phrase, Plotinus often expresses the view that the intelligibles are 'all together' (*homou panta*). The altogetherness of the intelligibles is no doubt connected to the claim here that they are grasped 'all at once'. For, as we have seen in previous chapters, the intelligibles exist in Intellect's thought; and Intellect is timeless; any apprehension in its case is therefore bound to be all at once: Intellect wouldn't grasp first this item and then that other one. What it thus grasps 'all at once' it grasps 'all together'.

The question, however, remains: how 'all together', how do the intelligibles appear when they are grasped 'all at once'? Pace Lloyd (1970; 1986), the intelligibles are not 'all together' in the sense of being all in one, blurred and indistinguishable, for there definitely is a quasi-space in Intellect allowing for distinctions between things: 'Place exists there in an intellectual mode in the presence of one thing in another' (V.9.10, 10). If they were entirely indistinct, there would not be any need for an intellectual space for them to reside in. Moreover, in V.9.6, 3 Plotinus explicitly remarks that even if all things are together in Intellect, 'they are nevertheless separate (*diakekrimena*)'. Actually, one of the stock adjectives he uses about Intellect, occurring pretty much in every passage where Intellect is treated at any length at all, is *poikilos*, 'many-coloured', 'variegated' (cf. e.g. V.3.10, 30; 41; VI.4.11, 12–15). The visual metaphor of the likenesses of the Egyptian priests helps elucidate this point: anybody who sees the likeness sees it as a whole all at once. Ordinary vision is such that it is both at once (temporally) and of a whole composed of parts. Analogously, I presume, non-discursive thought is at-once-of-a-whole, the instantaneousness and the togetherness being two related but distinguishable aspects of the act. Let us in the light of the foregoing posit two characteristics of non-discursive thought:

(2) Non-discursive thought is all at once.
(3) Non-discursive thought is of its objects all together.

Discursive thought, by contrast, is neither all at once nor of all its objects together. That is to say, discursive thought has some object, something that it seeks to ascertain, and perhaps eventually manages to ascertain. This, however, takes time, since it has to go through steps of reasoning piece by piece. This emerges from our passage in the contrast Plotinus makes between that which comes all at once [*athroon*], and that which is a discourse [*dianoêsis*] or deliberation [*bouleusis*]: discourse and deliberation are not all at once. Nor is discursive thought 'all together'. That is to say, what non-discursive thought grasps in a single blow, discursive thought has divided into steps, premisses, or reasons, for the fact to be ascertained (cf. VI.2.21, 32–7).

Yet another feature with regard to which discursive and non-discursive thought split company is the authenticity of the objects of non-discursive thought, as opposed to the images discursive thought deals in. In our passage this is not quite explicit. Although Plotinus does here associate discursive thought with images, it is not certain (though this may be the case) that he is thereby saying anything more than that discursive thought is an image of non-discursive thought. He need not be taken as affirming that non-discursive thought is thought of the ontologically primary things. As we saw in the previous chapter, however (see especially Sections 3 and 6), there is ample evidence that could be cited in support of the claim that Plotinus thought so. In the light of this and the previous discussion, let it be said that:

(4) Non-discursive thought is non-representational; it doesn't think in images.

Another characteristic of non-discursive thought, which is not explicitly in view in our passage, is its certainty and veracity. This is, however, implicitly present in Plotinus' denial that non-discursive thought employs reasoning or deliberation. For reasoning and deliberation are by themselves marks of uncertainty: nobody who really knew the outcome would be engaged in such modes of thought (cf. V.5.1, 1 ff.). Non-discursive thought, being directly engaged with true being itself, with no possibility of a deceitful veil between it and its object, cannot go wrong. So it is veridical. It is also subjectively certain because the object of this sort of thought is totally transparent and leaves no questions unresolved. Discursive thought, by contrast, is liable to error and uncertainty (V.5.1, 5–7). So:

(5) Non-discursive thought is veridical and certain.

Another difference between non-discursive and discursive thought, closely related to the previous one, is that non-discursive thought does not search for its object: it possesses it (this is implied by the internality of the intelligibles to Intellect); discursive thought, by contrast, must seek and is typically ambivalent and insecure (IV.4.17, 1–7). Again, this contrast is not quite explicit in our text, but it is there implicitly, as may be seen from what was said above about the veracity requirement. Let us lay down as our sixth and last item:

(6) Non-discursive thought doesn't search for its object, it possesses it.

There may be other features in regard to which discursive and non-discursive thought can be contrasted. I believe, however, that the preceding list captures the most significant ones. Readers at home in the literature may, however, be missing one interesting feature: isn't non-discursive thought arguably non-propositional as opposed to the propositional nature of discursive thought? Well, arguably. I have not forgotten this issue and will turn to it at some length below.

Some of the characteristics we have come up with are obviously interrelated. For instance (5), being veridical and certain, (6), being in possession of its object, and (4), being non-representational (immediate), are no doubt connected. Non-representational or unmediated thought is supposed to be thought that does not employ any kind of proxies, including words, for the things it apprehends. It grasps its object itself directly. What intuitively lies behind the idea of immediacy here is the view that, epistemically speaking, nothing can compare with direct exposure to the thing itself. As in the things of the senses, what the eyewitness experiences is epistemically superior to any kind of indirect knowledge, so here the one who has experienced the intelligible object itself is privileged in comparison with anyone who is acquainted with it merely through imperfect representations.[2] Thus, even if it is perhaps not a full guarantee of certainty, we may readily see non-representationality as a necessary condition of certainty. At least it has a clear intuitive appeal to claim that, compared with inspecting the thing itself, grasping it via some proxy or other invites lack of clarity, uncertainty, and error. The direct view must function as a standard against which any claims to cognition based on an indirect grasp are measured. With regard to certainty, there is nothing like a direct confrontation with the very thing at issue.

Plotinus wishes, however, to take this a step further and work out what he considers a full guarantee for the certainty of non-discursive thought. As we saw in the previous chapter, this is an important motivation behind the thesis that the Ideas, i.e. intelligible content as such, are internal to the universal mind: if external, the intelligibles will not be known in their own right. Intelligible content consists in the thoughts of Intellect and is constituted by its acts of thought. Intellect doesn't have to approach its own content via proxies: this content is there and is there in such a way as to make it impossible, or so Plotinus thinks, to put a veil between the thinking subject and it. Given the One and Plotinus' set-up for what happens after the One, there are indeed metaphysically good reasons for the objects of Intellect's thought to be internal to it. At the same time we may see the internalization of the intelligibles as an attempt to strengthen the sense of immediacy in the relations between thinker and object, so as to make Intellect immune to error. This sense is further strengthened by the self-constitutional aspect of its thought expounded in Chapter 2, Section 7: the beings thought by Intellect are self-identifying thoughts. In the absence of prior beings, such thoughts cannot go wrong.

The last item on our list, (6), the possessing and non-searching nature of non-discursive thought, is connected with timelessness, non-inferentiality, and veracity. Plotinus evidently believed that possession and freedom from the toil of search go hand in hand with freedom from time and inference:

---

[2] Burnyeat (1987) accounts impressively for the Platonically inspired role of directness of knowledge or understanding in Augustine's *De magistro*. In several respects his views on Augustine on knowledge and understanding are close to the views I advocate here for Plotinus.

if there is nothing you do not possess, what would you have to search for or infer? He apparently linked this to veracity and non-representationality as well: 'To possess' here means to have the very original item available to you in such a way that you cannot go wrong about it; if you had something less, an image, the question might arise whether what you have got and the real thing are the same or not, because no image 'says what it is' (cf. Chapter 3, Section 9).

We have seen that inferential thought or reasoning (*logismos, syllogismos, bouleusis*) is temporal. The converse, however, apparently doesn't hold: there seems to be room for a kind of thought that is successive and temporal and is indeed called discursive (*dianoia*) but is yet not inferential and is thus free from the uncertainty and search which, according to Plotinus, is typical of inferential thinking. That this is so is evident from the treatise III.7, 'On Eternity and Time,' especially chapters 11 and 12. The origin of succession, of a temporal 'before' and 'after', says Plotinus, lies in the World-Soul's successive thinking (*dianoia*) of the contents of Intellect. He contrasts the activity of the World-Soul with that of Intellect. The latter's atemporal activity is degraded into one act after another, its togetherness into continuity, the latter being an imperfect image of the former, and 'instead of a whole all together [*athroou holou*]' there is a whole which will come and always will be coming into being part by part'.[3]

There is no suggestion here that the World-Soul uses any sort of reasoning in eliciting any particular contents out of Intellect. On the contrary, the evidence indicates that not only Intellect itself but also the World-Soul and the star-souls are quite free from reasoning (IV.4.16; V.8.7; VI.7.1). Yet, at least in III.7.11, Plotinus is willing to describe the mental life of the World-Soul as *dianoia*, discursive thought. The upshot of this is that discursivity is not synonymous with reasoning or inference. There is successive thinking, described as *dianoia* that is not yet inferential reasoning, the latter apparently being a peculiarly human phenomenon (cf. IV.4.17). Reasoning is discursive, but not all discursive thought is characterized as reasoning.

How are we to make sense of this? Plotinus, as we have seen, describes the World-Soul's thought as successive acts, implying that not all the

---

[3] III.7.11, 55–6. Since the World-Soul's successive, discursive thought constitutes time, Plotinus is unwilling to say that it is in time, as if time were something prior to it (cf. III.7.11, 58–63). Being time itself, temporal attributes such as 'before' and 'after' are not applicable to it or at least not in the same way as they apply to the visible cosmos itself. See also IV.4.16 and Smith (1996).

contents of Intellect are activated at once in the soul. This contrasts with the state of affairs in Intellect itself, where everything is actual all at once. The soul's relation to Intellect is typically described by means of visual imagery: the soul 'sees' the Intellect and absorbs the content of what it sees. It cannot, however, absorb it all at once. It has to do it successively. This is why it is called discursive. But ordinary vision involves no inference either (cf. IV.5.4, 40–6 and Emilsson 1988: 46–7). The use of visual imagery in this context may suggest that the soul's successive and partial activation of the contents of Intellect is to be seen as analogous to a narrowing of focus, rather than, say, inferring particular facts from an undifferentiated experience (cf. IV.4.1, 27 ff.). It is as if the soul cannot absorb the whole in a single apprehension and must focus on a part or an aspect of what it sees.

Nor is it evident that the contrast in III.7.11 between the successive thinking in Soul and the 'all together' thinking in Intellect is necessarily a contrast between non-propositional thinking and propositional thinking. In V.1.4, at least, Plotinus describes the succession and temporality characteristic of Soul, in contrast to the all-togetherness and eternity (i.e. timelessness) in Intellect, as follows: 'For around Soul things come one after another: now Socrates, now Soul, always some one particular being. But Intellect is all' (V.1.4, 20–2). It seems that the succession he has in mind here is the succession from one particular living being to another, e.g. when one and the same soul is now Socrates' soul and later on the soul of a particular horse.[4] This sort of narrowing of focus is not at all what is at stake when some intelligible content which exists 'all together' in Intellect is elicited into distinct propositions. However, as our pilot passage on this issue, V.8.6, suggests and as we shall see more clearly later on, in the human case the transition from all-togetherness to an inferior kind of thought typically consists in transforming intelligible content into propositionally expressed thoughts.

In any case, Plotinus often bypasses this kind of discursive thought which is characteristic of the World-Soul. He frequently contrasts *noêsis* directly with the searching kind of thought that employs inferences and deliberation (cf. V.8.6–7; VI.2.21, 28–38; VI.7.1–3). So even if discursive thought is not essentially inferential, its defining characteristic being just succession, it would not be unfair to say that in practice inference, temporality, search,

---

[4] Plotinus subscribes to the doctrine of transmigration of souls (cf. e.g. III.2.13, 15; IV.3.8; IV.7.4, 8–14; VI.7.6–7), though it must be admitted that it does not fit very well into his view on the soul in general.

and piecemeal apprehension go hand in hand and are characteristics of discursive thought.

2. Is Non-discursive Thought Propositional?

We have seen, then, that non-discursive thought is all at once, atemporal, of all things together, non-representational, veridical, and possessive of its object. Ignoring what Plotinus says about the thought of the World-Soul, discursive thought is characterized by all the contrary features. Does this imply that non-discursive thought, so understood, is not propositional?

This question may seem to be anachronistic. Surely, Plotinus does not explicitly raise it. The notion of a proposition (as an abstract item with a certain structure as opposed to a sentence, a linguistic item, essentially materially expressed in one way or other) is not one that he had readily available. Nevertheless, the *Enneads* contain some interesting remarks that may have a bearing on his stance on this issue, and in any case the question whether non-discursive thought must be non-propositional has been a matter of a scholarly debate the relevance of which goes beyond the letters of this question. So let me pursue the issue.

It was argued by Lloyd (1970: 263; 1986) that for Plotinus non-discursive thought is so unified that it involves no complexity. Non-discursive thought is so unified that there is no distinction corresponding to the difference between the subject and the predicate essential to propositional thought. Lloyd (1986: 263; cf. 1987: 179), as we already have had occasion to note, takes Plotinus' insistence on the 'all together' and 'all at once' characteristics of non-discursive thought to imply that this type of thought is undifferentiated. For Lloyd, therefore, the 'all together' and the 'all at once' requirements for non-discursive thought amount to non-complexity and thereby to non-propositionality—for any proposition is composed of at least a subject and a predicate. So, according to Lloyd (1970: 261 and *passim*; 1986: 260), being non-inferential is indeed a necessary, but by no means a sufficient, condition of being a non-discursive thought.

Lloyd's position has been forcefully attacked by Richard Sorabji (1982; 1983: 152–6; cf. also Alfino: 1988), who argues that not only the passages in Plato and Aristotle, but also those in Plotinus, that have been taken as evidence of their belief in non-propositional thought, show no such thing. He does not thereby deny the distinction between *noêsis* and *dianoia* in these authors, but it seems to be reduced to the distinction between non-inferential and inferential thought, both of which, however, are propositional according to Sorabji. So non-discursive thought is always like the grasp of an essence in Aristotle, which indeed is non-inferential in the sense that it is not demonstrated, not deduced from superior premisses. The grasp of an essence, however, is the grasp of a proposition expressing an identity, e.g. the proposition 'Man is a rational animal'.

It seems to me that neither Lloyd's nor Sorabji's account is satisfactory. In fact it seems to me that they share a mistaken assumption that leads each of them onto a wrong path, though in different ways. The assumption consists in taking complexity of thought as equivalent to the propositional nature of thought and thereby also, of course, non-complexity as equivalent to non-propositionality. Lloyd reasons that since non-discursive thought is not complex, it has to be non-propositional. Sorabji, on the other hand, reasons that since non-discursive thought is complex, it has to be propositional. So each of them agrees on the equivalence of complexity and propositionality, but they disagree as to whether Intellect's thought is in fact complex or not.

As to Lloyd's view, his claim that the object of non-discursive thought must be undifferentiated is refuted by the numerous passages where Plotinus insists that Intellect's thought is indeed complex, is a thought of many. Statements to this effect occur in virtually every passage where Plotinus discusses Intellect at any length. As already noted, he typically expresses this by saying that Intellect is variegated (*poikilon*). The lines from V.3.10 which engaged us for quite a while in Chapter 2 are as good an example as any:

> Therefore, the thinker must grasp one thing as different from another and the object of thought must contain variety [*poikilon einai*]; or there will not be a thought of it, but only a touching and a sort of contact without speech or thought [*arrêtos kai anoêtos*], prethinking, because Intellect has not yet come into being and that which touches does not think.[5] (V.3.10, 40–4)

There is no doubt that this is Plotinus' standard doctrine. All these passages did not, of course, escape Lloyd's notice, fine and observant scholar as he was. When confronted with their evidence by Sorabji, he (1986: 262) readily admits that 'Plotinus often requires thought to be complex'. He insists (1986: 264), however, that thought in its highest form, when

---

[5] Greek text given in n. 20 to Chapter 2.

nous is most immediately related to the One, is undifferentiated thought. Evidently he wishes thereby to imply that only this highest form of thought is non-discursive, properly so called. Let us consider this more fully.

Disregarding the question whether Lloyd is right in holding that there are instances of undifferentiated thought in Plotinus—a conclusion clearly at odds with Plotinus' insistence in V.3.10 and elsewhere that the object of any thought must be complex (cf. Chapter 2, Section 2)—it remains unquestionable that for Plotinus there is differentiated thought in Intellect, a grasp of many, which he usually calls *noêsis* or *theoria*. This kind of thought he is liable to contrast with another, inferior form of thought, characteristic of the soul, which he describes as discursive (see e.g. III.7.11–12; V.3.4; V.8.6–7). The dichotomy between discursive and non-discursive thought is not at all a dichotomy between what is complex and what is not. As we saw in the passage we set out from, V.8.6, the Egyptian sages make likenesses that contain all at once and all together the properties of the non-discursive wisdom the sages wish to faithfully express. Even if these likenesses are considered to be more unified than a corresponding expression in language, the non-complexity of the likenesses is not at all at issue: we may safely assume that these likenesses are variegated. In general, thought in Intellect is variegated though not thereby propositional or linguistic.

Lloyd (1986: 263) identifies the non-differentiated non-propositional thought with Intellect's grasp of the genus of being, which according to him is undifferentiated in intension though multiple in extension. I simply fail to see clear evidence of this in the *Enneads*. As we saw in Chapter 2, Section 7, in V.3.13 Plotinus indeed makes a point of noting that Intellect's thought of being as such is complex. The passages Lloyd cites in support of his view about the undifferentiated nature of non-discursive thought need not be so understood. His best case is V.3.15, 18–21, which seems to assert that because the intelligibles are 'all together' in Intellect one could not distinguish (*diakrinein*) them.[6] Just a few lines after the ones Lloyd cites, however, Plotinus says: 'But it [the One] had them [the intelligibles] in such a way as not to be distinct: they are distinguished on the second level, in the rational

---

[6] 'Since that which comes [right] after it [the One] shows clearly that it comes [right] after it, because its multiplicity is a one-everywhere; for although it is a multiplicity, it is at the same time in the same, and there is no way you could divide it, because "all things are together".' (Ἐπεὶ δὲ τὸ μετ' αὐτὸ καὶ ὅτι μετ' αὐτὸ δῆλον ποιεῖ τῷ τὸ πλῆθος αὐτοῦ ἓν πανταχοῦ εἶναι· καὶ γὰρ πλῆθος ὂν ὅμως ἐν τῷ αὐτῷ καὶ διακρῖναι οὐκ ἂν ἔχοις, ὅτι ὁμοῦ πάντα.)

form (*logos*). For this is already actuality' (V.3.15, 31–2).[7] So it is peculiar to the One to possess the intelligibles as not distinct. At the second stage they are distinct. This second stage after the One itself is of course the stage of Intellect and being, as is seen from the remark here that 'this is already actuality'. Given these internal difficulties in the interpretation of V.3.15, where Plotinus seems within the space of a few lines to contradict what Lloyd attributes to him, I would not give much weight to these lines as evidence for Plotinus' view.[8]

Even more important than the lack of clear textual evidence, I fail to see how Lloyd's reading could meet the difficulty raised by the abundant evidence for thought in Intellect being variegated. For indeed when Plotinus insists that any object of any thought is variegated, he of course means the intentional object of the thought, the object as grasped—in Intellect there is no external object different from the one that is grasped, save, in a manner of speaking, the One, which strictly speaking is not an object. In saying that Intellect's thought is *poikilos*, variegated, he definitely does not mean that it is complex merely in the sense that many things fall under it extensionally.

So, on the issue of complexity of non-discursive thought I come down on Sorabji's side. Sorabji, however, in my view assumes too quickly that complexity of thought implies the propositional nature of thought. This becomes particularly precarious if thinking propositionally means entertaining a single proposition in one's mind, i.e. mentally asserting just one truth.[9] Thus, I wish to question at least one side of the equivalence statement, i.e. that complexity implies propositionality. As will become clearer in the discussion to come, it is not an altogether simple task to determine whether or not non-discursive thought is propositional for Plotinus. Partly this is

---

[7] V.3.15, 31–2: Ἀλλ᾽ ἄρα οὕτως εἶχεν ὡς μὴ διακεκριμένα· τὰ δ᾽ ἐν τῷ δευτέρῳ διεκέκριτο τῷ λόγῳ. Ἐνέργεια γὰρ ἤδη.

[8] I do not know for sure myself how the question of the inconsistency of V.3.15 with respect to the distinctness of the things in Intellect is best resolved. Perhaps Plotinus intends *diakrinein* in the former case, where he denies that it is possible to *diakrinai* the intelligibles since they are 'all together' (line 21), in the sense of 'separate' or even 'isolate'. He would then be asserting that they are not separated or isolated. This would be so because the intelligibles make up a whole in which every part implies every other. This, however, is compatible with holding that each intelligible is distinct. If this is so, there is no air of inconsistency with Plotinus' standard doctrine. The price is that Plotinus would be using the same word, *diakrinein*, (distinguish, separate), in different senses about the same topic within the space of ten lines.

[9] It is not clear to me whether Sorabji himself regards propositional thought as essentially the thought of a single proposition. His account of Plotinian intellection does in any case not explicitly recognize the kind of 'visual' plurality which (or so I shall argue) constitutes an integral aspect of it. He seems in fact to hold vision itself to be non-propositional, cf. Sorabji (1983: 143).

due to a lack of clarity in the texts but perhaps no less to the fact that we may not be quite clear about what propositional thought amounts to.

So it seems to me that it would be advisable to make a fresh start. As already noted, when talking about non-discursive thought, Plotinus frequently asserts that this kind of thought is variegated. It involves distinctions. It is, to put it briefly, an apprehension of many things. However, he does say things that may be taken to imply that non-discursive thought is non-propositional. In the long quote about the Egyptian sages from V.8.6 that we started this chapter with it is said that true wisdom is not properly expressed by 'statements' or 'propositions' (protaseis, axiômata) (cf. I.2.3, 27–31; V.1.3, 6–9). This looks like a denial of the propositionality of non-discursive thought. We also have the following passage, which indeed is in many ways ambiguous, but deserves laborious scrutiny:

[The intelligibles] are certainly not statements [protaseis] or propositions [axiômata] or sayables [lekta]; for also these would be saying something about other things, and would not be the beings themselves, as for instance 'Justice is beautiful', where 'justice' and 'beauty' themselves are something else.[10] (V.5.1, 38–41)

This translation is of course barely penetrable. This is intentional: I am trying not to prejudge its interpretation. So I shall begin by indicating how I understand it. The list 'statements or propositions or sayables' seems to be intended to include any sort of propositional item that the Aristotelian and Stoic traditions of logic had invoked.[11] Plotinus wants to make sure that the intelligibles are not to be identified with anything of that sort. The Greek of the latter half of the passage allows for different grammatical constructions. The two main alternatives that suggest themselves are: (1) The one given in the translation above; the implied understanding is that if the intelligibles were protaseis etc., they would, because protaseis etc. are essentially linguistic expressions, say something about other things without being these things,

---

[10] V.5.1, 38–41: οὐ γὰρ δὴ προτάσεις οὐδὲ ἀξιώματα οὐδὲ λεκτά· ἤδη γὰρ ἂν καὶ αὐτὰ περὶ ἑτέρων λέγοι, καὶ οὐκ αὐτὰ τὰ ὄντα εἴη, οἷον τὸ δίκαιον καλόν, ἄλλου τοῦ δικαίου καὶ τοῦ καλοῦ ὄντος.

[11] The terms come from Aristotelian and Stoic logic. Aristotle distinguishes between protaseis ('statements','propositions') and axiômata ('basic propositions', 'axioms'), see e.g. An. post. I 72a 8–18. For the Stoics, axiômata are what can be true or false, propositions (cf. Diogenes Laertius, VII, 65), whereas lekta ('sayables') are states of affairs that can be expressed in speech (cf. Sextus Empiricus, Adv. math. VIII, 12). Plotinus does not explicitly call protaseis and axiômata representations of the (true) intelligibles; but the eidôlon mentioned in V.8.6, 10, 'already unfolded and speaking discursively' is almost certainly to be identified with the protaseis and axiômata of lines 5 and 6.

i.e. without being the intelligibles themselves; the proposition 'Justice is beautiful' is an example of this; justice and beauty themselves would be something different from the expression 'Justice is beautiful'. (2) One might also understand these lines as saying that if the intelligibles were *protaseis* etc., they would be predicating something of a thing that is different from that thing, e.g. predicating beauty of justice; thus, a proposition such as 'Justice is beautiful' fails to be a true intelligible because it is a composite, for obviously justice and beauty are two different intelligibles each in their own right. I believe that this latter paraphrase captures Lloyd's (1986: 261–2) understanding of these lines. We may summarize the difference between the two interpretations as follows: the former rejects *protaseis* etc. as the true intelligibles because they are representations, they stand for something else; the latter rejects them because they are essentially complex.

Lloyd (1986: 261–2) has the following argument going for his reading: the Stoic *lekta* are included among the items Plotinus says the intelligibles cannot be; the Stoic *lekta*, however, are never expressions, always what is or can be expressed; so Plotinus' point cannot be that the intelligibles are not expressions. Plotinus does not use the word *lekton* elsewhere, but it is clear from his other uses of *protasis* and *axiôma* in contexts similar to the one here that he takes them to be representations, things that express something other than themselves (see e.g. I.3.4–5 and V.8.5–6). But if Plotinus holds that *protaseis* and *axiômata* are kinds of expressions, he most likely holds the same of *lekta*, since he deals with all three at once in the same critical comment. Lloyd is of course right in holding that such an understanding of the *lekton* is hardly correct Stoicism. But as Lloyd himself notes, *lekta* came to be confused with thoughts.[12] And, contra Lloyd (1986: 262, n. 6), they were even confused with mere expressions: Philoponus attributes such a view to the Stoics (*In* An. pr., 2, 243, 4). So it is not at all impossible that Plotinus understands *lekton* as an expression of some sort.

So we should beware of being overly hasty in attributing to Plotinus the denial of propositionality to non-discursive thought on the basis of its not being *protaseis*, *axiômata*, or *lekta*. Thought by means of language is representational and it is also propositional. Might not such passages as we have been considering from V.8.6 and V.5.1 that seem to deny the propositionality of non-discursive thought really rather be denials of representationality?

---

[12] See Lloyd (1986: 262). He refers to Ammonius, *In* De Int. 17, 24–8 and Simplicius, *In* Cat. 10, 3–4.

Certainly the issue of the non-representational character of the intelligibles is a point in the context of both these passages. Plotinus' main point is to insist that the intuitive grasp of the intelligibles is a grasp of the very intelligibles themselves without the aid of proxies; hence, the rejection of statements, propositions, and sayables as the true intelligibles: these are all proxies in his view.

I don't suppose Plotinus had a clear distinction between sentences and propositions. For all I know he may have taken statements, propositions, and sayables to be essentially something linguistic, e.g. a sentence. Sentences are certainly representations but, it may be retorted, they express propositions. Might it not be the representational nature of sentences rather than propositional structure as such that Plotinus wished to deny to non-discursive thought?

An affirmative answer to this question would open up the following possibility: non-discursive thought, being the grasp of the things themselves as opposed to images or representations of these things, is the grasp of propositions, unmediated by language or other proxies. This proposal of course presupposes that Intellect itself, the true Platonic universe, is propositionally structured, that it is made up of propositions. This is a possible view, but I don't think it is Plotinus'. He normally talks about the intelligible world in substance terms: the primary items there are always thing-like (even if these 'things' are parts of a whole), not states of affairs or propositions. As we have seen, he himself admittedly uses propositions to describe the content of Intellect, and sometimes he metaphorically uses verbs such as 'to speak' about Intellect's thinking. However, as V.8.6 makes clear, Intellect's thinking does not rely on the order of words or anything essentially linguistic—on this I am in perfect agreement with Lloyd. So I conclude that in the passages we have seen that may seem to reject the propositional nature of non-discursive thought, Plotinus is really denying that they are linguistic expressions. But I don't think that he conceives of ultimate reality as a set of propositions either.

3. Non-discursive Thought and Perceptual Imagery

Plotinus resorts to highly metaphorical language when attempting to account for Intellect's mode of thought. As we have seen in previous chapters, he regularly uses the vocabulary of vision to describe the Intellect and its activities. Not only is its thinking often called 'seeing', the intellect itself is 'sight' (*opsis*) in its inchoate state and 'vision' (*horasis*) in its active mode.

Plotinus is of course not the first Greek philosopher to employ ocular metaphors in connection with thinking and knowledge. Plato and Aristotle too abound in them. We are here confronted with the famous ocular metaphors that Richard Rorty (1979: 162–3 and *passim*), following Heidegger and Dewey, makes so much of in his account of the history of Western philosophy and how it all went wrong. It is well known to scholars of ancient philosophy, but apparently not appreciated by philosophers generally, that the perceptual imagery for the mind in the Platonic-Aristotelian tradition is by no means confined to vision. Nor are the metaphors that are called upon to describe knowledge and the methods of getting it all perceptual: they are of all sorts.[13] Although his account of the intellect is primarily modelled on vision, Aristotle appeals significantly to touch as well to account for how knowledge of essences cannot go wrong.[14] The language of touch is also quite conspicuous in some Platonic passages describing our contact with ultimate reality such as *Symposium* 212c, and even more clearly in *Republic* VI, 490a–b. The kind of touch Plato has in mind is fairly explicitly sexual contact: the wisdom-lover's most intimate knowledge of the truly real, the Ideas, is likened to having a sexual intercourse with it, and this is naturally a contact that is bound to bear fruit (true virtue). In Plotinus too we find tactual, erotic language, mostly in connection with contact with the One, not in connection with thinking and knowledge as such (cf. V.3.10, 40–4; V.3.17, 25–36; VI.7.39, 15–20; VI.9.11, 24). In the light of this, Rorty's (1979: 39) ironical remark, presumably pointing at the arbitrariness of philosophical visual metaphors, that 'some nameless pre-Socratic, is responsible for viewing [knowledge of universals] as *looking* at something (rather than, say, rubbing up against it, or crushing

---

[13] In Plato the search for the definition of justice in *Republic* II–IV as well as that for the definition of the sophist in the *Sophist* are described with the aid of metaphors from hunting: the search for knowledge is like pursuing a wild animal; getting the knowledge is then presumably like locating the animal, if not killing it. Then there is the famous midwifery metaphor in the *Theaetetus*, which seems to equate the acquisition of knowledge with the birth of a healthy child. In Stoicism the main metaphors tend in the direction of grasping things and getting a solid hold of them, cf. the famous story about Zeno's gestures with his hands reported by Cicero, *Acad.* II, 145 = Long and Sedley (1987), 41. The central term in Stoic epistemology is *katalêpsis*, which contains the root of *lambanein*, 'to take'.

[14] *Meta.* IX, 1051b 23–4. Cf. also XII, 1072b 21, where Aristotle appeals to contact in explaining how thought and its object are the same.

it underfoot, or having sexual intercourse with it', somehow misses the mark. The Greeks had a variety of metaphors to describe 'the better sort of knowledge', some of which were indeed fairly explicitly erotic.

It is not my purpose here to enter into a general discussion of perceptual imagery in Greek philosophy, still less into a discussion of the consequences of this imagery for the subsequent philosophical tradition and the way we all think about knowledge and reality today. Let it be said, though, that the Platonic–Aristotelian tradition has no single sphere that serves as a source of metaphors for knowledge. Although visual metaphors are quite prominent, they are by no means alone on the scene. It does not strike me that the Greek philosophers were unwitting in their choice of metaphorical language. In general they knew well what they were doing, and there is no reason to suppose that they were in general misled by their metaphors or unaware of their limitations. They would use visual ones to describe certain things, when it seemed to them that these fitted best. On other occasions some other metaphors were deemed more apt.

According to a plausible view of ordinary vision, which Plotinus in fact seems to endorse, vision's grasp of sensible objects is immediate (cf. IV.5.4, 36–44 and Emilsson 1988: 123–4), it is of these objects themselves (cf. Chapter 3, Section 1), and it is of a manifold of them (or their parts) at once (cf. IV.4.7, 7 ff.). Plotinus does not directly address the question whether vision is primarily propositional or a grasp of an object, whether it is 'seeing *that* p' or seeing an object. He seems to take it for granted that the primary object of vision is qualified things or colours and shapes (II.6.2, 17; II.8.1, 13–16). In general, to perceive is to receive the form of an external object in one's soul (IV.4.23, 3; 32). So far this looks like an object-oriented doctrine. He, however, also identifies sense-perceptions with *kriseis*, judgements (III.6.1, 1–3; IV.4.23, 38 ff.). This may rather suggest a propositional account. I suspect that he never pondered the question which of these alternatives is the more basic but thought that one could both see a thing and see that the thing is such and such, as indeed ordinary language suggests. Much, however, speaks in favour of supposing that if pressed, he would have said that a direct exposure to a variegated object is the basic form of vision and sense-perception generally. At least the idea that the object of vision is laid out for us with all its qualities together but yet spatially separated plays an important role for him in comparing and contrasting ordinary and intellectual vision (cf. V.3.9, 30; V.9.9, 14–16).

Let us follow this up by an example. When I enter a room for the first time, for instance, I may see a table with a fruit bowl on it; there are four chairs around it, a carpet on the floor, walls and a ceiling, a window; and much more. I see all these things right away. I might even leave the room or close my eyes and respond correctly to questions about what was in the room and how it was arranged. We have seen that non-discursive thought accomplishes something analogous. It thinks the intelligibles themselves without mediation and it thinks them as a whole all at once.

Prompted by the foregoing considerations, I now wish to lay down two hypotheses. The first, and the more general one, is that Plotinus transfers the above-mentioned features of ordinary vision to the thought of the intelligibles, *mutatis mutandis*. That is to say, the complexity of vision, its all-at-once character, and its immediacy are taken to be characteristics of non-discursive thought. The fact that much of the language Plotinus uses about Intellect's apprehension of the intelligibles is directly taken over from vision makes this hypothesis prima facie plausible: visual language metaphorically applied to the grasp of intelligibles should follow the logic of non-metaphorical visual language at least so long as we don't have a specific reason to think otherwise. Furthermore, this hypothesis seems reasonable in the light of the fact that Plotinus goes in for a theory that posits intelligible objects that are essentially complex as what is ultimately real. If these objects are to be known, themselves as they are, the knower should grasp them as they are in their complexity without any mediation. Thus, there should be at the intelligible level something analogous to the vision at the sensible level. For vision manages something tantamount with respect to sensible objects.

This is not to say that the analogy between vision and non-discursive thought is perfect: for, as we have seen in the two previous chapters, there is a much more intimate relationship between thinker and object of thought than there is of sight and the object of vision; secondly, the intelligible object is after all a rather different sort of thing than the sensible one; seeing the former all at once in its complexity is not the same thing as seeing the sensible object all at once in its complexity. I shall explore some of the salient differences in this regard here below.

The second hypothesis, which in fact may be seen as a particular instance of the first one, is that non-discursive thought is just as propositional or non-propositional as ordinary vision is. Given the prominence of visual language in Plotinus' accounts of Intellect's thought, it strikes me as an initially plausible assumption that intellection should be like vision in this respect. That this should be so also gets some support from the passage from V.8.6 about the Egyptian sages that we started this discussion with. Having explained that the sages didn't bother about writing down their wisdom in a form reflecting language and made likenesses instead, Plotinus says that 'they manifested the non-discursiveness of the object, since each likeness would then be a kind of knowledge and wisdom, an underlying subject which comes all at once, and not a discourse or deliberation.' The sense in which the likeness is all at once and not a discourse or deliberation is the sense in which visible objects in general come all at once non-discursively and are so grasped by the power of sight. So we should expect that the intelligible object, which the likeness is relevantly similar to—this is the very point of bringing it in at all—is non-discursive in a similar way.

It is tempting to take this thought one step further, even if there is, so far as I can tell, not any explicit evidence for exactly this point in the *Enneads*. A reason for using vision as a metaphor for non-discursive thought is to convey the idea that the grasp of the conceptual relations between a whole array of concepts may be analogous to the grasp of spatial relations in vision: somehow the very experience of thinking non-discursively has about it a clarity and immediacy concerning multiple conceptual relationships that vision has about spatial ones. As already said, Plotinus never says anything of this sort directly. It seems to me, however, that some thought like this must lie behind his insistence on the holism of the intelligible world: the relations between the items in it are laid out for thought and they are clear to the subject as the spatial relations between the things in ordinary vision are clear. This must be the deep point of the visual imaginary combined with holism. It is this kind of distinctness and clarity about relations Plotinus wishes to insist on for Intellect, while at the same time asking us to remove spatial associations from the picture. In a different mood and context Plotinus is like other Platonists liable to contrast thought (including discursive thought) and sense-perception: in comparison with the former, vision is unclear and confused, and doesn't reveal the reasons for its objects being as they are (VI.3.18, 1–15), objects that are in any case ontologically derivative. Such denigrations of vision are, however, primarily due to vision's poor performance in conceptual relations. They do not affect the fact that vision's grasp of multiple spatial relations can be used as an analogy to suggest salient features of the non-discursive grasp of intelligible relations. It is tempting to borrow Sellars's phrase 'the space of reasons' to communicate this. We should then say that non-discursive thought sees everything in its proper place in a space of reasons, and it sees this whole space.

There is a noteworthy passage in VI.4.11, 12–17 that brings forth some of Plotinus' views on perceptual metaphors applied to intelligibles. Interestingly, this passage does not appeal to vision as such as a model for understanding the thought of Intellect, but rather to the unity of experience provided by different senses:

For the eye perceives the colour, the smell, the fragrance, and other different senses different things, coming from the same [sensible object], which exist all together, but not separately. Is that first [Intellect], then, variegated and many? Yes, but the variegated is also simple, and the many one.[15] (VI.4.11, 12–17)

As is evident from the surrounding lines, 'that first' in this context is Intellect. The fragrance and the colour of an apple, say, come from the same body, the apple. In the apple they are not spatially distinct. Nevertheless, there is a distinct perception of each. Plotinus is suggesting that these facts can shed light on Intellect's thought. It seems that by this analogy Plotinus is in one breath denying the spatiality of the intelligibles, as it is natural for him to do, since the intelligibles are not in space, while at the same time insisting on their distinctness: even if 'all are in one' spatially speaking, they are perceived as distinct, as indeed they are; they are 'all together', yet distinct. The passage suggests an epistemic distinctness that is not at the same time a spatial distinctness, but one that invokes a 'phenomenological region' that contains an array of distinct items that may be grasped all together. Thus, the passage avoids the spatiality of vision, while retaining its variedness. Perhaps this result is obtained at some expense to the feature of integrity of experience in which the relations between the apprehended items are all clearly laid out. Nevertheless, this passage taken together with purely visual metaphors is quite suggestive about how Plotinus wishes to conceive of Intellect's thought.

My vision of the room in the example above is an integrated experience in which all the spatial relations form a single but variegated whole.

---

[15] VI.4.11, 12–17: Ἐπεὶ καὶ ἀπὸ τοῦ αὐτοῦ ὁ μὲν ὀφθαλμὸς εἶδε τὸ χρῶμα, ἡ δὲ ὄσφρησις τὸ εὐῶδες, ἄλλη δὲ αἴσθησις ἄλλο, ὁμοῦ πάντων, ἀλλ' οὐ χωρὶς ὄντων. Οὐκοῦν ἐκεῖνο ποικίλον καὶ πολύ; Ἢ τὸ ποικίλον ἁπλοῦν αὖ, καὶ τὰ πολλὰ ἕν. Λόγος γὰρ εἷς καὶ πολύς, καὶ πᾶν τὸ ὂν ἕν.

But couldn't it still be propositional? This is indeed a tricky question. Somebody might point out that there is more than one type of 'ordinary vision'. Entering a room without looking for, or expecting, anything in particular and just seeing what meets the eye there may be rather different from opening the door and looking for a matchbox and eventually noticing one on the windowsill. The latter seems to be more singular than the less specific experience of just looking into the room. We might express the content of the experience of seeing the matchbox by a single proposition: 'The matchbox lies on the windowsill.' I may see *that* the matchbox is on the windowsill. This too is, of course, a case of quite ordinary vision. Should we say that this type of vision, 'seeing that', is propositional while the former kind perhaps isn't? I don't think so. Ordinary vision, whether indefinite or catching sight of a specific state of affairs, is variegated. When I notice that a matchbox lies on the windowsill, I also see many other things and am aware of many more facts: facts about colours, shades, sizes, relations, and usually some other objects as well that are not included in the proposition that the matchbox is on the windowsill. The visual experience is not exhausted by any proposition that expresses a single fact that I see. I might of course try to pack all this additional content into a grammatically or logically single proposition (however complex). Still, the possibility of doing so does not constitute a sufficient reason for holding that the vision itself is propositional. At any rate, when we see we do not consciously go through a complex proposition in our minds expressing all the facts that we see. We may of course do that, but that would be afterwards and it would be something done in addition to mere seeing.

Could we then instead describe seeing as the grasp of a number of propositions all at once? I suppose we could. The problem is, however, that this doesn't conform well to ordinary experiences of vision. Although there is no denying that propositions can be elicited from vision, and granting even that a proposition may be an object of vision, as when we see that something is the case, the underlying visual experience itself seems to lack the elements most naturally associated with entertaining propositions: to entertain a proposition in one's mind involves entertaining a subject term and a predicate term of one or more places; this is done by means of language either expressly or tacitly in one's mind. Vision itself, on the other hand, doesn't seem to involve any of this. The visual experience of seeing a white and brown matchbox doesn't break into the different components 'matchbox', 'white', and 'brown' related in such a way as to form a well-formed proposition. So, if it still seems tempting to insist that vision must be propositional, this has nothing to do with the conscious experience of seeing. Its propositional nature must be unconscious. This would be claimed for theoretical reasons alone, the primary one no doubt being that since a typical way of learning the truth of propositions is by seeing certain things, therefore, it is felt, the experience by means of which we learn this must itself be propositional. However, it seems to me that such an inference is by no means necessary and is, in fact, rather implausible.

If, as I have hinted, vision is not propositional, would it follow that it isn't conceptual either? Again, the very meaning of the question is unclear. Some philosophers understand 'propositional' and 'conceptual' as twin notions that are bound to go hand in hand, concepts understood as essentially being elements in propositions and propositions as concepts structured in a certain way. This is hard to quarrel with, if the terms are so defined. As I see it, however, there is no good, intuitive, non-question-begging reason for supposing the conceptual should be so limited. In any case, *intellectual vision* as I interpret it is definitely conceptual, which is tantamount to saying that it has an intelligible content, and of course intellectual vision has that: its objects, the intelligibles, are something of the order of concepts. What is question-begging is the view that conceptual relations must have a propositional structure. In fact, what Plotinus seems to be suggesting is a vision-like experience of the region of concepts or intelligibles that is not structured in the manner of propositions.

In Plotinus we find a notion of non-discursive thought that explicitly has all the features I have been laying out. It is directed at the things themselves rather than at proxies; it is directed at these things in their totality. Indeed, seeing any given such thing is seeing it in relation to everything else—this is what constitutes 'seeing' it (cf. V.8.4, 21–7; IV.9.5, 12–22). Its apprehension of these things is not broken up into separate components so that e.g. grasping the intelligible Horse is a matter of identifying the Horse independently and then entertaining about it any or all of the predicates that are true of it. Rather, grasping beauty is a matter of 'seeing' a lot of things, 'all together'. We shall inquire further into just how in the next section.

4. The Holism of Intellect

In the previous section we have seen how ordinary vision takes a manifold object and we have given some hints about how this may have served as a model for what Plotinus wishes to say about the intelligible world and the vision of it. At the very least vision presents us with several things at once and shows us how they are related in space. Intellectual vision shares the feature of presenting many at once in a fixed order and place. The holism Plotinus claims for Intellect, however, goes well beyond what can be said of any ordinary sight. In this section, I wish to inquire into the nature of this holism. Let us start by looking at a passage from V.8 that belongs to the same discussion as the Egyptian priests passage we set out from.

For all things there [in the intelligible world] are transparent, and there is nothing dark or opaque; everything and all things are clear to the inmost part to everything; for light is transparent to light. Each there has everything in itself and sees all things in every other, so that all are everywhere and each and every one is all and the glory is unbounded. ... the sun there is all the stars, and each star is the sun and all the others. A different kind of being stands out in each, but in each all are manifest.[16] (V.8.4, 4–11)

The view expressed here that 'each is all' certainly looks strange. It is however perhaps less queer than it may at first sight seem. Plotinus says here that each of the intelligibles is all the others, but 'a different kind of being stands out in each'. I take it that this is the same doctrine as he elsewhere expresses by saying that each of the intelligibles implicitly contains all the others (VI.2.20, 20–3). Even if he nowhere gives us all the details, it is not at all difficult to follow his thought here in general outline. He evidently believes in a thoroughgoing holism about the intelligible world, which he expresses quite forcefully e.g. in VI.7.2. This means that if we were to understand any one item in it, we should have to bring in all the rest. So when he says that the sun is all the stars, he presumably means that

---

[16] V.8.4, 4–11: διαφανῆ γὰρ πάντα καὶ σκοτεινὸν οὐδὲ ἀντίτυπον οὐδέν, ἀλλὰ πᾶς παντὶ φανερὸς εἰς τὸ εἴσω καὶ πάντα· φῶς γὰρ φωτί. Καὶ γὰρ ἔχει πᾶς πάντα ἐν αὑτῷ, καὶ αὖ ὁρᾷ ἐν ἄλλῳ πάντα, ὥστε πανταχοῦ πάντα καὶ πᾶν πᾶν καὶ ἕκαστον πᾶν καὶ ἄπειρος ἡ αἴγλη· ἕκαστον γὰρ αὐτῶν μέγα· ἐπεὶ καὶ τὸ μικρὸν μέγα· καὶ ἥλιος ἐκεῖ πάντα ἄστρα, καὶ ἕκαστον ἥλιος αὖ καὶ πάντα. Ἐξέχει δ' ἐν ἑκάστῳ ἄλλο, ἐμφαίνει δὲ καὶ πάντα.

an account of what the sun really is would have to bring in the stars: an exhaustive account of the sun, 'the sun is ...', where the blank was filled with everything that pertains to the nature of the sun, would include a reference to the stars; the stars are a part of what makes the sun what it is. He is not suggesting, I take it, that in the intelligible world to be the sun is the very same thing as to be e.g. the Evening Star or that the Evening Star is an attribute of the sun (for this claim seems to imply that the sun would just as much be an attribute of the Evening Star, which is absurd). The claim here must rather be that an account of each thing involves all the others; that 'a different kind of being stands out in each' just means that we could put the focus on anyone we like and say what it is, all the rest would enter into that account. This is very much the kind of world Leibniz envisaged in e.g. *Discourse on Metaphysics* §9 and *Monadology* §59. In Intellect, however, not only is it the case that the stars would enter into an account of the sun; in intellectually seeing the sun intellect sees the stars.

Plotinus' holism is tied to a certain view about causes or reasons in Intellect. To see how this comes about, let us consider the following lines from VI.7.2:

> For we [with our limited sight of the intelligible] grant that it [Intellect] has the 'that' but not the 'why', or, if we do grant it the 'why', it has it as separate [from the 'that']. And we see man or, if it happens so, an eye, as an image or something pertaining to an image. But in reality there [in the intelligible] there is man and the reason why there is man, if the man there must also be intellectual, and an eye and the reason why there is an eye; or they would not be there at all, if the reason why was not. ... But there [in the intelligible] all are in one, so that the thing and the reason why of the thing coincide.[17] (VI.7.2, 3–12)

I take it that the main claim here is that the questions 'Why is there man?' or 'Why does man have eyes?' coincide with the questions 'What is man?' or 'What is an eye?' Following Aristotle, Plotinus notes himself that even in the sensible realm there are cases where the 'that' (*hoti*) and the 'why'

---

[17] VI.7.2, 3–12: Τὸ μὲν γὰρ ὅτι δίδομεν αὐτὸν ἔχειν, τὸ δὲ "διότι" οὐκέτι, ἤ, εἰ δοίημεν, χωρίς. Καὶ ὁρῶμεν ἄνθρωπον ἢ ὀφθαλμόν, εἰ τύχοι, ὥσπερ ἄγαλμα ἢ ἀγάλματος· τὸ δέ ἐστιν ἐκεῖ ἄνθρωπος καὶ διὰ τί ἄνθρωπος, εἴπερ καὶ νοερὸν αὐτὸν δεῖ τὸν ἐκεῖ ἄνθρωπον εἶναι, καὶ ὀφθαλμὸς καὶ διὰ τί· ἢ οὐκ ἂν ὅλως εἴη, εἰ μὴ διὰ τί. Ἐνταῦθα δὲ ὥσπερ ἕκαστον τῶν μερῶν χωρίς, οὕτω καὶ τὸ "διὰ τί". Ἐκεῖ δ' ἐν ἑνὶ πάντα, ὥστε ταὐτὸν τὸ πρᾶγμα καὶ τὸ "διὰ τί" τοῦ πράγματος. Πολλαχοῦ δὲ καὶ ἐνταῦθα τὸ πρᾶγμα καὶ τὸ "διὰ τί" ταὐτόν, οἷον τί ἐστιν ἔκλειψις.

(*dioti*) coincide, e.g. in the case of the eclipse: an eclipse is, in Aristotle's words, 'the privation of the moon's light by the interposition of the earth' (*An. post.* II, 90a 15–18; cf. *Meta.* VIII, 1044b 9–15). In addition to saying what an eclipse is, this account also states its cause, the reason why there is an eclipse. In the intelligible world everything is supposed to be such that the 'what' and the 'why' coincide.

The intuitive idea here is no doubt considerations to the effect that an account of what a given object is must bring in the whole of which it is a part. If one is to say what an eye is or what a given type of eye is, one would have to say something about the nature of an animal and, in the particular case, say something about the nature of the kind of animal which has the given kind of eye. Such considerations answer the question what the given kind of eye is. Is it for instance an eye fit for hunting or an eye that catches a wide horizon so as to make the animal fit to notice and flee from a predator? These considerations, however, also answer the question why there is such an eye: this is explained by the kind of animal in question. Now the Intellect as a whole is, according to Plotinus, an organism of a kind. So the same sort of considerations that apply to parts and wholes of ordinary animals apply to the intelligibles and Intellect at large. So what is here asserted about animals and their parts holds for the intelligible world at large: the causes or reasons for the parts are immanent in the wholes; so if one knows the wholes, and especially if one knows a given whole and its intelligible context, one knows that it will contain such and such parts.

In the passage from V.8 we started this section with, it was said that the sun is all the stars; it was suggested that this means that the stars would have to enter into an account of what the sun is. In the second passage cited we saw that in Intellect each thing contains its reasons or that the reasons for it are contained in what it is. If we put the two passages together, we get the picture that the way a given intelligible, F, is everything according to the former passage, is by having everything else among the reasons for its being such as it is, reasons which in fact constitute what F is. So what F is is determined by F's place in the system of intelligibles. This obviously raises the question whether the being of F is exhausted by these relations to the others or whether F is something in and of itself independently of these relations. So far as I can tell there is no text that settles the matter.

Plotinus sometimes uses an analogy of a science and its theorems to illustrate the holism of Intellect: each theorem of a science implicitly contains the whole science (III.9.2, 1–3; IV.3.2, 50–5; IV.9.5, 12–21; V.9.8, 5–7; VI.2.20).[18] In VI.2.20 he discusses this analogy at considerable length. I think it is worthwhile to consider what he has to say in some detail:

Let us then grasp that the intellect which in no way applies itself to partial things and is not active about anything in particular exists, so that it may not become a particular intellect, like the science before the specific, partial sciences, and the science in specific form before the parts of it. No science is [the science of] any of its specific [contents] but the power of all of them; each is actually science and potentially each specific content. And the same is true of universal science: the specific sciences, which lie potentially in the whole, those, that is, which grasp the specific contents, are potentially the whole; for the whole is predicated of them, not a part of the whole; yet it must certainly be pure and independent. Thus, we can certainly say that universal intellect exists in one way—that is the one before those which are actually the particular intellects—and particular intellects in another, those which are partial and filled from all. But Intellect ranging over all of them leads the particular intellects, but is the power of them and contains them in its universality. They, on the other hand, in their partial selves contain the universal intellect, as a particular science contains the science.[19] (VI.2.20, 1–16)

This passage seems to invoke three levels of science: (1) The universal science which is not of anything in particular; (2) particular sciences such as geometry or musical theory; and (3) particular scientific knowledge, or theorems. The relationship between (1) and (2) and between (2) and (3) is such that the more particular contains the more general, which is predicated of it; and the more general contains the more particular in the sense of being the power of producing them or containing them potentially. The same kind of relationship is supposed to hold between the universal intellect and the particular intellects.

---

[18] For illuminating discussions of this analogy, see Tornau (1998) and Nikulin (2005).

[19] VI.2.20, 1–16: Λάβωμεν οὖν τὸν μὲν εἶναι νοῦν οὐδὲν ἐφαπτόμενον τῶν ἐν μέρει οὐδ᾽ ἐνεργοῦντα περὶ ὁτιοῦν, ἵνα μὴ τὶς νοῦς γίγνοιτο, ὥσπερ ἐπιστήμη πρὸ τῶν ἐν μέρει εἰδῶν, καὶ ἡ ἐν εἴδει δὲ ἐπιστήμη πρὸ τῶν ἐν αὐτῇ μερῶν· πᾶσα μὲν οὐδὲν τῶν ἐν μέρει δύναμις πάντων, ἕκαστον δὲ ἐνεργείᾳ ἐκεῖνο, καὶ δυνάμει δὲ πάντα, καὶ ἐπὶ τῆς καθόλου ὡσαύτως· αἱ μὲν ἐν εἴδει, αἲ ἐν τῇ ὅλῃ δυνάμει κεῖνται, αἱ δὴ τὸ ἐν εἴδει λαβοῦσαι, δυνάμει εἰσὶν ἡ ὅλη· κατηγορεῖται γὰρ ἡ πᾶσα, οὐ μόριον τῆς πάσης· αὐτήν γε μὴν δεῖ ἀκέραιον ἐφ᾽ αὐτῆς εἶναι. Οὕτω δὴ ἄλλως μὲν νοῦν τὸν ξύμπαντα εἰπεῖν εἶναι, τὸν πρὸ τῶν καθέκαστον ἐνεργείᾳ ὄντων, ἄλλως δὲ νοῦς ἑκάστους, τοὺς μὲν ἐν μέρει ἐκ πάντων πληρωθέντας, τὸν δ᾽ ἐπὶ πᾶσι νοῦν χορηγὸν μὲν τοῖς καθέκαστα, δύναμιν δὲ αὐτῶν εἶναι καὶ ἔχειν ἐν τῷ καθόλου ἐκείνους, ἐκείνους τε αὖ ἐν αὐτοῖς ἐν μέρει οὖσιν ἔχειν τὸν καθόλου, ὡς ἡ τὶς ἐπιστήμη τὴν ἐπιστήμην. The text seems to be somewhat corrupt, though not so as to affect the sense in a very serious way. What is given here is the H-S² text as usual.

Before proceeding any further, let me clarify what is meant by 'universal intellect' and 'particular intellect' in this passage. The first lines of the next chapter, VI.2.21, make clear that the universal intellect is the thought that comprises the highest kinds (see Chapter 2, Section 6), whereas the particular intellects are equivalent with more particular intelligibles. The question may be raised whether the account of the relationship between the universal science and the partial ones, and the universal intellect and the particular ones doesn't add support to Lloyd's view that at its peak Intellect's thought is undifferentiated and simple (cf. p. 187) for Plotinus says here in VI.2.20, 1–3 that it isn't about anything in particular; it may seem that differentiation first comes with the particular intellects. But this is not so. The universal intellect may in a sense not be directed at anything in particular. It is, however, *per se* directed at being as such (cf. VI.2.8, 14–16): being as such, however, is in a sense nothing in particular. But if the universal intellect is directed at being as such, it also involves the thought of the other primary genera (see Chapter 2, Section 6). So the thought of being as such is indeed complex.

Two important questions that arise in connection with our passage are in what sense the part is potentially in the whole and in what sense the whole is potentially in the part. The key to the answer to both of them lies in another and earlier passage, where Plotinus uses the science analogy, but this time to explain the relationship between the hypostasis Soul and individual souls, IV.9.5. This latter relationship is in fact closely related to the relationship between Intellect and partial intellects, so that it is in itself not surprising that the same analogical explanation is used for both (cf. IV.3.2, 50–5). Here Plotinus explains that when a geometer holds a given theorem in his mind, 'Also there [in the science of geometry] what is brought forth for use is indeed by its activity/actuality (*energeiai* [dat.]) a part, and this stands out; but the others [i.e. the other theorems] follow unnoticed in virtue of the power but they are all there in the part' (IV.9.5, 13–15). He explains this further by noting that holding a particular theorem in mind in isolation from the rest of the science, 'will no longer be by art or scientific, but like a child was talking' (21–2).

It emerges from this that the sense of science Plotinus has in mind is not geometry or grammar abstracted from anybody's mastery of it. On the contrary, it is the science as incorporated in the scientist's soul. Accordingly, the sense in which the whole is in the part is a sense which brings in the mind of the scientist engaged in the science. But, even so, how are we to think of the whole science as all at once actual in the scientist's mind, as Plotinus suggests (IV.9.5, 17; IV.3.2, 50–5)? In a recent article Christian Tornau (1998) sheds much light on this question. What I have to say about the science analogy here below largely reflects his conclusions.

What the geometer possesses is according to Plotinus a power (*dynamis*) in the sense of a capacity to produce particular theorems. As generally in Plotinus, however, a power is at the same time an *energeia*: considered as the cause of something else it is liable to be described as a power, considered in itself it is an activity (cf. Chapter 1, Section 1, (6)). Tornau (99) notes that mastering geometry implies the equal mastery of all the propositions it contains at once and that 'it is in this sense that Plotinus says that inside the scientist's soul all the propositions are active and actual'. They are all equally ready for use. There is surely a certain twist of Aristotle's *dynamis/energeia* relationship taking place here: as we noted in Chapter 1, Plotinus takes it that the exercise of a capacity presupposes a prior level of activity in which the capacity consists, whereas for Aristotle the exercise seems to be prior (cf. Chapter I, Section 7). But what might this activity be? Tornau (102) mentions 'die Beherrschung der Wissenschaft'. That seems reasonable. But how are we to conceive of the mastery of a science as an activity?

Plotinus says nothing very explicit about this, but it could be argued that the mastery of a science constitutes a determinate state in the scientist's soul: the scientist's soul is such that not merely is the scientist prone to think certain particular propositions, he thinks them by virtue of already being active in thinking some other thoughts from which these particular propositions flow. These other thoughts would be something like the thoughts of the principles of the science. By this I do not mean to suggest an express thought of a given axiom or set of axioms of the science from which the scientist deduces the particular thought. Rather I am thinking of a more general state of mind, the state of mind which constitutes general understanding of the principles of the science. Being in such a state is not to think particular propositions of the science, but being in a state that allows the scientist to think any proposition he chooses with scientific understanding.

So, to return to our two questions: for the one who is in the state of mind of mastering a science, the particular theorems are readily available. They can be brought forth at will. This shows that they are present in the mastery of the science in general though they may not be explicitly activated. And conversely, for one who masters the science in this way the entertainment of a single theorem brings with it, for almost trivial reasons, the whole science: nobody who doesn't master the whole science could entertain the theorem in *this* scientific way, with *this* understanding of it. So the particular thought of this theorem contains the thoughts that constitute the mastery of the science in general, which in turn contains the thought of any other theorem of the science.

I suppose that Plotinus' remark in VI.2.20 that 'The specific sciences ... are potentially the whole; for the whole is predicated of them' is to be seen in the light of the same view of science. That is to say, the point is not, or not merely, that geometry is science or a science. It is rather that the one who really masters the science of geometry also masters scientific knowledge in general. If not, his general geometrical thoughts would be like 'a child talking'. So to master, say, geometry, is to master scientific knowledge in general, i.e. to master geometrical knowledge is to master general scientific knowledge. That is the sense in which science as such is predicated of a branch of science.

Two interesting points in addition emerge from the preceding discussion: (1) The passage from IV.9.5 speaks about the relationship between a science as a state of the scientist's soul and the thought of a particular theorem in such a way that the latter emerges as an offshoot, a kind of second act, of the former.[20] (2) The passage we started out from, VI.2.20, is to be interpreted along the same lines: the partial science incorporates the whole science in the same way as suggested in IV.9.5, that is to say, when the part is active it is active by a general power that is the same for all the parts. Hence, it contains the power or capacity that can produce all the others and thus may be said to be potentially any of the others.

The foregoing comparison with the sciences is supposed to shed light on the way the intelligibles are 'all together' and on the way each can be said to contain all. One question that arises here is whether Plotinus thinks that the part/whole relationships in Intellect work in every respect just like in the sciences according to his view of science, or whether the

---

[20] Tornau (98 ff.) links the relationship between the possession of a science and individual theorems to the Stoic doctrine of the *prophorikos logos* in contradistinction to the *logos en tēi psychēi*. Cf. Sextus Empiricus, *Adv. math.* VIII, 278. See also Plotinus, V.1.3, 6–10, where the relationship between Intellect and soul is compared with the relationship between *logos* in soul and what he calls *logos en prophorai*, cf. also I.2.3, 26–8.

science analogy is merely intended to shed light on certain aspects of the relationships in Intellect. In other words, is the science analogy genuinely an analogy or is scientific knowledge, as Plotinus conceives of it, really just a familiar case of what it is supposed to throw light on? Are we here faced rather with an instance than a mere analogy?

The suspicion that it is more than a mere analogy is strengthened by the fact that the conception of science involved is 'science as known by scientists' and that at the level of Intellect the intelligibles are essentially something thought and known. So in both cases a knower is a crucial part of the picture: in either case, when the whole is said to be contained in the part the meaning is that the one who knows the part in the relevant way also knows the whole, that the knowledge of the whole is brought to bear in the way the part is known. Thus, the question can be rephrased as the question whether human scientists, as Plotinus conceives of them, instantiate the same intellectual powers as Intellect itself.

I do not doubt that the science analogy/example is meant to provide us with a genuine instance of something that is the case in Intellect, i.e. that a so-called part is or contains the whole of which it is a part and for the reasons that we have seen. Moreover, I don't think this is just a handy coincidence: the scientist's knowledge exhibits this feature because it is the same sort of thing as the knowledge of Intellect. In this sense Plotinus' comparison of Intellect with sciences is more than an analogy. The scientist's knowledge may nevertheless fall short of divine knowledge in various ways. It is not that scientific knowledge is necessarily discursive, whereas Intellect has non-discursive knowledge: even if Plotinus presumably conceives of the individual theorems that are brought forth as discursive and propositional, the level above, at which the whole science is active and actual, is presumably non-discursive. The main qualitative difference between scientific knowledge and Intellect lies in the fact that Intellect's vision of the whole is simply much stronger than the scientist's. We noted above that Plotinus says about the sciences that a given part is active but the others follow unnoticed (IV.9.5, 14–15). This is a considerably weaker claim than is implied by his descriptions of Intellect such as the one quoted above from V.8.4, 5–8: 'Each there has everything in itself and sees all things in every other, so that all are everywhere and each and every one is all and the glory is unbounded ...' I don't suppose Plotinus expects human sciences ever to reach this sort of clarity. His somewhat idealized picture of human science is suitable to give us a hint about what the truly ideal knowledge of Intellect is like. The kind of insight he wishes to attribute to Intellect, however, surpasses even idealized human science.

5. Discursive Thought's Dependence on Intellect

It is plausible enough to conceive of the individual theorems of an axiomatic science, such as people in antiquity supposed sciences ideally to be, as parts of a larger structure in which the theorems have a fixed place and relations to the other parts. We may even suppose that the very truth and meaning of a given theorem is determined by its place in this larger structure (cf. IV.9.5, 12–22). The truth and meaning of such theorems will only be evident when other parts of the structure are taken into account. However this may be, one may wonder why it should be necessary that somebody, Intellect in particular, actually thinks the whole science in order for me to infer piecemeal from true premises to a conclusion. To repeat the question in a slightly different form: why is it not enough that the conceptual structure exists; why does someone have to think it all at once in a single gaze?

Such reflections raise the question about the relationship between discursive and non-discursive thought.[21] As the passage about the Egyptian priests in V.8.6 suggests, the primary kind of thought is the non-discursive type. That is to say, the non-discursive type of thought is seen as ideal thought, what all thought strives but usually fails to be. This is understandable enough: I really and fully understand something only if I have a clear grasp of it in all its relations, if I see the thing itself as it is in the context of the other things in virtue of which it gets its distinctive marks. Consider a mind that only has a partial grasp of what in principle is graspable; it knows a part, but is unable to activate the vision of the whole at once, though it can make

---

[21] A full treatment of the issues relating to the relationship between Intellect and our souls' discursive thought would naturally take us to topics such as the relationship between individual souls and Intellect, and in particular to the relationship between the human intellect (the highest part of the individual human soul) and Intellect. From this there is but a short path to the controversial topic of Ideas of individuals in Plotinus, which has been much debated among scholars over the past decades (see e.g. Rist 1963, Blumenthal 1966, Mamo 1969, Armstrong 1977, Gerson 1994, Kalligas 1997, and Remes [forthcoming]). I shall resist the temptation of going into all this. It seems to me that whatever conclusions I might come up with on these issues, they would risk being less certain than anything I have advanced about the relationship between non-discursive and discursive thought.

a transition to the other parts that it fails to see clearly at the loss of the one it actually has. Such a mind is clearly less powerful and less lucid than the one that sees everything in a single gaze. Its understanding is less complete. It is at every moment in need of some further insight that it presently lacks. It will still have to seek and rely on its memory in making the connections that bring it the knowledge and understanding it is capable of.

That such a perfect kind of grasp, free from the above-mentioned shortcomings, is what all understanding strives to be, is of course not a good argument for claiming that such understanding actually exists, still less for holding that other forms of thought actually depend on such understanding. This may, however, go some way towards establishing non-discursive thought as the primary sort of thought in the sense that it is against non-discursive thought so understood that claims to understanding must be measured. Understanding will be seen as complete or not relative to the extent to which it approaches this ideal.

One reason why Plotinus takes the further step of claiming that discursive thought actually depends on non-discursive thought is surely the following: as we have seen, Plotinus was convinced that the intelligible structure, the realm of the Platonic Ideas, was the thought of a universal mind, Intellect, and had no prior existence outside such a mind. This is what we labelled the Internality Thesis in Chapter 3. According to this view, there is no possible conceptual structure that is not also a thought or thoughts. Hence, if the force of ordinary discursive reasoning is seen to depend on there being a complex structure of intelligibles on which the ordinary reasoning draws, that structure has to be a structure consisting of thought. In the previous chapters we have indeed seen Plotinus insisting that the intelligibles are thoughts. So one way to account for the claim that discursive thought depends on non-discursive thought is just to point out that discursive thought presupposes a prior intelligible structure and that structure is indeed a structure of thought: it cannot be made sense of in any other way. Since the images non-discursive thought deals in are images of the intelligibles and the intelligibles are thoughts, the images depend on thought.

This may be all there is to the claim that discursive thought depends on non-discursive thought. I suspect, however, that it is possible to dig deeper. Isn't there a sense, according to Plotinus, in which *my* discursive thoughts depend on Intellect's thinking the intelligible counterparts of these thoughts in such a way that Intellect's *thinking* plays an essential role in the affair?

In order to get clearer about this, let us consider some actual passages where Plotinus discusses the relationship between our souls' discursive thoughts and Intellect. In V.3.3 he says in connection with discursive reason's judgement in relation to a perceptual image of a human being who has been identified as Socrates:

And if it [the soul] says whether he is good, its remark originates in what it knows through sense-perception, but what it says about this it has already from itself, since it has a norm of the good in itself. How does it have the good in itself? Because it is like the good, and is strengthened for the perception of this kind of thing by Intellect illuminating it; for this is the pure part of the soul and receives the reflection of intellect coming down upon it.[22] (V.3.3, 6–12)

In the same discussion of how we are related to Intellect, Plotinus states that 'We can be in accord with it [Intellect] in two ways, either by having something like its writing written in us like laws, or by being as if filled with it and able to see it and be aware of it as present' (V.3.4, 1–5). In the latter case, we have become Intellect (V.3.4, 7). A few lines below he reiterates this writing metaphor saying that 'the one who writes and has written' what appears in us like laws is in the intelligible world (V.3.4, 22–3).

It emerges from these passages about discursive reason's relation to Intellect that in order to engage in its cognitive activities, discursive reason depends on being informed by Intellect (cf. also I.6.2, I.4.10, 3–16, and IV.3.30, 7–16). What it receives, however, is mere images of the true intelligibles, images that have broken up and separated what in the nature of things is unified.

It is important not to overinterpret the claims made here. Plotinus is for instance not saying that every state of affairs or event in the sensible realm is as such an image of an intelligible counterpart. The sensible realm has an intelligible counterpart only in so far as the former incorporates intelligible content. This only applies to the concepts instantiated in the sensible realm and perhaps some of their relations (e.g. 'horses are animals'); it does not mean that every combination has a counterpart in Intellect: there are no doubt lots of contingent, arbitrary relationships in the sensible realm which

---

[22] V.3.3, 6–12: εἰ δέ, εἰ ἀγαθός, λέγοι, ἐξ ὧν μὲν ἔγνω διὰ τῆς αἰσθήσεως εἴρηκεν, ὃ δὲ εἴρηκεν ἐπ' αὐτοῖς, ἤδη παρ' αὐτῆς ἂν ἔχοι κανόνα ἔχουσα τοῦ ἀγαθοῦ παρ' αὐτῆς. Τὸ ἀγαθὸν πῶς ἔχει παρ' αὐτῇ; Ἡ ἀγαθοειδής ἐστι, καὶ ἐπερρώσθη δὲ εἰς τὴν αἴσθησιν τοῦ τοιούτου ἐπιλάμποντος αὐτῇ νοῦ· τὸ γὰρ καθαρὸν τῆς ψυχῆς τοῦτο καὶ νοῦ δέχεται ἐπικείμενα ἴχνη.

may be captured by discursive thought; nothing intelligible corresponds to them as such, although something intelligible corresponds to the different notions used to express them.

Another warning about a possible misinterpretation: the claim that cognition of images presupposes intellectual knowledge of the things themselves doesn't mean that in order to have any mundane thought we must ascend to Intellect. The example just considered about seeing Socrates and judging that he is good shows this very well. Clearly Plotinus holds that discursive reason is self-sufficient in the sense that it more or less adequately judges what it judges by means of the images it receives from Intellect and the senses without having a direct vision of Intellect. True that its judgements are fallible and it doesn't have a complete understanding of the notions it employs, but it can manage its tasks nevertheless, more or less. Ascending to Intellect itself is rather the exceptional case. It follows from these considerations that the primacy of Intellect does not consist in its being a kind of arbiter in our discursive reasoning. We do not normally use Intellect in order to check our frailer discursive thoughts.

In V.3.4, 1−5 quoted above Plotinus describes the case in which we have become Intellect as one in which we are 'filled with it [Intellect] and able to see it and be aware of it as present'. It is clearly implied by the context here that in the discursive case we do *not* see it and are *not* aware of it as present. If we generalize from this, it emerges that the sense of image at stake in discursive reason is a sense which presumes that the originals are present to some knowing subject; the images are, as it were, what is left in the absence of a grasp of the original. As we saw, he also describes the case of Intellect itself as that of the one who 'writes and has written', in contrast to the case of discursive reason which merely has something written in it. So the thinker engaged in non-discursive thought is the author of his thoughts and understands fully what he thinks. He is like a lawgiver who makes the law and supposedly has an inside understanding of it, as opposed to the subject who merely knows the law as something imposed that must be followed. The contrast drawn here between discursive reason and non-discursive thought is not merely a contrast between images and originals in a purely ontological sense, but a contrast between *knowing* images and *knowing* originals. This may suggest that just as the cognition of sensible events from reports about them presupposes an eyewitness to the original events, discursive reason's grasp of images is like knowledge by hearsay presupposing a direct view. In other words: in the context of discursive reason, an image is not merely contrasted with an original of which it is the image, it is contrasted with the apprehension of that original itself.

So the suggestion is that the images involved in discursive reason are not merely contrasted with the originals that non-discursive thought grasps: they contain an implicit reference to Intellect's clear view of the originals. If this is so, it becomes understandable that cognition of images is supposed not only to presuppose an intelligible structure of which the images are images, but to presuppose direct knowledge of this structure. Its status is like that of the report of an event or a state of affairs. In its case it always seems appropriate to ask: 'But who did actually see it?'

I suspect that Plotinus thought about these issues along the lines just suggested. As in the case of sensibles, there is an important distinction between the eyewitness and the one who believes something merely on the basis of a report, so in the case of intelligibles, there is a difference between the one who directly apprehends the intelligibles and the one who makes do with subsequent representations of them. If such a distinction is granted, it is fairly obvious that the direct grasp must be seen as the prior kind of thought. Talk of reports is meaningless in the absence of somebody who saw the actual event, or at least in the absence of the possibility of seeing it: if it wasn't clear what it would take to see the act itself, the notion of 'reports' would lose its meaning. Similarly, the notions of representation or image are, in Plotinus' view, mere empty words in the absence of clarity about what direct exposure to what is represented would be. In this sense, I believe, Plotinus comes close to a kind of verificationism about the intelligibles. That is to say, if the verificationist thesis that the meaning of a statement is equivalent to the method of its verification is taken to imply that for a statement to have meaning, there must be something that counts as verifying it empirically, Plotinus' attitude towards the intelligibles can be seen to be kindred in spirit: unless there is something like a direct exposure to the intelligibles, talk of apprehending images of them would lose all sense.

Behind such a view there are of course philosophical presuppositions that not everyone is ready to embrace. For instance, somebody might say that dealing in representations is all we can strive for, it helps us cope and that is all we need. To respond to such a view would take us back to the beginnings of Plotinus' philosophy and indeed of the Platonic approach to human beings and the world. I shall resist that temptation. It might also be claimed, more plausibly, that thought that only deals in images may reach out to the things themselves; the representations somehow transcend themselves and manage to refer to something beyond them. To this Plotinus' response would presumably be: well, how is that credible? Mustn't there be something like a direct exposure to the thing itself, if there is to be any assurance that such reference hits its mark?

Even if Plotinus' notion of an image here may derive its sense from the contrast with direct exposure, we have not yet fully explained how discursive thinking by means of images depends on non-discursive thinking of the things themselves. We have considered ways in which this dependence is not supposed to be, and we have seen something about how Plotinus may have thought that discursive thinking in images presupposes the direct thought of originals. This, however, does not quite explain how my discursive thought relates to Intellect: how am *I* personally better off with my images, if Intellect thinks the originals?

The problem is this: how am I better off epistemically speaking if somebody else, in this case Intellect, has grasped something directly? Well, the one who grasped the thing directly might tell me! Is that the situation in the relationship between Intellect and discursive reason? Yes, arguably: this is just what the imagery of the lawgiver and the abiding citizen suggests. Intellect has 'told' discursive reason what to think by 'writing' something in it. The moral authority of the law, as it were, depends on the fact that someone got it right. Luckily, in the present case, that someone was Intellect, which is one with the law, so that the same problem of getting it right doesn't arise with respect to it.

A difficulty nevertheless presents itself: is discursive reason then a mere recipient of the thoughts of an alien master? Plotinus clearly wishes to say 'no, not really', because he thinks that in some sense Intellect and us, 'us' understood as our discursive reason (cf. I.1.7, 16–17; V.3.3, 35–7), are not as estranged as that. As is clear from the quotation above saying that we may become Intellect, in some sense we are Intellect all along. Plotinus also holds that something of our soul never descends into the body (IV.8.8), and that the individual soul has 'an amphibious life', one present to Intellect, and another directed at the sensible (IV.8.4, 31–5; on this passage, see Schniewind 2005). It is, however, a vexed question that I shall not enter into, how exactly Plotinus conceives theoretically of this 'halfway' identity between us and Intellect.

References

Ackrill, J. L. (1997) 'Aristotle's Distinction between Energeia and Kinêsis'. In J. L. Ackrill, *Essays on Plato and Aristotle*. Oxford: Oxford University Press. Originally published in R. Bambrough (ed.), *New Essays on Plato and Aristotle*. London: Routledge, 1965.

Alfino, J. L. (1988) 'Plotinus and the Possibility of Non-Propositional Thought', *Ancient Philosophy* 8: 273–84.

Anscombe, G. E. M. (1975) 'The First Person'. In S. Guttenplan (ed.), *Mind and Language*. Oxford: Oxford University Press, 45–65.

Armstrong, A. H. (1937) 'Emanation in Plotinus', *Mind* 46: 61–6.

——— (1960) 'The Background of the Doctrine "That the Intelligibles are not Outside the Intellect"'. In *Les Sources de Plotin*. Geneva: Fondation Hardt, 393–413.

——— (ed.) (1967) *The Cambridge History of Late Greek and Early Medieval Philosophy*. Cambridge: Cambridge University Press.

——— (1977) 'Form, Individual and Person in Plotinus', *Dionysius* 1: 49–68.

Atkinson, M. (1983) *Plotinus: Ennead V.1 On the Three Principal Hypostases*. Oxford: Oxford University Press.

Beierwaltes, W. (1972) *Platonismus und Idealismus*. Frankfurt am Main: Vittorio Klostermann.

——— (1991) *Selbsterkenntnis und Erfahrung der Einheit*. Frankfurt am Main: Vittorio Klostermann.

——— (2002) 'The Legacy of Neoplatonism in F. W. J. Schelling's Thought'. *International Journal of Philosophical Studies* 10(4): 393–428.

Blumenthal, H. J. (1966) 'Did Plotinus Believe in Ideas of Individuals?', *Phronesis* 11: 61–80.

——— (1971) *Plotinus' Psychology*. The Hague: Martinus Nijhoff.

——— (1974) 'Nous and Soul in Plotinus: Some Problems of Demarcation'. In *Plotino e il Neoplatonismo in Oriente e in Occidente*. Rome: Accademia Nazionale dei Lincei, 203–19.

Bréhier, E. (1924) *Plotin: Ennéades* II. Paris: Les Belles Lettres.

——— (1931) 'Notice' to V.5. in *Plotin: Ennéades* V. Paris: Les Belles Lettres.

Brisson, L. (1991) 'Comment Plotin interprète-t-il les cinq genres du *Sophiste*?' In P. Aubenque (ed.), *Études sur le* Sophiste *de Platon*. Naples: Bibliopolis.

Burnyeat, M. F. (1982) 'Idealism and Greek Philosophy: What Descartes Saw and Berkeley Missed', *Philosophical Review* 91: 3–41.

—— (1987) 'Wittgenstein and Augustine's *De Magistro*', *Proceedings of the Aristotelian Society*, Supplementary Volume 61: 1–24.

Bussanich, J. R. (1987) 'Plotinus on the Inner Life of the One', *Ancient Philosophy* 7: 163–89.

—— (1988) *The One and its Relation to Intellect in Plotinus*. Leiden: E. J. Brill.

—— (1996) 'Plotinus' Metaphysics of the One'. In Gerson 1996: 38–65.

Charles, D. (1984) *Aristotle's Philosophy of Action*. Ithaca, NY: Cornell University Press.

Charrue, J.-M. (1978), *Plotin: lecteur de Platon*. Paris: Les Belles Lettres.

Chiaradonna, R. (2002) *Sostanza, movimento, analogia: Plotino critico di Aristotele*. Naples: Bibliopolis.

Corrigan, K. (1996) 'Essence and Existence in the *Enneads*'. In Gerson 1996: 105–29.

Crystal, I. M. (1998) 'Plotinus on the Structure of Self-Intellection', *Phronesis* 43: 3.

—— (2002) *Self-Intellection and its Epistemological Origins in Ancient Greek Thought*. Aldershot: Ashgate.

D'Ancona Costa, C. (1996) 'Plotinus and Later Platonic Philosophers on the Causality of the First Principle'. In Gerson 1996: 356–85.

Davidson, D. (1980) 'The Individuation of Events'. In D. Davidson, *Actions and Events*. Oxford: Oxford University Press, 163–80. Originally in N. Rescher (ed.), *Essays in Honor of Carl G. Hempel*. Reidel: Dordrecht, 1969.

De Groot, J. (1983) 'Philoponus on *De Anima* II.5, *Physics* III.3, and the Propagation of Light', *Phronesis* 28: 177–96.

Dodds, E. R. (1928) 'The *Parmenides* of Plato and the Origin of the Neoplatonic "One"', *Classical Quarterly* 22: 129–42.

—— (1961) '*Plotins Schriften* edd. Harder, Beutler, Theiler. 5', *Gnomon* 33: 706–10.

—— (1963) *Proclus: The Elements of Theology* (text, translation, and commentary), 2nd edn. Oxford: Oxford University Press.

Emilsson, E. K. (1988). *Plotinus on Sense Perception*. Cambridge: Cambridge University Press.

—— (1991). 'Plotinus on Soul-Body Dualism'. In S. Everson (ed.), *Psychology, Companions to Ancient Thought*. Cambridge: Cambridge University Press.

—— (1995) 'Plotinus on the Object of Thought', *Archiv für Geschichte der Philosophie* 77.

—— (1996) 'Cognition and its Object'. In Gerson (1996).

—— (1999) 'Remarks on the Relation between the One and Intellect in Plotinus'. In J. J. Cleary (ed.), *Traditions of Platonism*. Aldershot: Ashgate, 271–90.

Emilsson, E. K. (2003) 'Discursive and Non-Discursive Thought'. In Fossheim et al. (eds.), *Non-conceptual Aspects of Experience*. Oslo: Unipub, 47–66.

Frede, M. (1987) 'The Original Notion of a Cause'. In M. Frede, *Essays in Ancient Philosophy*. Minneapolis: University of Minnesota Press, 125–50. Originally published in M. Schofield, M. F. Burnyeat, and J. Barnes (eds.), *Doubt and Dogmatism: Studies in Hellenistic Epistemology*. Oxford: Oxford University Press, 1980.

—— (1992) 'On Aristotle's conception of the Soul'. In M. C. Nussbaum and A. O. Rorty (eds.), *Essays on Aristotle's* De Anima. Oxford: Oxford University Press, 93–107.

Gerson, L. P. (1994) *Plotinus*. London: Routledge.

—— (ed.) (1996) *The Cambridge Companion to Plotinus*. Cambridge: Cambridge University Press.

—— (1997) 'Introspection, Self-Relexivity, and the Essence of Thinking according to Plotinus'. In J. J. Cleary, *The Perennial Tradition of Neoplatonism*. Leuven: Leuven University Press, 153–73.

Gill, M. L. (1991) 'Aristotle on Self-Motion'. In L. Judson (ed.), *Aristotles's Physics*. Oxford: Oxford University Press, 243–65.

Goldman, A. I. (1970) *A Theory of Human Action*. Prentice Hall: Englewood Cliffs, NJ. Available at: **http://tabula.rutgers.edu/disciplines/philosophy/goldman/Goldman.pdf**

Graeser, A. (1972) *Plotinus and the Stoics: A Preliminary Study*. Leiden: E. J. Brill.

Gurtler, G. M. (1988) *Plotinus: The Experience of Unity*. New York: Peter Lang.

Hadot, P. (1968) *Porphyre et Victorinus*. 2 vols. Paris: Études Augustiniennes.

—— 'Neoplatonist Spirituality: Plotinus and Porphyry'. In A. H. Armstrong (ed.), *Classical Mediterranean Spirituality*. New York: Herder & Herder, 230–49.

—— (1987) *Plotin: Traité 38: VI.7*. Paris: Les Éditions du Cerf.

—— (1999) 'Être, vie et pensée chez Plotin et avant Plotin'. In P. Hadot, *Plotin, Porphyre: Études néoplatoniciennes*. Paris: Les Belles Lettres, 127–81. First published in *Entretiens sur l'antiquité classique 5: les sources de Plotin*. Geneva: Fondation Hardt, 1960.

Halfwassen, J. (1994) *Geist und Selbstbewusstsein: Studien zu Plotin und Numenios*. Akademie der Wissenschaften und der Litteratur, Mainz. Stuttgart: Franz Steiner Verlag, 1994.

Ham, B. (2000) *Plotin: Traité 49: V.3*. Paris: Les Éditions du Cerf.

Heiser, J. H. (1991), *Logos and Language in the Philosophy of Plotinus*. Studies in the History of Philosophy 15. Lewiston, NY: The Edwin Mellen Press.

Holladay, A. (2000) **www.wonderquest.com/ExpandingUniverse.htm**.

Jones, R. M. (1926) 'The Ideas as the Thoughts of God', *Classical Philology* 21: 317–36.

Kal, V. (1988) *On Intuition and Discursive Reasoning in Aristotle*. Leiden: E. J. Brill.

Kalligas, P. (1997) 'Forms of Individuals in Plotinus: A Re-Examination', *Phronesis* 42: 206–27.

Kant, I. (1787) *Kritik der reinen Vernunft*, 2nd edn.

Kosman, A. (1969) 'Aristotle's Definition of Motion', *Phronesis* 14: 40–62.

—— (2000) 'Metaphysics Lambda 9'. In M. Frede and D. Charles (eds.), *Aristotle's Metaphysics Lambda: Symposium Aristotelicum*. Oxford: Oxford University Press, 307–26.

Kripke, S. A. (1982) *Wittgenstein on Rules and Private Language*. Cambridge, Mass.: Harvard University Press.

Lloyd, A. C. (1970) 'Non-discursive Thought—an Enigma of Greek Philosophy', *Proceedings of the Aristotelian Society* 70: 261–74.

—— (1986) 'Non-propositional Thought in Plotinus', *Phronesis* 31: 258–65.

—— (1987) 'Plotinus on the Genesis of Thought and Existence', *Oxford Studies in Ancient Philosophy* 5: 155–86.

—— (1990) *The Anatomy of Neoplatonism*. Oxford: Oxford University Press.

Long, A. A., and Sedley D. N. (1987) *The Hellenistic Philosophers*. 2 vols. Cambridge University Press: Cambridge.

Mamo, P. S (1969) 'Forms of Individuals in the *Enneads*'. *Phronesis* 14: 77–86.

Narbonne, J.-M. (2001) *La Métaphysique de Plotin*. Paris: Vrin.

Natali, C. (1999) 'La critica di Plotino ai concetti di attualità e movimento in Aristotele'. In C. Natali and S. Maso (eds.), *Antiaristotelismo*. Amsterdam: Hakkert, 211–29.

Nikulin, D. (2005) 'Unity and Individuation in the Soul in Plotinus'. In R. Chiaradonna (ed.), *Studi sull'anima in Plotino*. Naples: Bibliopolis, 275–304.

Norman, R. (1969), 'Aristotle's Philosopher-God', *Phronesis* 14: 63–74.

O'Brien, D. (1991) *Plotinus on the Origin of Matter*. Naples: Bibliopolis.

O'Daly, G. J. P. (1973) *Plotinus' Philosophy of the Self*. Shannon: Irish University Press.

—— (1974), 'The Presence of the One in Plotinus'. In *Plotino e il Neoplatonismo in Oriente e in Occidente*. Rome: Accademia Nazionale dei Lincei, 159–69.

O'Meara, D. J. (1985) 'Plotinus on How Soul Acts on Body'. In D. J. O'Meara (ed.), *Platonic Investigations*. Washington, DC: Catholic University of America Press, 247–62.

—— (1993) *Plotinus: An Introduction to the Enneads*. Oxford: Oxford University Press.

—— (2000) 'Scepticism and Ineffability in Plotinus', *Phronesis* 45: 242–51.

Oosthout, H. (1991) *Modes of Knowledge and the Transcendental*. Amsterdam: B. R. Grüner.

Rappe, S. (2000) *Reading Neoplatonism: Non-discursive Thinking in the Texts of Plotinus, Proclus, and Damascius.* Cambridge: Cambridge University Press.

Remes, P. (forthcoming) *Plotinus on Self and Person: The Philosophy of the 'We'.* Cambridge: Cambridge University Press.

Rich, A. N. M. (1954) 'The Platonic Ideas as the Thoughts of God', *Mnemosyne* 4(7): 123–33.

Rist, J. M. (1963) 'Forms of Individuals in Plotinus', *Classical Quarterly* 13: 223–31.

——— (1967) *Plotinus: The Road to Reality.* Cambridge: Cambridge University Press.

——— (1989) 'Back to the Mysticism of Plotinus: Some more Specifics', *Journal of the History of Philosophy* 27, 183–97.

Rorty, R. (1979) *Philosophy and the Mirror of Nature.* Princeton: Princeton University Press.

Rutten, C. (1956) 'La Doctrine des deux actes dans la philosophie de Plotin', *Revue philosophique* 46: 100–6.

Santa Cruz, M. I. (1997), 'L'Exégèse plotinienne des ΜΕΓΙΣΤΑ ΓΕΝΗ du *Sophiste* de Platon'. In J. J. Cleary (ed.), *The Perennial Tradition of Neoplatonism.* Leuven: Leuven University Press.

Schniewind, A. (2005) 'Les Âmes amphibies et les causes de leurs différences: à propos de Plotin, Enn. IV 8 [6], 4. 31–35'. In R. Chiaradonna (ed.), *Studi sull'anima in Plotino.* Naples: Bibliopolis, 179–200.

Sedley, D. (1998) 'Platonic Causes', *Phronesis* 43(2): 114–32.

Sellars, W. (1963) *Science, Perception and Reality.* London: Routledge & Kegan Paul.

Sharples, R. W. (1982) 'Alexander of Aphrodisias on Divine Providence: Two Problems', *Classical Quarterly* 32: 198–211.

Sleeman, J. H., and Pollet, G. (1980) *Lexicon Plotinianum.* Leiden: E. J. Brill.

Smith, A. (1974) *Porphyry's Place in Neoplatonic Thought.* The Hague: Martinus Nijhoff.

——— (1996) 'Eternity and Time'. In Gerson 1996: 196–216.

Solmsen, F. (1960) 'Platonic Influences in the Formation of Aristotle's Physical System.' In I. Düring and G. E. L. Owen (eds.), *Aristotle and Plato in the Mid-Fourth Century.* Gothenburg: Elanders.

——— (1960) *Aristotle's System of the Physical World: A Comparison with His Predecessors.* Ithaca, NY: Cornell University Press.

Sorabji, R. (1982) 'Myths about Non-Propositional Thought'. In M. Schofield and M. C. Nussbaum (eds.), *Language and Logos.* Cambridge: Cambridge University Press, 295–314.

——— (1983) *Time, Creation and the Continuum.* London: Duckworth.

Strange, S. K. (1992) 'Plotinus's Account of Participation in *Ennead* VI. 4–5', *Journal of the History of Philosophy* 30, 479–96.

Szlezák, T. A. (1979), *Platon und Aristoteles in der Nuslehre Plotins*. Basle: Schwabe & Co.

Tornau, C. (1998) 'Wissenschaft, Seele, Geist: Zur Bedeutung einer Analogie bei Plotin (*Enn.* IV 9, 5 und VI 2, 20)', *Göttinger Forum für Altertumswissenschaft* 1: 87–111.

Trouillard, J. (1955) *La Purification plotinienne*. Paris: Presses universitaires de France.

——— (1961) 'Valeur critique de la mystique plotinienne', *Revue philosophique de Louvain* 59: 431–44.

Vieillard-Baron, J.-L. (1979) *Platon et l'idealisme allemand (1770–1830)*. Paris: Beauchesne.

Wagner, M. F. (1996) 'Plotinus on the Nature of Physical Reality'. In Gerson 1996: 130–70.

Wallis, R. T. (1987) 'Skepticism and Neoplatonism'. In W. Haase (ed.), *Aufstieg und Niedergang des römischen Welt* II, 36, 2. Berlin: Walter de Gruyter, 911–54.

Waterlow, S. (1982) *Nature, Change, and Agency in Aristotle's Physics*. Oxford: Oxford University Press.

Index of Cited Texts

General Index

One (the) 1, 5–6 and passim
  and the inchoate intellect, see inchoate
    intellect
  as Intellect's intended object, see desire
    for the Good and (intellectual) vision
  as beyond thought or being 22 n. 2, 25,
    78, 92
  as a kind of psychological entity 70–1,
    174–5
Oosthout, H. 88 n. 21, 154 n. 19
otherness, see plurality
ousia, see Being

paradigm 27, 61, 68
paschein, see undergoing
patiency, see undergoing
phantasma, see image
Plato 36 n. 22, 52, 60–8, 80, 88 n., 106,
    118, 126, 149 n., 161, 169 n. 36, 185,
    192
Platonism 27, 35 n. 20, 44, 54, 60–7, 126,
    162, 167 n. 34, 168, 171–2, 174, 176,
    182 n., 191–3, 195, 212
plurality 2, 72, 79, 81–4
  of the object of thought 83–91, 98–100,
    104–7, 111–13, 119, 122, 180, 185–9,
    194, 203
  as duality of subject and object 69, 79,
    85, 88–9, 103, 105–6, 111–12, 157
poiein, see making
poikilos (variegated) 86, 180, 186, 188
Porphyry 7, 17, 101 n. 31, 120, 130
potentiality, see power
power (dynamis) 28–30, 35 n. 20, 36 n. 21,
    38, 40, 54–8, 61, 70, 108, 147–8,
    151–5, 162–3, 169, 175, 202–6
principles 1–2, 8–11, 16, 27, 29, 33, 51, 54
    n., 59–60, 62, 64–8, 72 n. 2, 124,
    134–6, 140, 153, 168–9, 174, 176,
    200–1
procession (proodos) 26, 69, 70, 74–5, 122,
    134, 156 n. 25, 162–4
Proclus 63 n. 49
proodos, see procession
propositional thought 117, 177, 181, 184,
    185–91, 193–4, 197–8, 204, 206

qualities, see form

Rappe, S. 19

Reason 5–6
Remes, P. 91, 207 n.
representation, see image
Rich, A. N. M. 167 n. 34
Rist, J. M. 92 n., 102–3, 207 n. 21
Rorty, R. 192
Rutten, C. 25, 54–56

Santa Cruz, M. I. 106 n. 35
scepticism 4, 13, 124, 129, 131 n. 4, 139,
    144, 169–73
Schniewind, A. 213
Sedley, D. 60
self-knowledge, see self–thinking
self-sufficiency (autarkeia) 51, 72, 84,
    108–9, 113, 126, 154, 175, 210
self-thinking 70, 82, 87, 104, 173–4
  as primary thinking 107, 122, 142, 144,
    146
  and the first person 107, 109–14,
    117–18, 121–3, 146–50, 173
  and thinking that one thinks 118–22
Sellars, W. 170–1, 196
sense-perception (aisthêsis) 2, 98,
    124–5, 127–8, 129–40, 193, 195,
    209
sensible objects 1–2, 76, 124–5, 128–9,
    131–6, 139–41, 168, 174, 193–4, 196,
    210–11, 213
Sextus Empiricus 39 n. 27, 144, 146 n.,
    170, 189 n. 11, 205 n.
Sharples, R. W. 52 n. 43
skepticism 4, 13, 124, 129, 131 n. 4, 139,
    144, 169–70, 171–3
Smith, A. 25 n. 8, 26, 183 n.
Solmsen, F. 60
Sorabji, R. 14, 110, 185–188
Soul; souls 2–3, 28, 31, 32 n. 13, 40, 44,
    50, 53, 62–3, 65–7, 85, 134, 142–3,
    203
  World-Soul 16, 62, 63 n. 40, 183–5
  and discursive reason 125, 129, 183–5,
    187, 207 n.
Spinoza 5, 177
Stoicism 10, 37, 52–4, 189–90, 192 n. 13,
    205 n.
Strange, S. K. 139 n.
subject of thought, see thinker
sympatheia 136
Szlezák, T. A. 83 n. 16, 110, 148, 149 n.,
    167 n. 33–4